IMAGES
of America

SHIPWRECKS OF CURRY COUNTY

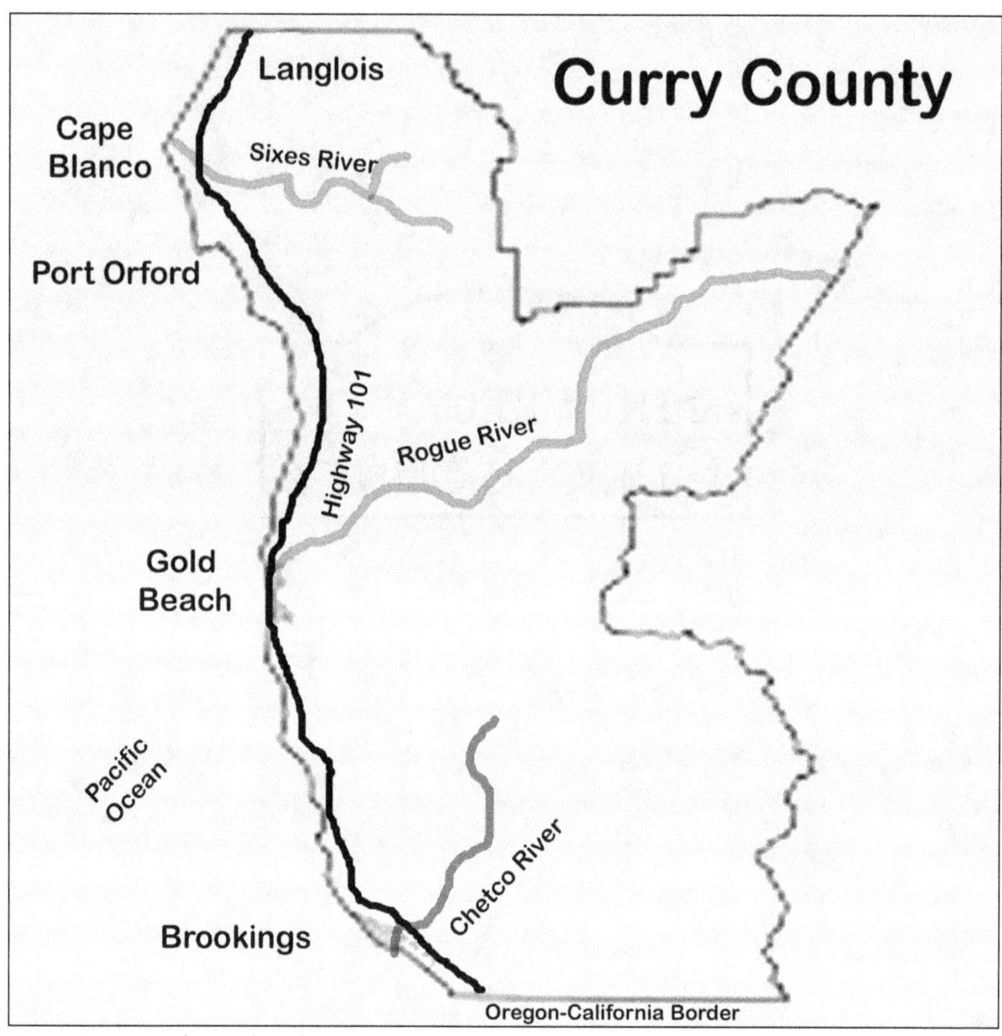

Curry County is located in the southwestern corner of Oregon. Due to the Pacific Ocean on the west and the mountains to the east, the coastal communities are geographically isolated from the rest of the state. Historically, settlers were forced to rely on the waterways for the transportation of both people and supplies. Although not to scale, this map provides a general overview of the area. The largest towns, rivers, and geographical locations that are discussed in the book have been labeled. (Author's collection.)

On the Cover: The steam schooner *Lakme* became waterlogged during a storm off the southern Oregon coast in January 1911. The crew spent an uncomfortable night clinging to the forecastle, which was the only portion of the ship out of reach of the waves. They were rescued the following evening by the crew of the steamer *Nann Smith*. The *Lakme* was later towed to San Francisco and repaired. (CHM 007-25.530.)

IMAGES
of America

SHIPWRECKS OF CURRY COUNTY

H.S. Contino

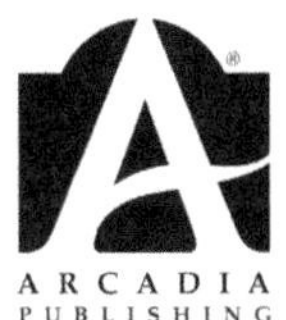

ISBN 978-1-5402-1693-9

Published by Arcadia Publishing
Charleston, South Carolina

Library of Congress Control Number: 2017940140

For all general information, please contact Arcadia Publishing:
Telephone 843-853-2070
Fax 843-853-0044
E-mail sales@arcadiapublishing.com
For customer service and orders:
Toll-Free 1-888-313-2665

Visit us on the Internet at www.arcadiapublishing.com

In memory of my grandfather, John Dauray, from whom I inherited my appreciation for history

Contents

ACKNOWLEDGMENTS

This project would not have been possible without the encouragement of my family and friends. In particular, I would like to thank June Contino, Laura Cantrell, Karen Lind, and Betty Pratt. I would also like to thank Debbie Newman for keeping me company while tracking down shipwreck locations and taking photographs when the battery in my camera died.

I'm thankful for the support of my coworkers at the North Bend Public Library. I would especially like to thank Gary Sharp, Lyn Johnston, Kimie Wright, Becky Martin, and Clara Piazzola.

I'm grateful to Alan Mitchell for loaning me several of the amazing photographs from his personal collection. I appreciated the help of Bill McNair of Jerry's Rogue Jets for answering some of my shipwreck related questions.

I'm indebted to Jim Proehl at the Bandon Historical Society and Michelle Nash at the Coos History Museum (CHM) for allowing me to search through their archives and use photographs and objects from their museum collections in the book.

Although we never met, I would like to acknowledge the late Victor West. His extensive research binders have been invaluable to the completion of this project.

Finally, I would like to thank Arcadia Publishing for giving me the opportunity to write this book. I'm grateful for the assistance of Katelyn Carter and Stacia Bannerman.

INTRODUCTION

The rugged Oregon coast is one of the most beautiful and dangerous coastlines in the world. Curry County is located in the southwestern corner of the state. Although early explorers visited the area as early as the 1500s, European settlement did not begin until the 1850s. Most of the early communities were located along the coastline. This was partially due to the discovery of gold and other precious metals by explorers in 1852. These resources could be found in the rivers and along the beaches.

Historically, the residents of Curry County's coastal communities were forced to rely on the waterways for transportation. This was due to their geographic isolation from the rest of the state. With the Pacific Ocean to the west and mountains to the east, traveling by water was the only practical option for early settlers. It took many years for inland transportation routes to be built. This kept the area isolated from the rest of the state until the mid-1900s.

Among mariners, the Oregon coast has the reputation of being dangerous to navigate. Hundreds of ships of varying sizes have run into trouble along the Curry County coastline over the years. One of the earliest known wrecks was a Russian whaling ship that stranded near Port Orford in the 1830s.

The southern Oregon coastline holds many potential hazards for mariners. For instance, there are numerous partially submerged offshore rocks (sometimes referred to as "sea stacks"). The weather can change rapidly. The area often experiences thick fog (which can drop the temperature 20 degrees or more), and it is known for its impressive winter storms that can produce wind gusts of 50 miles per hour and higher. Ships caught in storms often found both the wind and waves working against them. Together, these two forces could break a ship apart. To make matters worse, the ocean temperatures average 50 degrees Fahrenheit. Tragically, passengers and crew that survived the actual shipwreck often died of exposure while waiting to be rescued.

Not all shipwrecks are caused by the forces of nature. Accidents can be caused by human error as well. During the peak era of sailing ships, many vessels lost their bearings and inadvertently traveled too close to the rugged coast where the winds and currents forced them onto rocks. In other cases, shipwrecks were blamed on a captain's poor knowledge of the Oregon coast's dangers, incomplete charts, or the captain's underestimation of Oregon weather. Navigational errors could cause the ships to wander too close to shore. Once in trouble, the remote region (with few places to find refuge) played a role in many shipwrecks.

Port commissioners requested a US Life-Saving Station (precursor to the modern Coast Guard) to be built in the county in 1889. Although their request was authorized in 1891, the Cape Blanco Life-Saving Station was not constructed until 1934. The community waited 43 years. According to David Pinyerd, author of *Lighthouses and Life-Saving on the Oregon Coast*, they were forced to wait "longer than any other Oregon coastal community." The lifeboat station was decommissioned in 1970 after 36 years of service. The residents of Curry County spent more time waiting for a station to be built than the station remained in operation.

While they waited, the closest station was located on the Coquille River—55 miles to the north. Ships in distress, along with their passengers and crew, were forced to wait extended periods of time for help to arrive. The Coquille River Life-Saving Station crew could be gone for days on a single rescue. This was the case after the gas schooner *Washcalore* struck a reef near Island Rock, just south of the Rogue River, during a storm. The ship was eventually pounded to pieces, but the crew managed to get off the disabled vessel. They found partial shelter on the island while they awaited rescue. Fortunately, they managed to salvage some supplies—including plenty of whiskey. It took the life-saving crew 36 hours to rescue them. First, they caught a ride south on the tug *Klihyam*. They then used their small lifeboat to approach the rock island. With its shallow draft, it could safely approach and transport the *Washcalore*'s 14 crew members back to the tug. The exhausted life-saving crew escorted the survivors to the nearest port before finally returning home.

Although it shares some features with neighboring counties—rocky outcroppings, hidden reefs, and sand bars—the area is also unique. Curry County is home to Port Orford, which is the only open water port on the Oregon coast. Historically, ships could find some shelter at the dock, but it was a relatively exposed location. Over the years, numerous docks, breakwaters, and jetties were built to try to provide ships with some protection. Unfortunately, these structures were often damaged or destroyed by storms. As a result, they were rebuilt numerous times. Eventually, the port district was established, and they developed an unusual setup. They built a high dock. Every day, boats are lowered to and raised from the ocean using giant cranes. This makes Port Orford one of only six "dolly" ports in the world.

In modern times, Highway 101 runs parallel with the coastline and provides numerous scenic overlooks of the Pacific Ocean. According to one promotional brochure, the ocean provides "year-round air conditioning." The temperatures rarely rise above 70 degrees in the summer or reach freezing temperatures in winter. The area draws thousands of visitors every year. They come to marvel at the beauty in the summer, and they are awed by the powerful storms in the winter.

Modern technology, harbor improvements, and navigational aids have reduced the number of marine accidents along the southern Oregon coast, but shipwrecks still occur. Better communication has also decreased the number of accidents. It is hard to imagine the early ships traveling along the coast without radios. When things went wrong, all they could do was fire flares or hang signal flags in the slim hope that another ship would be close enough to see and respond to their call for help.

Since the construction of bridges and the completion of Highway 101, there has been less need for maritime travel. Most cargo in Curry County is now transported overland using semi-trucks, which eliminates the risk associated with shipping cargo by sea. The ports are mostly used by small fishing boats and the famous jet boats that transport tourists up the Rogue River.

There are several rivers on the Curry County coastline, including the Rogue, Chetco, and Sixes. They were often the site of maritime accidents. The main issue was trying to cross the bar. In maritime terms, a bar is where a river meets the sea. It can cause many problems for mariners. For instance, there can be large differences in the water depth, which can cause ships to ground. In addition, sand and silt can build up at the mouths of rivers, and objects can be carried downstream and deposited there. All of these factors presented the risk of ships striking objects and damaging their hulls.

Tragically, many of the casualties during the shipwrecks discussed in this book could have been prevented if the accidents had occurred in modern times. In particular, the Coast Guard helicopters are quite literally lifesavers. They are capable of arriving at the scene quickly and approaching wrecks with relatively little risk to their crew. Compare this to the early lifesaving crews that were equipped with little more than a small rowboat and a Lyle gun (a small cannon that could be used to fire a line to the disabled vessel in order to bring the passengers and crew ashore).

Finally, it is important to remember that maritime accidents are not just about the ships—there is also the human factor. Traumatic and life-threatening situations tend to bring out both the best and worst in people. Some people behaved heroically when their ships ran into trouble, while others thought only of themselves and their own survival. There's a maritime tradition that captains should be the last to leave their ship during a disaster. However, there are several incidents described in this book during which captains chose to board a lifeboat before their ships had been safely evacuated. In these cases, there were usually investigations afterwards. Captains that lived while passengers died were often faced with public criticism.

On the flip side, it is easy to imagine how difficult it would be for the captains when faced with a potential disaster. West Coast storms, in particular, have been responsible for damaging many ships en route. Can you imagine standing on the bridge knowing that your ship has become disabled or is sinking and trying to decide whether or not you should send the women and children to the lifeboats? During storms, it was sometimes safer to remain on board and continue to try to pump out the water rather than risk launching the lifeboats. There were several reasons for this. For instance, launching the boats was a several-step process. First, the boats had to be unstowed, which usually involved lowering them to the side of the ship. The passengers could then be loaded. Finally, the boats had to be lowered down to the water.

Several things could go wrong during this process: the boats could strike the side of the ship, they could capsize, and the occupants could be forced into the rough surf. Many of the early ships had wooden lifeboats that could be smashed into bits against the side of the ship. And then, even if the lifeboats made it safely away from the ship, there was no guarantee that they would make it safely to shore or that the passengers would be picked up by other ships. The small boats did not stand much of a chance in the open sea. Many times, the lifeboats capsized, causing the occupants to drown—or their passengers died from exposure while awaiting rescue. In some cases, such as the *South Coast*, the fate of the ship and its crew remain a mystery. Some wreckage, including an empty lifeboat was discovered, but the ship itself was never found, and there were no survivors.

All of these factors and potential problems would be running through the captains' minds as they contemplated the right course of action. It put the captains in a difficult position. Which would be more dangerous for their passengers—staying on board the disabled vessel or risking the lifeboats in the open sea?

It is also important to remember the people on shore that were affected by the shipwrecks. Early settlers were reliant on ships to bring them supplies. They often took advantage of wrecks close to shore. There was always the chance of looting, but in many cases, people could legally purchase salvaged supplies from shipwrecks at a discounted price. For example, after the wreck of the *Bawnmore*, several gallons of Pacific Rubber paint were salvaged and purchased by area residents. An early pioneer reminisced in the *Curry County Echoes* about most of the buildings in town having a coat of the yellow paint.

This book does not cover all of the wrecks that have occurred in Curry County. However, it does include a variety of vessel types that range from old wooden sailing ships to steel hulled steamships to modern fishing boats. The shipwrecks and maritime mishaps span a nearly 200-year period. The chapters have been organized based upon the locations where the wrecks occurred. These "problem areas" are locations where, for different reasons, large numbers of vessels have run into trouble. Beginning in the northern portion of the county, the first chapter focuses on Cape Blanco, the Sixes River, and Floras Lake. Moving south, the next few chapters cover accidents in Port Orford, Gold Beach, and the Rogue River. The final chapter discusses shipwrecks along the coastline in general. It also includes accidents at Brookings, the Chetco River, and Harbor.

Some ships were hard to place if they ran into trouble in more than one location or on more than one occasion. Some had trouble in southern Oregon but technically wrecked elsewhere. For instance, in 1865, the side-wheel steamer *Brother Jonathan* ran into trouble near the Oregon-California state line. The captain made the decision to turn around and return to Crescent City, California in search of shelter from the storm. They never made it. The ship struck a submerged reef and sank. Due to a variety of reasons—the ship sank quickly, there were not any ships nearby to witness the accident, and there were few survivors—the exact wreck location remained a mystery until the 1990s. Although we now know that the ship sank in northern California, the wreck is included in this book because the only lifeboat came ashore in Curry County.

One

Cape Blanco and the Sixes River

Cape Blanco is a headland on the southern Oregon coastline that is estimated to be 80,000 years old. It is the second most westerly point in the continental United States. Cape Blanco has been the location of many shipwrecks. There are many submerged rocks and reefs in the area that ships could strike. Fog could be especially dangerous. The reduced visibility often caused captains to lose their bearings and stray too close to shore.

Accidents in the area often occurred during storms. At such times, it was dangerous and difficult for would-be rescuers to reach disabled ships. Storm conditions could also make it hard for survivors to get safely to shore because the rough surf could capsize lifeboats or smash them against the rocks.

Over the years, there have been several improvements to the area designed to prevent accidents and assist distressed mariners when they do occur. For instance, the Cape Blanco Lighthouse was constructed in 1870. As the name suggests, it was built on Cape Blanco, which is located just south of the mouth of the Sixes River. The lighthouse is located between Port Orford and Bandon. In addition to the lighthouse, local port commissioners requested a US Life-Saving Station (the precursor to the modern Coast Guard) to be built in the county in 1889. Although their request was authorized in 1891, the Cape Blanco Life-Saving Station was not constructed until 1934. The community waited 43 years for it to be completed. According to David Pinyerd, author of *Lighthouses and Life-Saving on the Oregon Coast*, they were forced to wait "longer than any other Oregon coastal community." The lifeboat station was decommissioned in 1970 after 36 years of service. In other words, the residents of Curry County spent more time waiting for a station to be built than the station remained in operation.

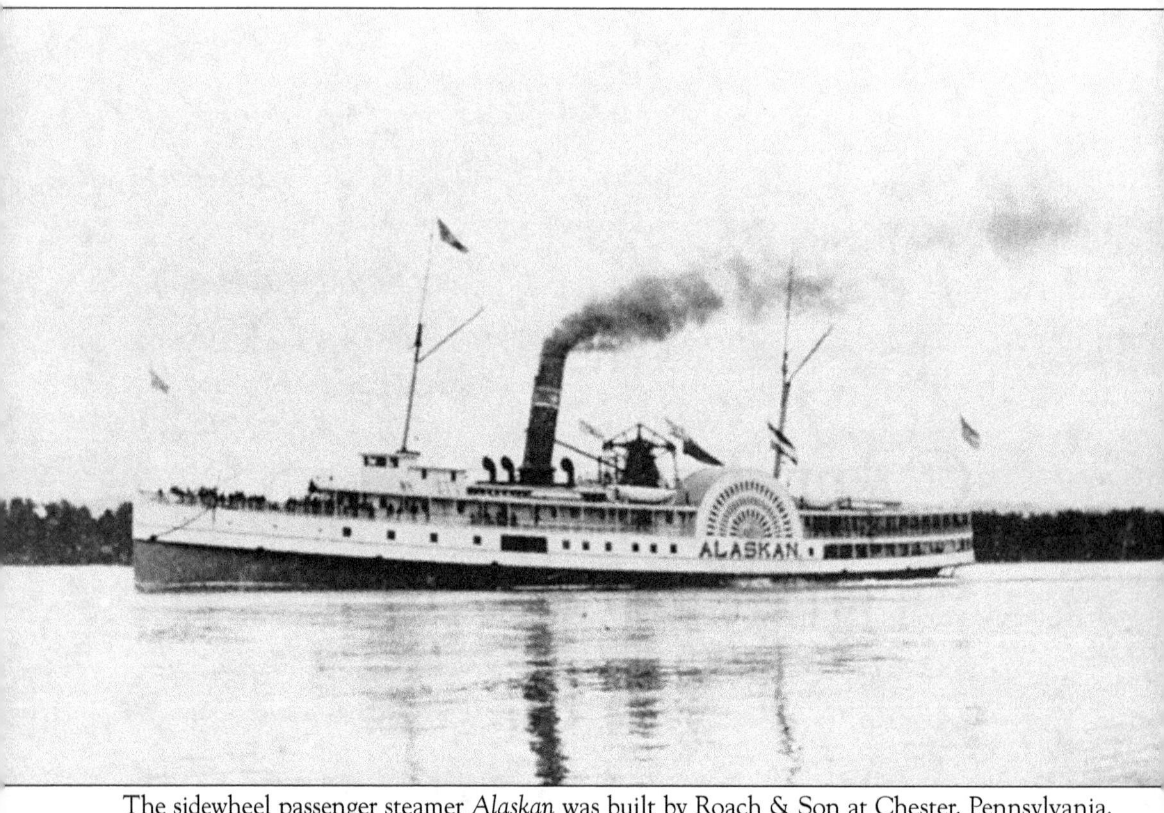

The sidewheel passenger steamer *Alaskan* was built by Roach & Son at Chester, Pennsylvania, in 1883. The 1,919-gross-ton ship was iron hulled, 280 feet long, with a 40-foot-wide beam and a 13-foot depth. Although it was built for inland water service, the *Alaskan* was considered a good sea boat. It was owned by the Oregon Railway & Navigation Company. The ship departed Portland on Friday, May 10, 1889, under the command of Capt. R.E. Howes, on its way to San Francisco for dry-docking and repairs. The following day, it made a brief stop at Astoria before continuing south. On Sunday, May 12, they encountered a storm. The ship was approximately 18 miles offshore of Cape Blanco. As conditions continued to deteriorate, the ship struggled to make progress. By afternoon, it began taking on water. The crew tried to stop the leaks by stuffing them with bedding. Despite their efforts, the water extinguished the fires in the boilers. Around 11:00 p.m. that night, the captain gave the order to launch the lifeboats. (CHM 009-16.1198.)

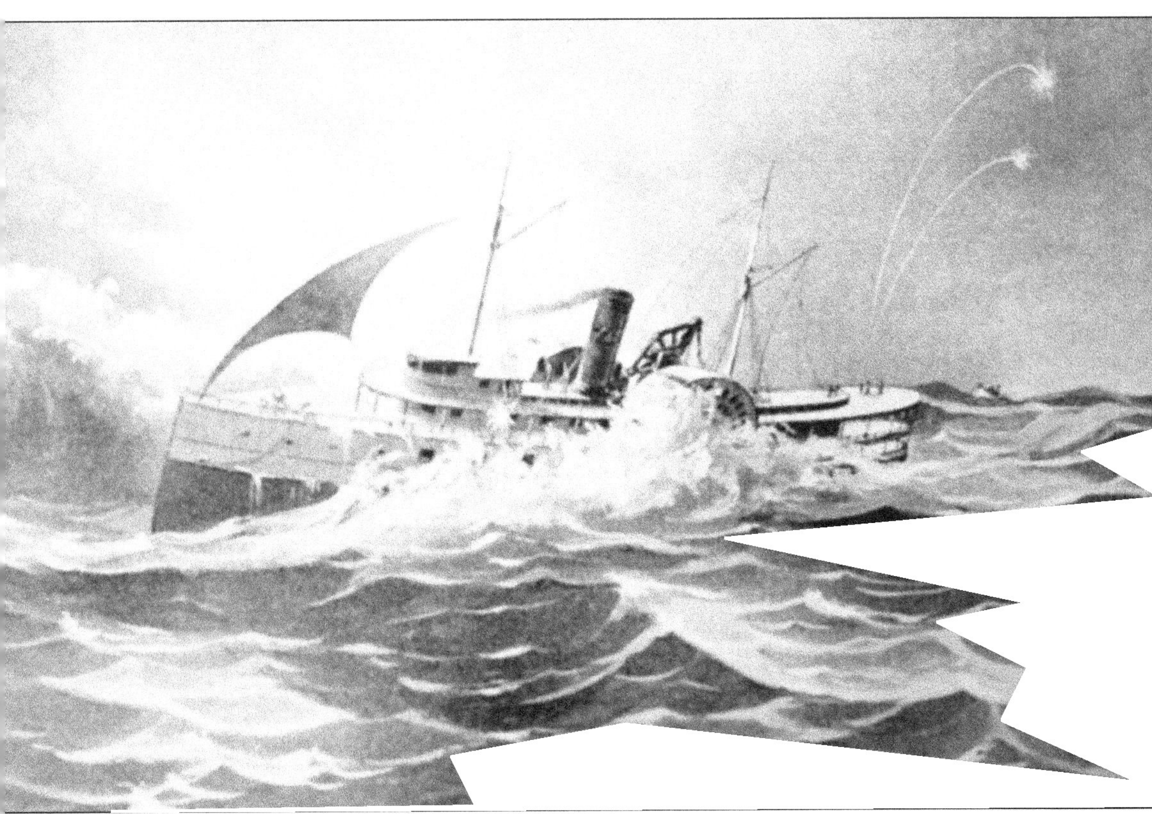

As the conditions at sea continued to worsen, the *Alaskan* began to leak. It managed to travel as far south as Cape Blanco before it began to break up, and the crew made the decision to abandon ship. Four lifeboats were launched, and several crewmen made rafts in an attempt to make it to shore. Of the 47 crewmen, only 17 survived. The tug *Vigilant* picked up a few survivors, including the captain. He and three other men clung to wreckage for more than 30 hours. One man came ashore above Ten Mile Creek after drifting off the coast for about a week. Another crewman, also clinging to wreckage, was picked up a week later by the British bark *Kattie* on its way to Hong Kong. His family believed that he was dead for several months. They did not receive word of his survival until October. This painting depicts the ship in distress on rough seas. (CHM 009-16.383.)

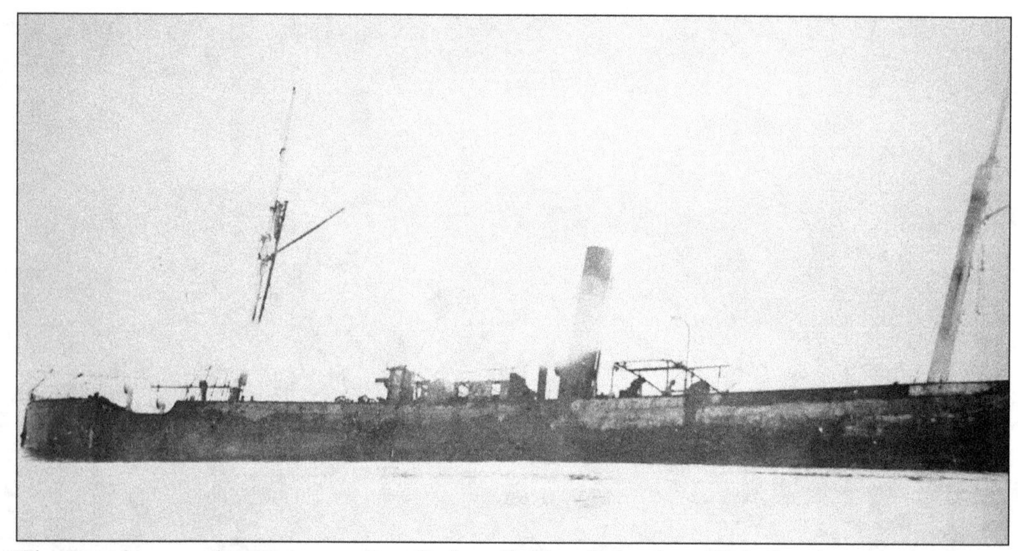

The British steamship *Bawnmore* was built at Belfast, Ireland in 1889. On August 28, 1895, it grounded near Floras Lake (north of Cape Blanco) due to a faulty compass and a dense fog. The 1,430-ton iron hulled vessel's cargo included lumber, building supplies, streetcars, and purebred cattle. The crew secured a lifeline to drift logs on the beach. All of the passengers and crew used it to safely cross the 700-foot span to shore. Although the *Bawnmore* became a total loss, most of cargo was salvaged before the hull caught on fire. Numerous cans of salvaged Pacific Rubber Paint were sold at a discount. Many buildings featured a coat of the yellow paint. This table, which was salvaged from the shipwreck, is on display at the Bandon Historical Society Museum. (Above, CHM 009-16.329; below, Bandon Historical Society.)

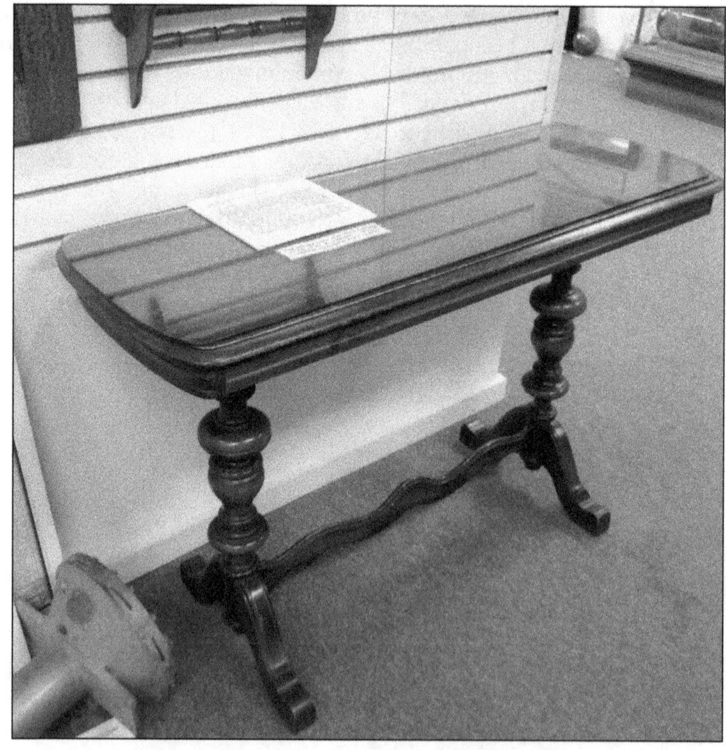

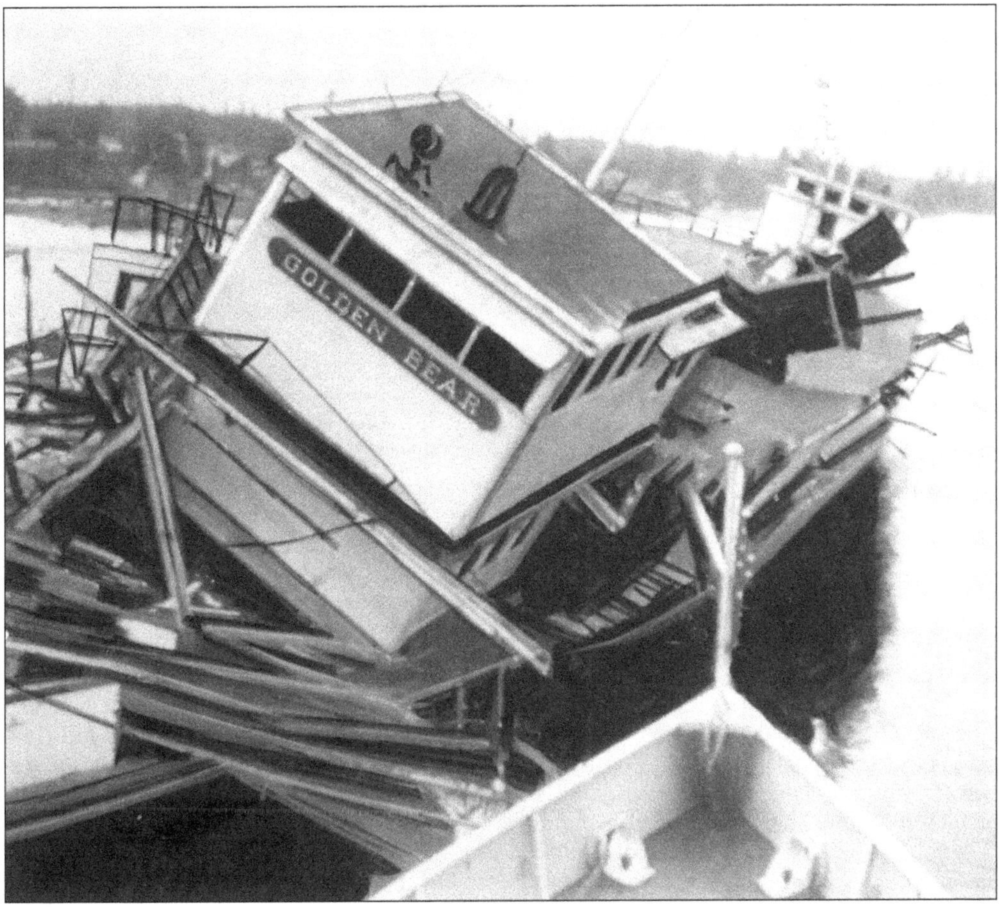

The wooden diesel electric ferryboat *Golden Bear* was built between 1926 and 1927. The Puget Sound Navigation Company purchased it in 1937. On November 12th, the tug *Active* started towing it from San Francisco Bay to Puget Sound. On the 15th, they encountered bad weather, which caused the hawser (tow line) to part off of Cape Blanco. While adrift, the ferry became damaged in the rough seas. The deckhouse became loose and leaned over on one side, causing part of it to wash overboard. The *Active* took the ferry's seven-man crew on board overnight. On the 16th, the *Active* crew worked with the crew of the Coast Guard cutter *Pulaski* to get another hawser on the *Golden Bear*. Both photographs on this page show the damaged ferry at dock after the accident. (Above, CHM 007-25.240; below, CHM 007-25.247.)

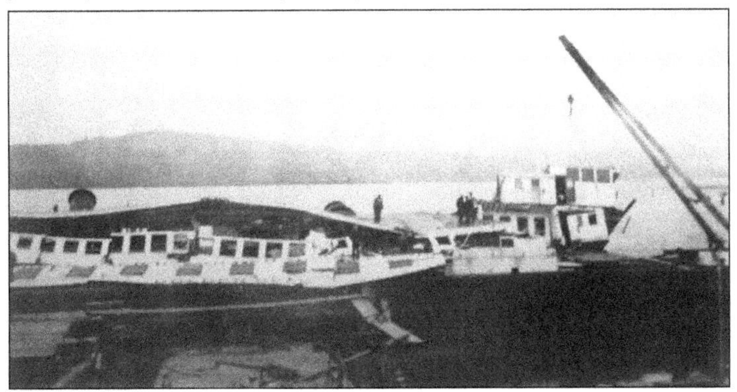

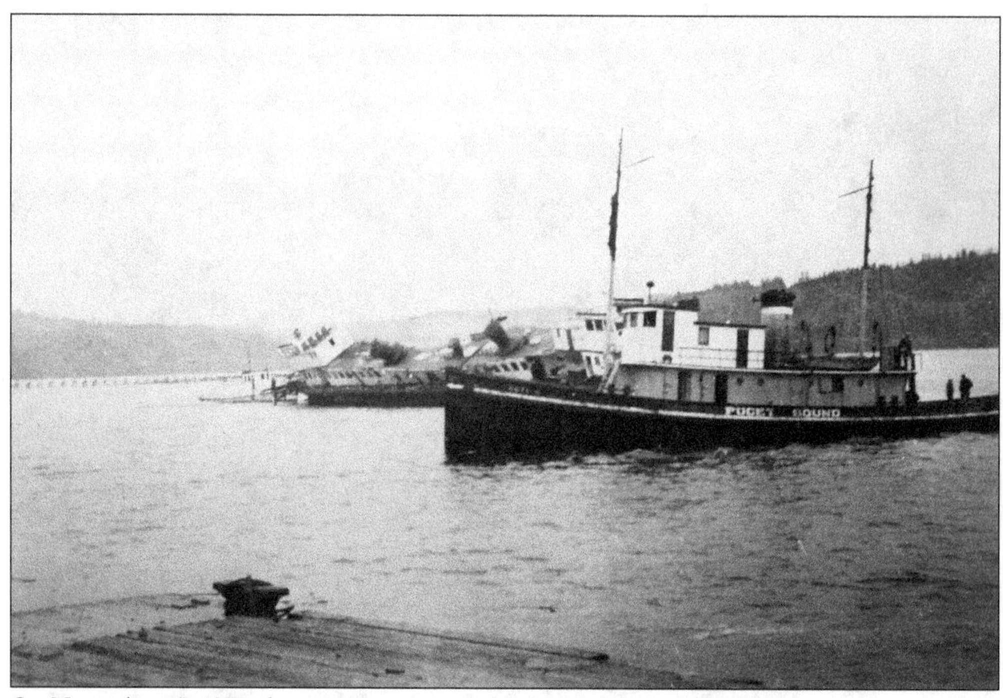

On November 17, 1937, the tug *Active* towed the disabled ferry *Golden Bear* into the Coos Bay. The damaged deckhouse and other wreckage were cleared away at Kruse & Banks Shipyard. The hull of the ferry was later towed to Puget Sound, where the machinery was removed, and it was converted into a cement barge. Eventually, the hull of the *Golden Bear* was incorporated into a breakwater in British Columbia. In the photograph above, a boat (bearing the name of the ferry's original destination) passes the wrecked *Golden Bear* at dock. In the image below, two men stand among the wreckage after the deckhouse was removed from the disabled ferry. (Above, CHM 009-16.919c; below, CHM 007-25.246.)

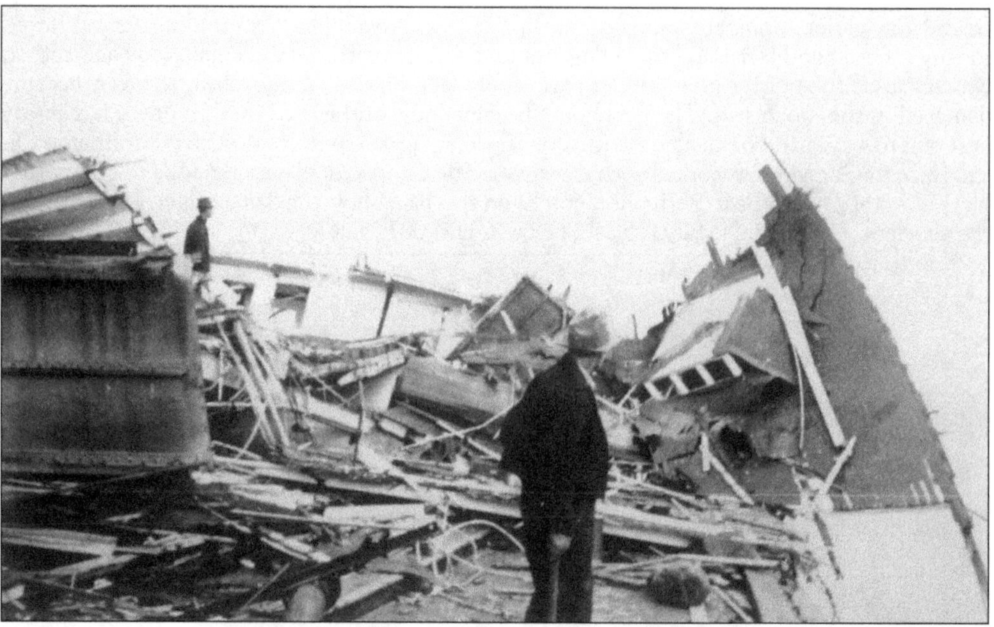

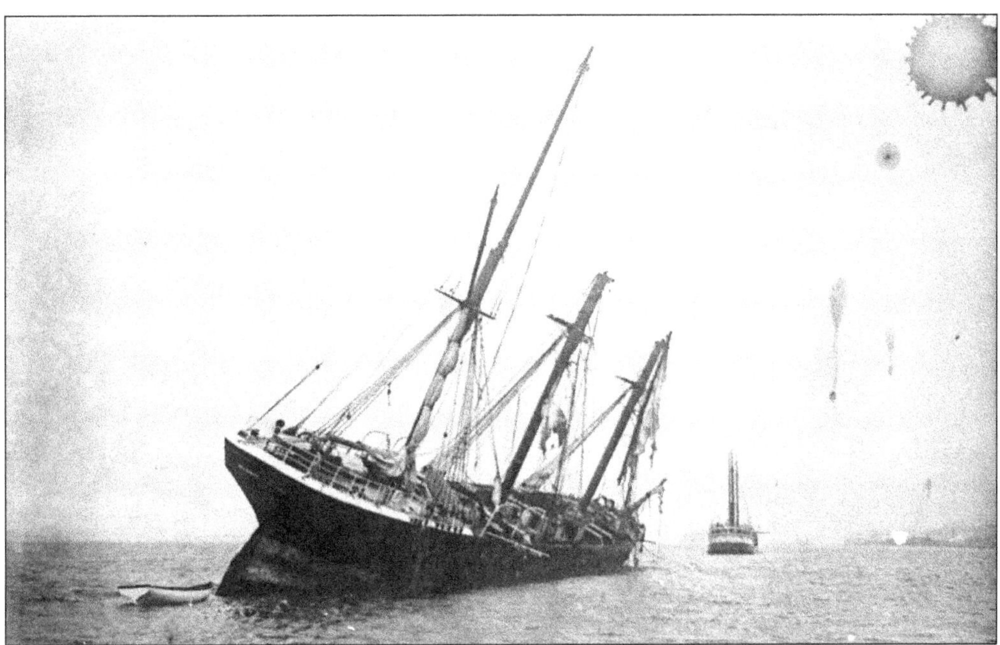

The iron-hulled *Melanope* was built in Liverpool in 1876. On December 6, 1906, the British sailing vessel's ballast shifted, forcing the ship "on beam ends." The maritime term refers to a vessel listing (leaning) 45 degrees or more. The crew, including Capt. N.K. Wills and his family, was forced to climb into the rigging to avoid being swept overboard. The following morning, they succeeded in lowering a lifeboat over the side of the ship. A passing vessel picked up the survivors, but the hull of the *Melanope* continued to drift without sinking. Several days later, the steamer *Northland* found it. After securing a towline, the crew towed the wreck to Astoria, where they collected a salvage fee for their efforts. The ship was pumped out, sold, and converted into a barge. (Above, CHM 009-16.9491; below, CHM 009-16.7395.)

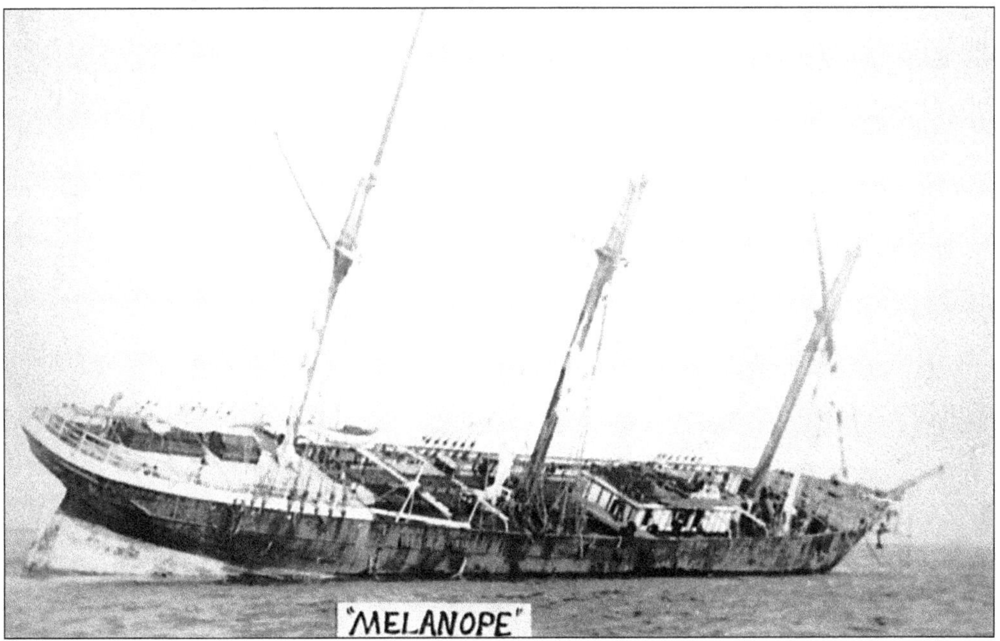

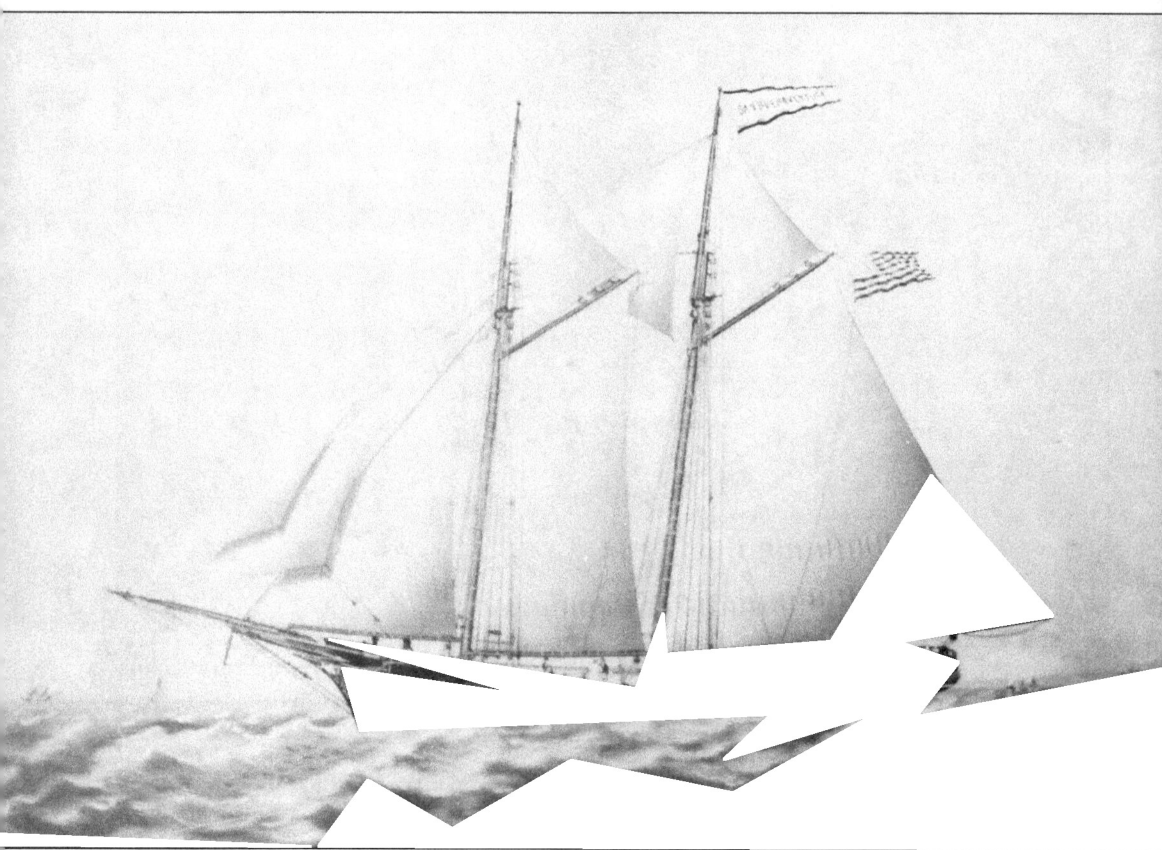

H.D. Bendisen built the two-masted schooner *San Buenaventura* at Fairhaven, California, in 1876. The 180-gross-ton vessel was 107 feet long with a 30-foot beam and an 8-foot depth. Despite the name, which loosely translated means "good fortune" or "good adventure," the *San Buenaventura* ran into trouble on at least four different occasions during its 34 years of service. The first incident occurred on April 25, 1903. The ship grounded near the Coos Bay jetty and was in danger of being broken up in the rough surf. Fortunately, the lifesaving crew succeeded in refloating the ship using a kedge anchor. A tugboat then towed the disabled ship into port. The schooner sustained a damaged keel and lost some of its rigging. The second incident occurred on February 15, 1906. The hawser parted while the tug *Triumph* was towing the *San Buenaventura* out of the Coquille River. The schooner drifted into the breakers near the north spit. The ship was again refloated. (CHM 009-16.1257.)

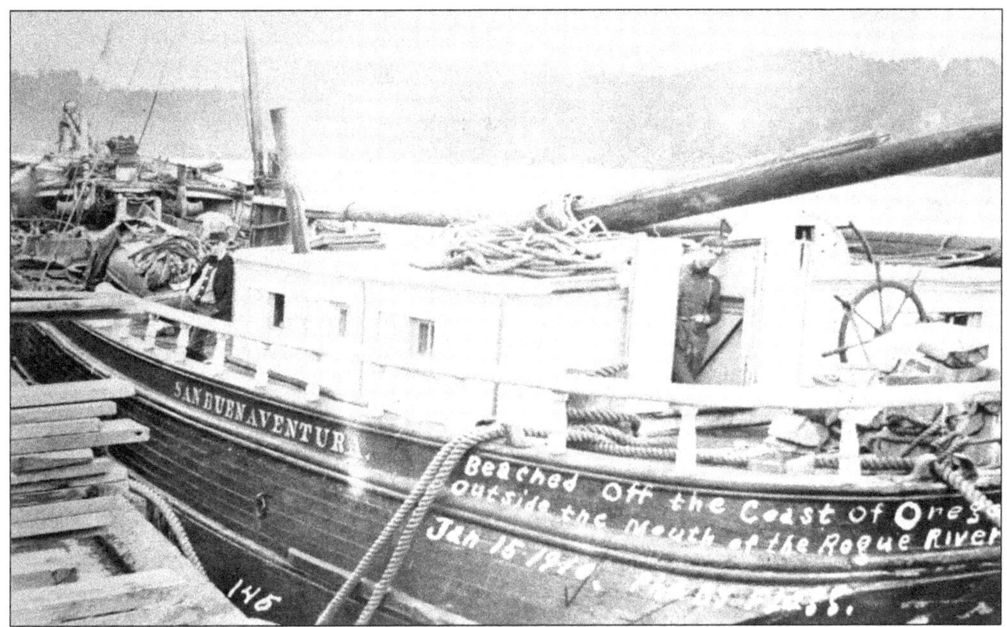

On December 21, 1908, the *San Buenaventura* encountered a gale off of Cape Blanco while being towed from San Francisco to the Coquille River. The strong winds stripped the schooner of its masts. The tug *Columbia* towed the damaged ship to the Coos Bay, where it was repaired at Kruse & Banks Shipyard. This photograph shows the damaged *San Buenaventura* at dock. (CHM 009-16.417.)

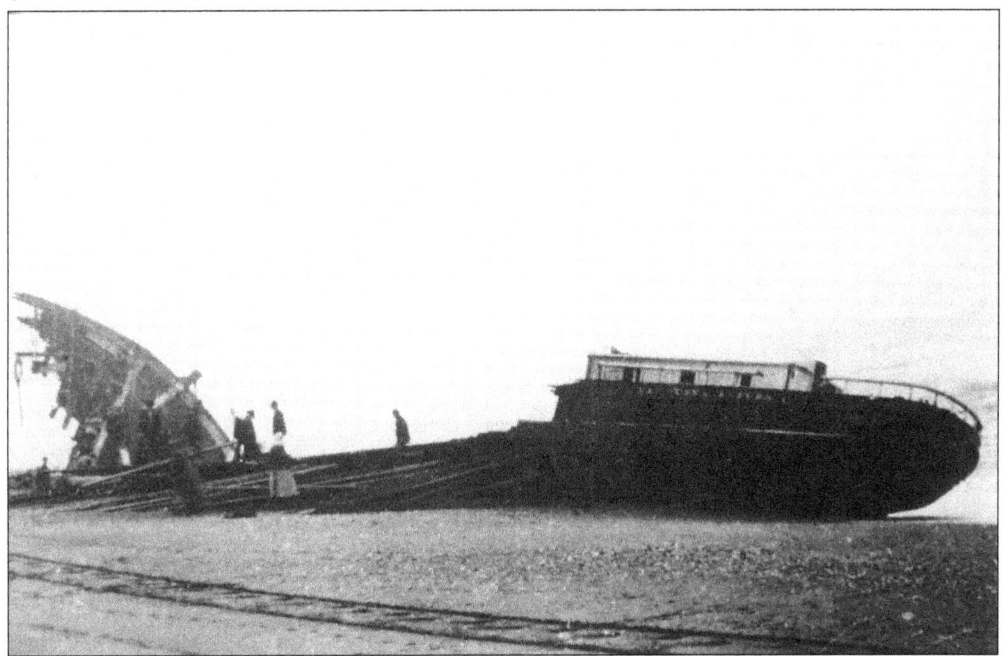

The *San Buenaventura* ran into trouble for the final time on January 13, 1910. The schooner became waterlogged during a storm. The crew of the steam schooner *Fairhaven* rescued the crew. The abandoned ship drifted ashore south of the Rogue River. In this photograph, the partially broken hull is on the beach. Several people can be seen exploring the wreckage. (CHM 007-25.533.)

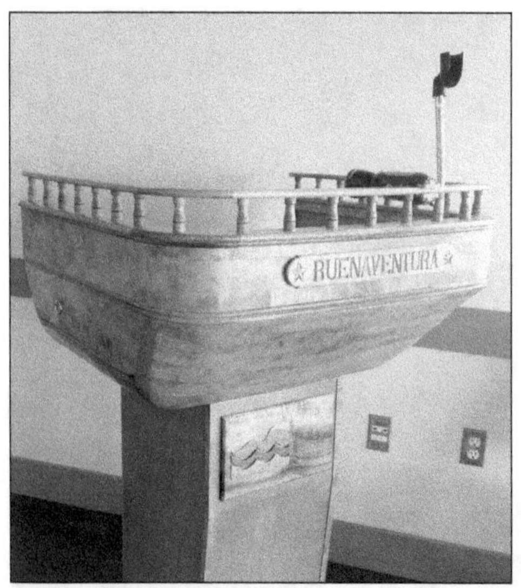

This podium, which belongs to the Coos History Museum in Coos Bay, has been carved to look like the stern of a wooden ship. The nameplate reads "Buenaventura." Inmates at the Shutter Creek Correctional Institution in Hauser carved the podium. The minimum-security prison is located in a former Air National Guard radar station. It provides the inmates with programs that help them earn their GED, gain life and work skills, and learn anger management. Woodworking is one of the classes they offer, and the inmates offered to make the podium. They were inspired by historical photographs of ships that operated on the West Coast, including the *San Buenaventura*. The project allowed them to work on job skills while giving something back to the community. (Both, author's collection.)

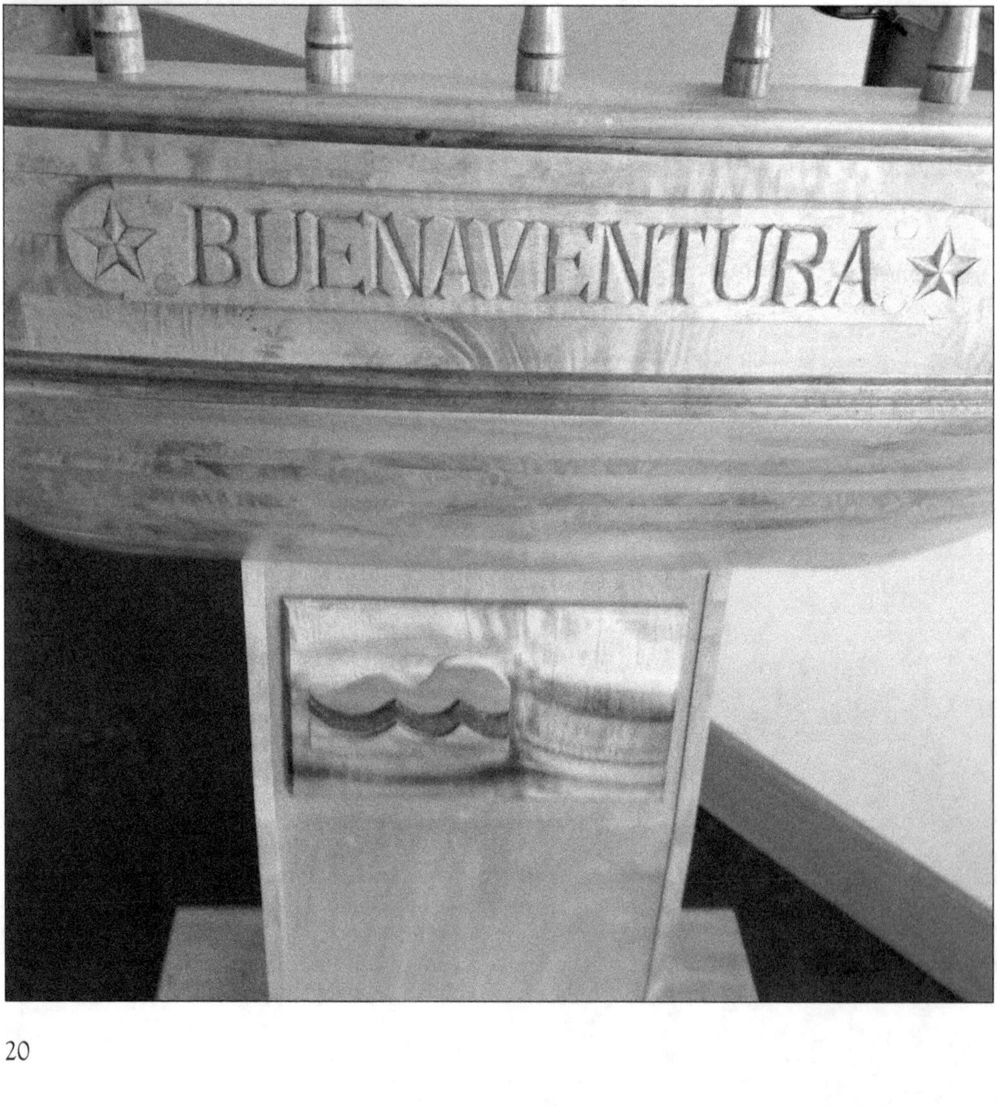

The steam schooner *Bertie M. Hanlon* was built by E. Heuckendorff at Marshfield (now Coos Bay), Oregon. The ship was originally named *Marshfield*. The 146-foot wooden-hulled vessel was launched on October 26, 1901. It was 388 gross tons and measured 148 feet long by 33 feet wide with an 11-foot depth. The ship, which worked in the coastal lumber trade, usually employed a 12-person crew. It had a capacity of 400,000 board feet of lumber. The name was changed in 1924. During Prohibition, the Anza Trading Company ran the ship to San Francisco as a rum carrier. In 1932, the ship was seized by the US Marshals Service, who later sold it. (Above, CHM 009-16.221B; below, CHM 992-8-2627.)

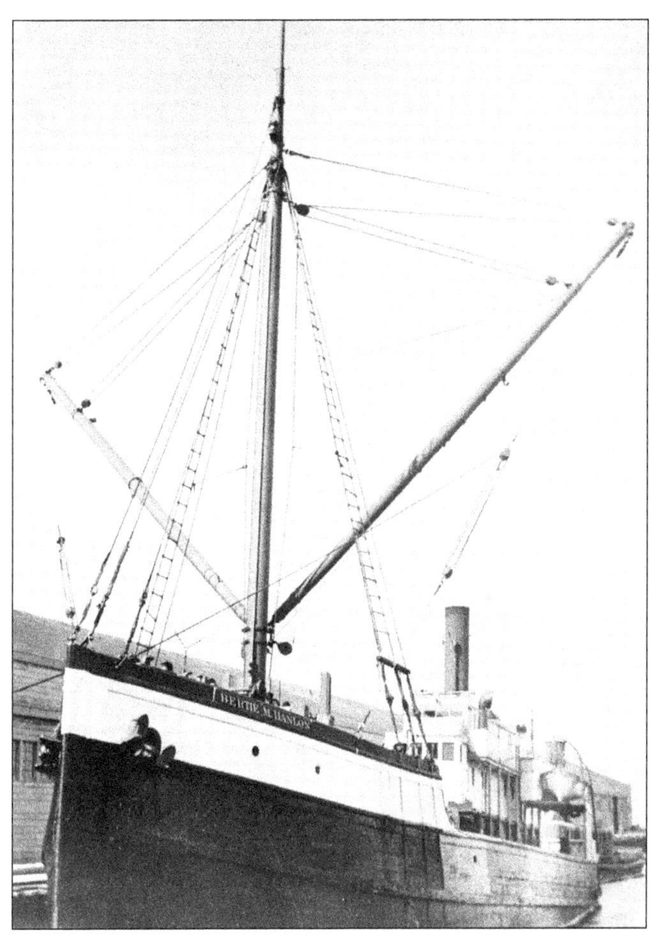

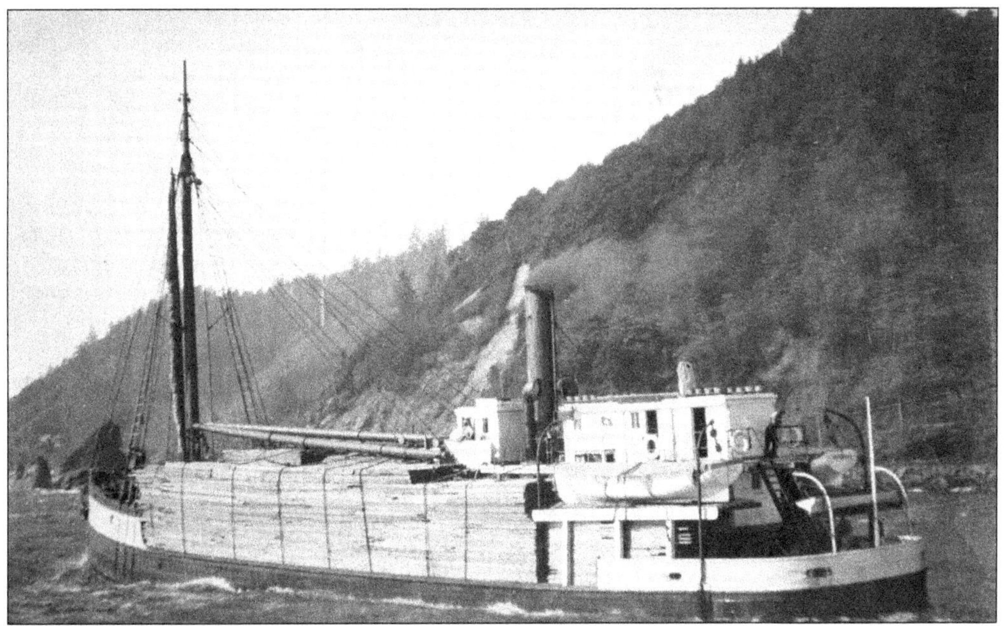

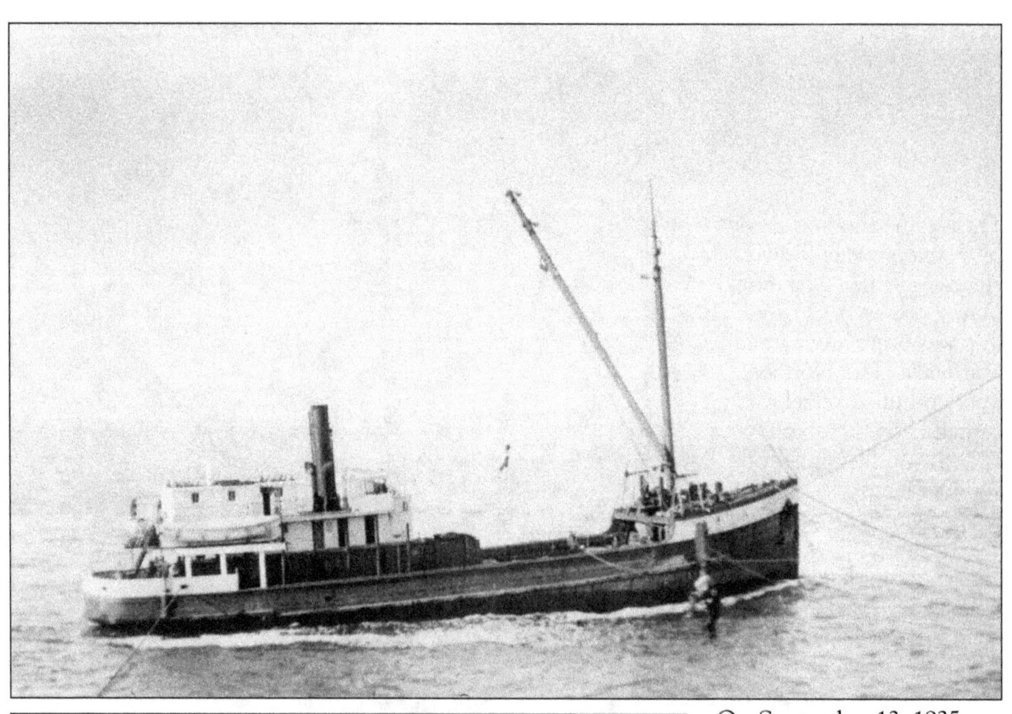

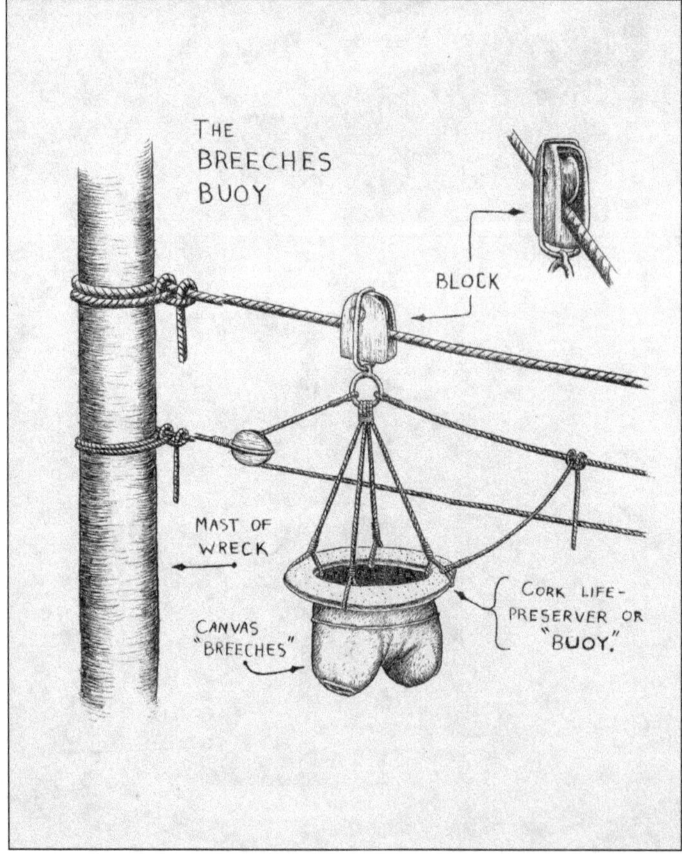

On September 13, 1935, the *Bertie M. Hanlon* ran into strong winds and began leaking near Cape Blanco. The crew was successfully evacuated from the disabled vessel. The ship was later repaired and returned to service. Here, a man is being transported off of the ship using a breeches buoy device. (CHM 009-16.221C.)

The breeches buoy device consisted of a pair of short-legged canvas breeches attached to a buoy. It was suspended from a line stretched from ship to shore (or ship to ship, if the accident occurred at sea). It worked like a zip line and provided a relatively safe rescue method when a rough surf or debris made it difficult to approach a ship. (Bandon Historical Society 28063.)

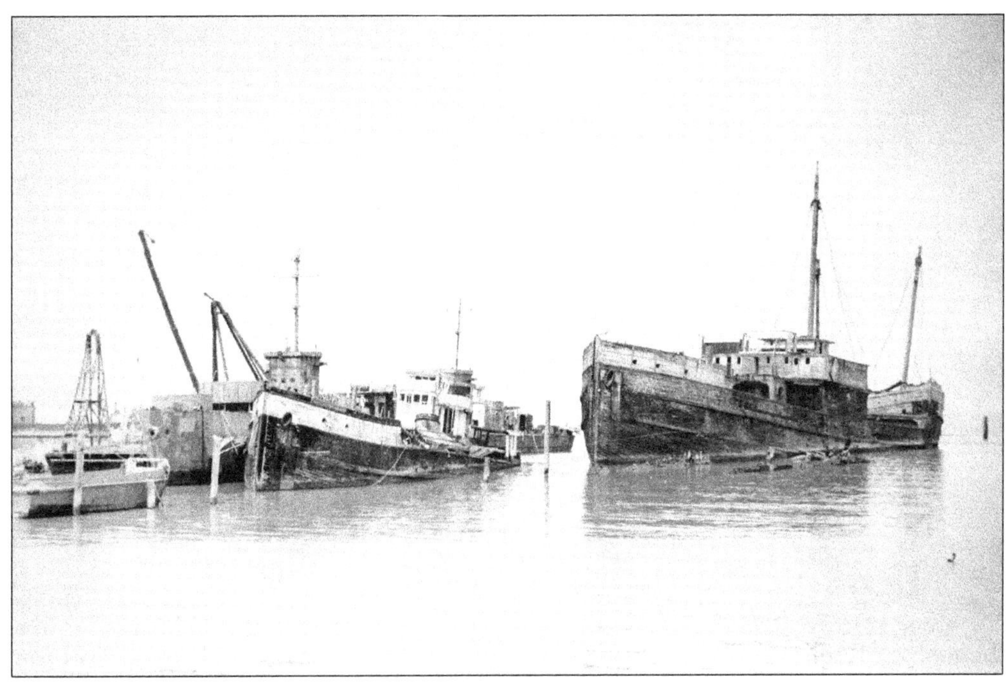

After the accident at Cape Blanco in September 1935, the *Bertie M. Hanlon* was successfully refloated, repaired, and put back in service. The *Bertie M. Hanlon* was abandoned around 1940. Here it is shown laid up with several other steam schooners that have outlived their purpose. Eventually, the old ship was towed to San Pablo, California, and sunk. It was incorporated into a yacht harbor breakwater. (Above, CHM 009-16.221a; below, CHM 009-16.221.)

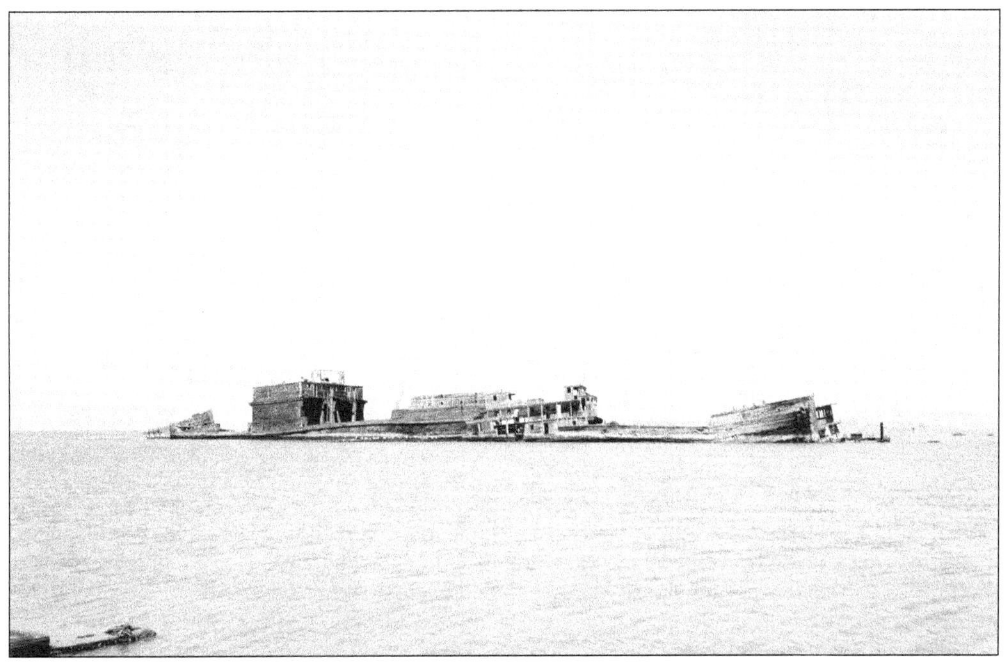

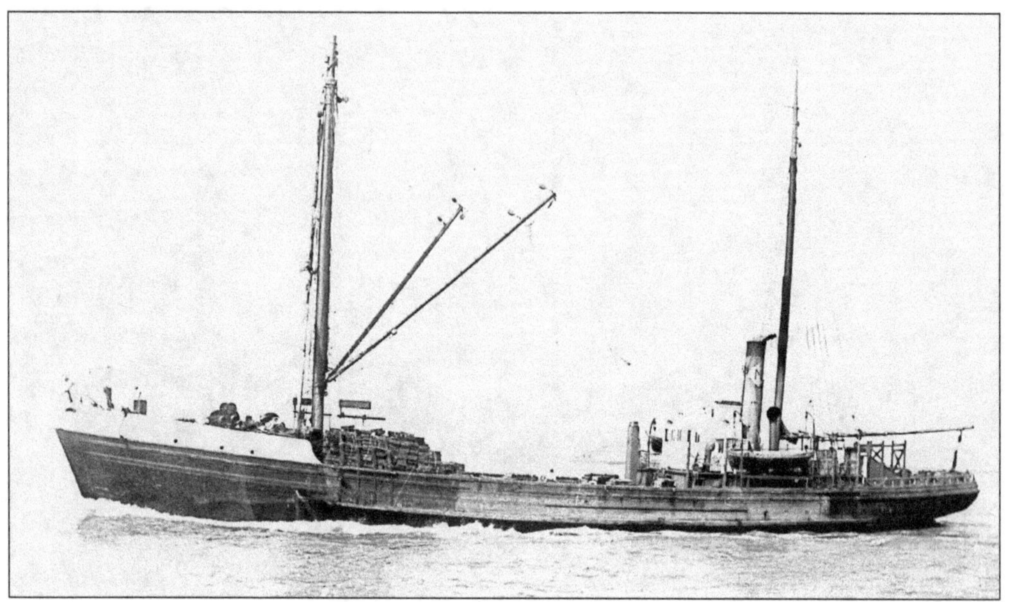

The wooden steam schooner *Lakme* was built by Thomas Peterson at Port Madison in the Washington Territory in 1888. The ship was built by T.A. Peterson for G.H. Hinsdale of San Francisco. The vessel was 529 gross tons and 177 feet in length with a 39-foot beam and a 12-foot depth. It was equipped with a 366-indicated horsepower (IHP) engine. (CHM 009-16.1936.)

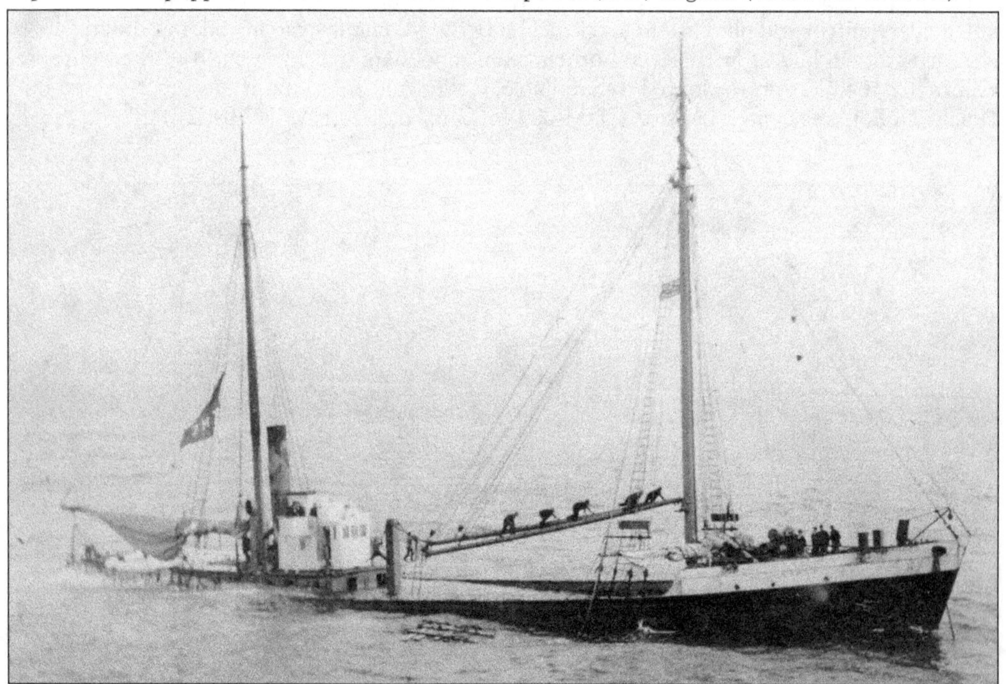

On January 15, 1911, the *Lakme* departed Coos Bay under the command of Capt. William Malmgren. It encountered a storm off Cape Blanco. Several waves washed over the decks and extinguished the fires in the boilers. The helpless vessel came close to striking Fox Rock. Fortunately, the storm subsided the next day. Above, the crew is moving toward the front of the ship, which is still above the waterline. (CHM 007-25.530.)

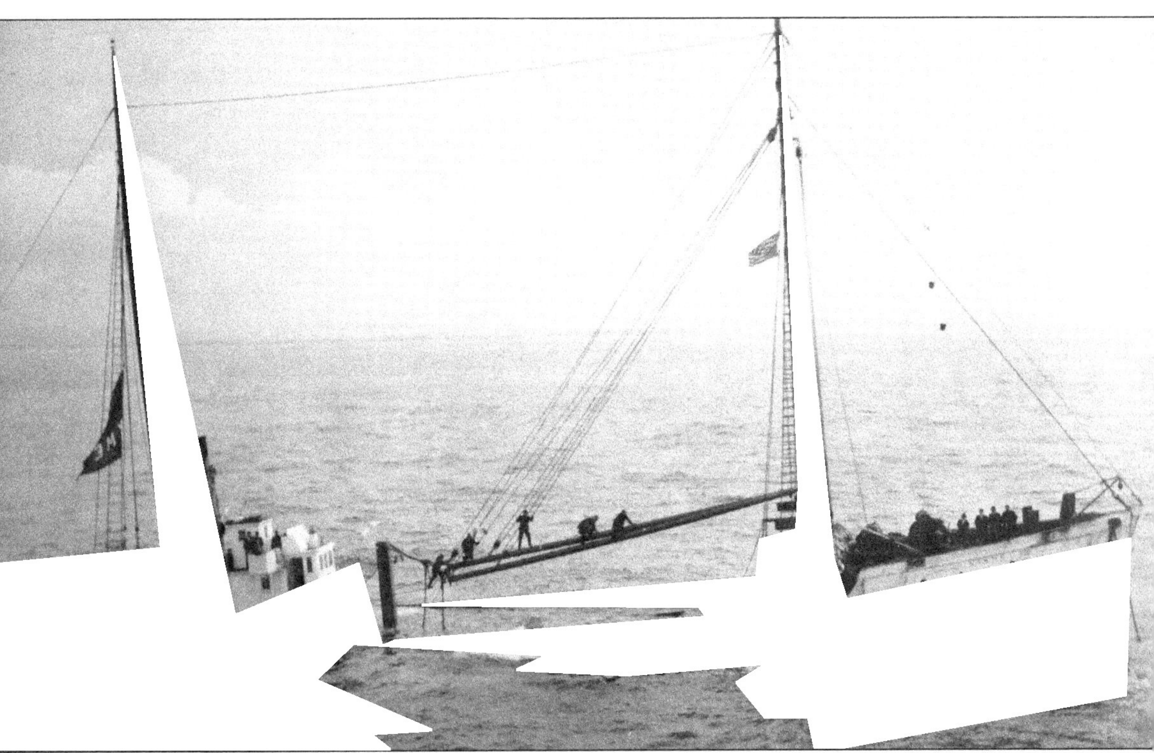

During a severe storm in January 1911, the *Lakme* lost her deck load of lumber, and the waves washed away the ship's lifeboats. The loose lumber became a hazard as the waves continued to smash it against the ship. The crew was forced to spend the night clinging to the forecastle, which was the only portion of the ship out of the reach of the waves. They had some food but no water. It was reported that the crew survived for 36 hours without drinkable water. The following day, the steamer *Watson* encountered the *Lakme*. The crew tried unsuccessfully for three hours to shoot a line to the disabled ship. Later that day, the *Nann Smith* found the waterlogged steam schooner *Lakme* drifting and powerless off Cape Blanco. The American flag has been hung upside down as a signal of distress to other ships. (CHM 992-8-2804a.)

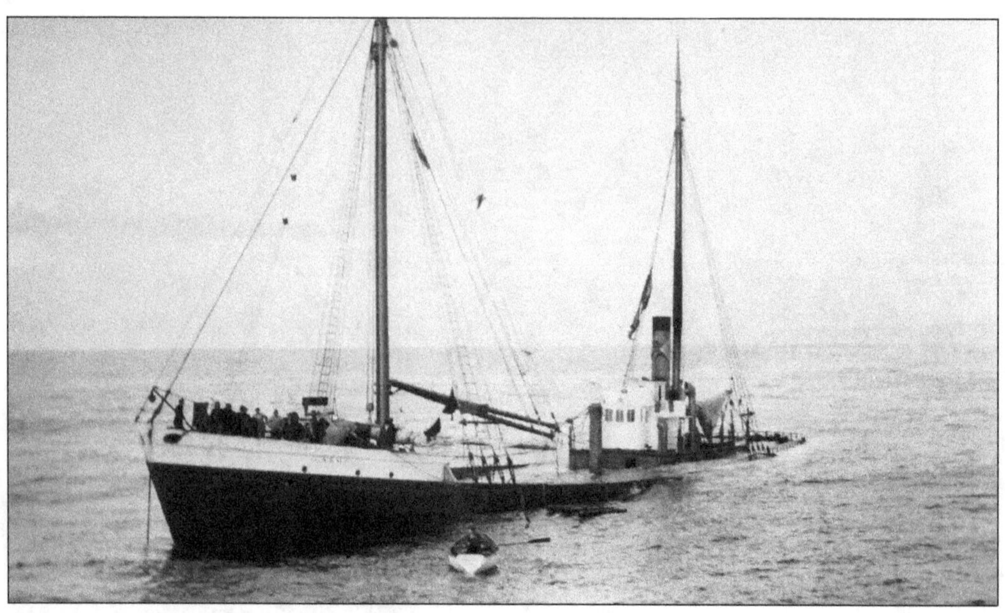

The photograph above depicts a man in a lifeboat rowing toward the disabled ship whose crew can be seen crowded in the bow. Fortunately, by the time the *Nann Smith* arrived, the seas were relatively calm. They were able to rescue the crew from the waterlogged vessel using one of the *Nann Smith*'s lifeboats. In the photograph below, the *Lakme* crew is posed on the *Nann Smith*'s deck after their rescue. The entire crew was rescued without incident. They also succeeded in securing a line to the disabled ship. On January 19, 1911, the *Lakme* was taken in tow for San Francisco. The ship was pumped out, repaired, and returned to service. The ship continued to operate on the West Coast until it was scrapped in 1927. (Above, CHM 992-8-2804b; below, CHM 009-16.1173B.)

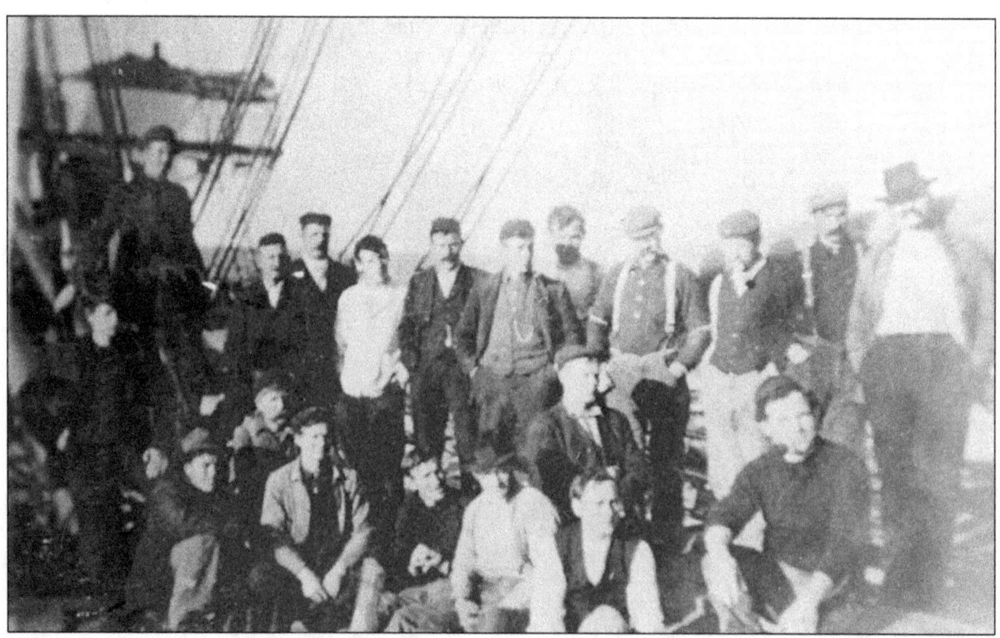

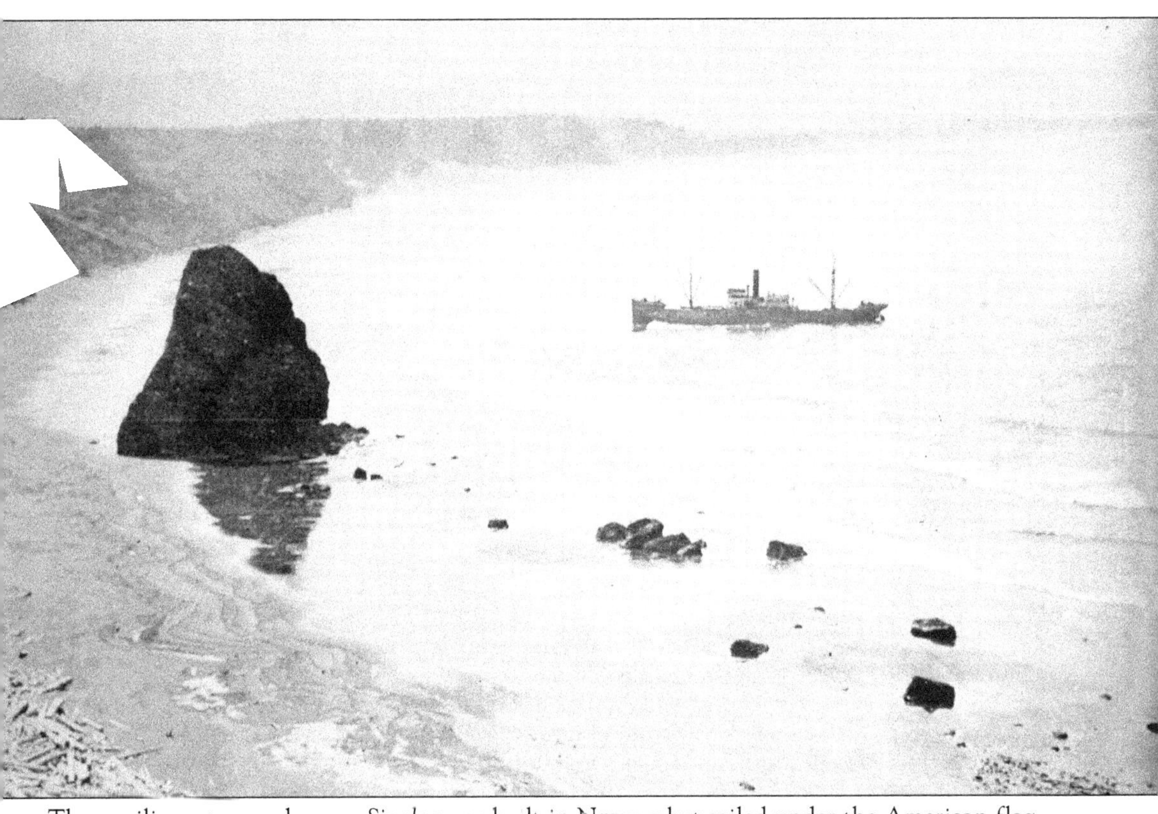

The auxiliary steam schooner *Sinaloa* was built in Norway but sailed under the American flag. On June 15, 1917, the 1,648-ton vessel encountered heavy fog while traveling near Cape Blanco. The ship was under the command of Capt. James Sannaes and on the San Francisco to Astoria leg of its trip, which began in Chile. The *Sinaloa* struck a reef in the vicinity of Blacklock Point, just north of Cape Blanco, and ran aground. Although the crew was saved, the ship and most of its cargo was lost. This photograph shows a bird's-eye view of the wreck off the coast in the surf. (CHM 009-16.392.)

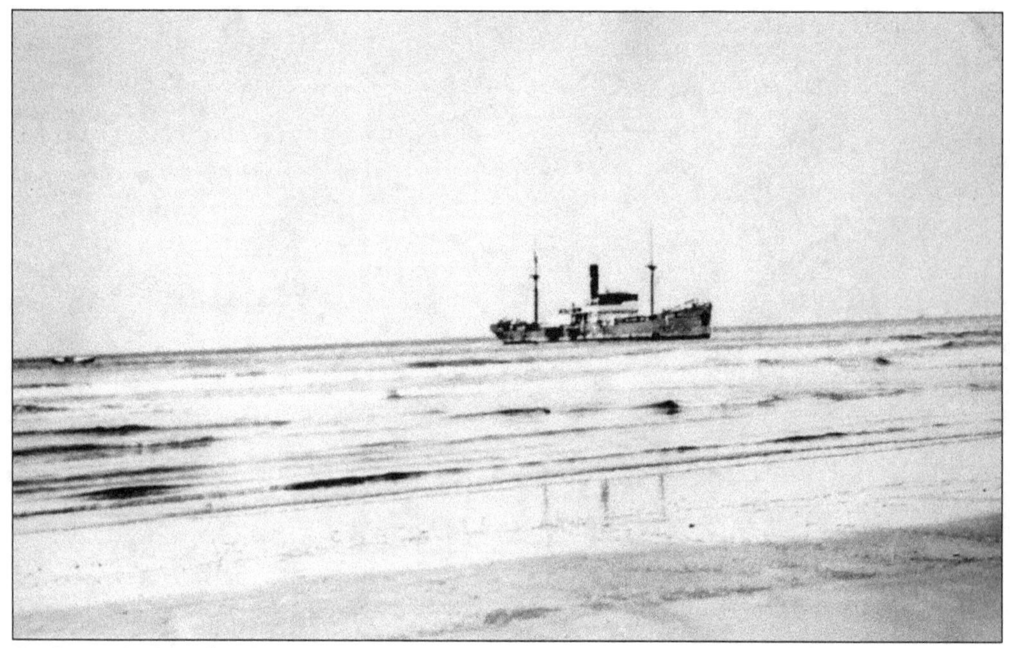

On June 15, 1917, the Norwegian steamer *Sinaloa* was stranded near Cape Blanco in a thick fog. The ship was five miles off course when it struck a reef and ran aground. The *Sinaloa* was on its way to Astoria with a cargo of 2,500 tons of nitrate for the Dupont Powder Company. The crew was safely rescued from the disabled ship. On July 19th, the tug *Oneonta* succeeded in refloating the *Sinaloa*. It was towed to Port Orford, where it was temporarily repaired. The ship sustained an eight-foot hole in its aft hold. The *Oneonta* later towed the *Sinaloa* to the Columbia River. (Above, CHM 009-16.842; below, Alan Mitchell.)

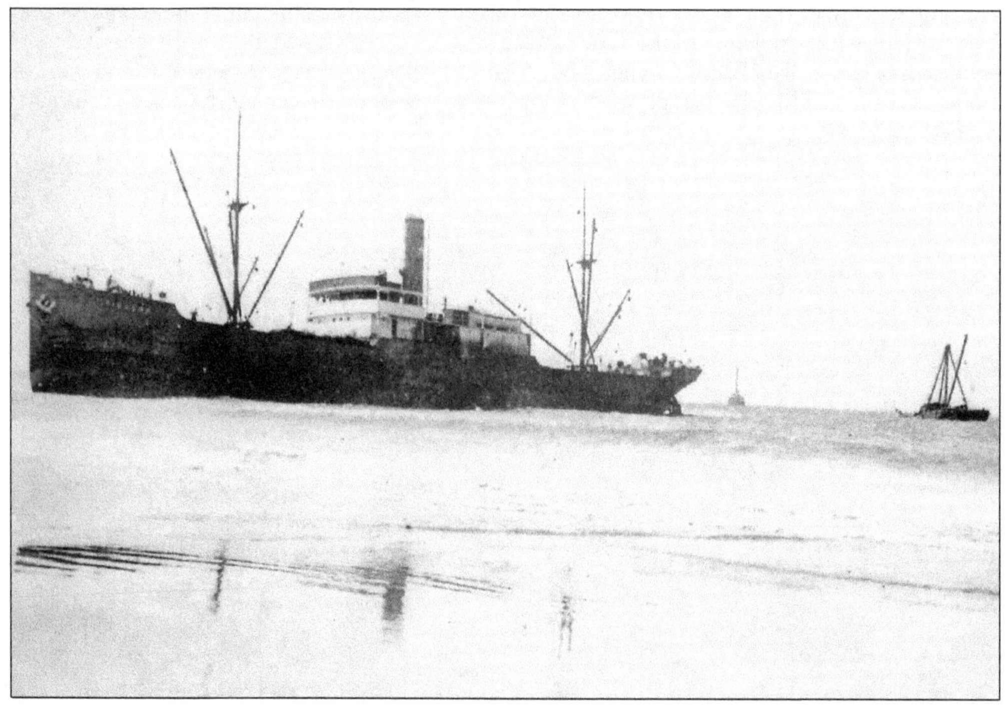

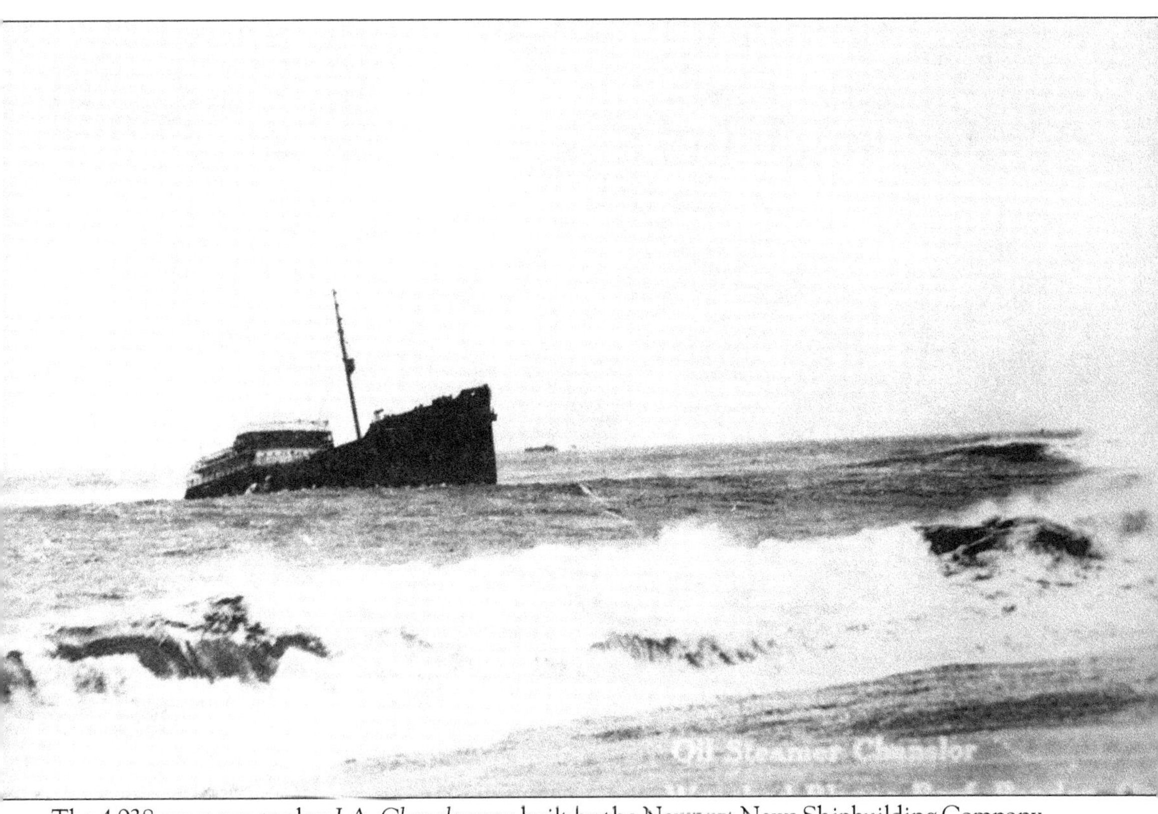

The 4,938-gross-ton tanker *J.A. Chanslor* was built by the Newport News Shipbuilding Company in Virginia in 1910. The steel-hulled ship was 378 feet long with a 52-foot breadth and 29-foot depth. On December 19, 1919, it struck a rock near Cape Blanco in a thick fog. The ship quickly broke into two pieces, causing the stern to sink. The accident happened so quickly that most of the crew lost their lives. They did not have enough time to escape the sinking portion of the ship. The 13 crewmen in the fore-section of the ship managed to escape in a lifeboat. Two of them died of exposure while the boat drifted north for a day and a half. Seven crewmen drowned when the group attempted to land the lifeboat near Whiskey Run (near Bandon). Out of the entire crew, only three survived the wreck. The fore-section of the *J.A. Chanslor* drifted ashore near the Sixes River. The Associated Oil Company owned the ship at the time of its loss. (CHM 009-16.857.)

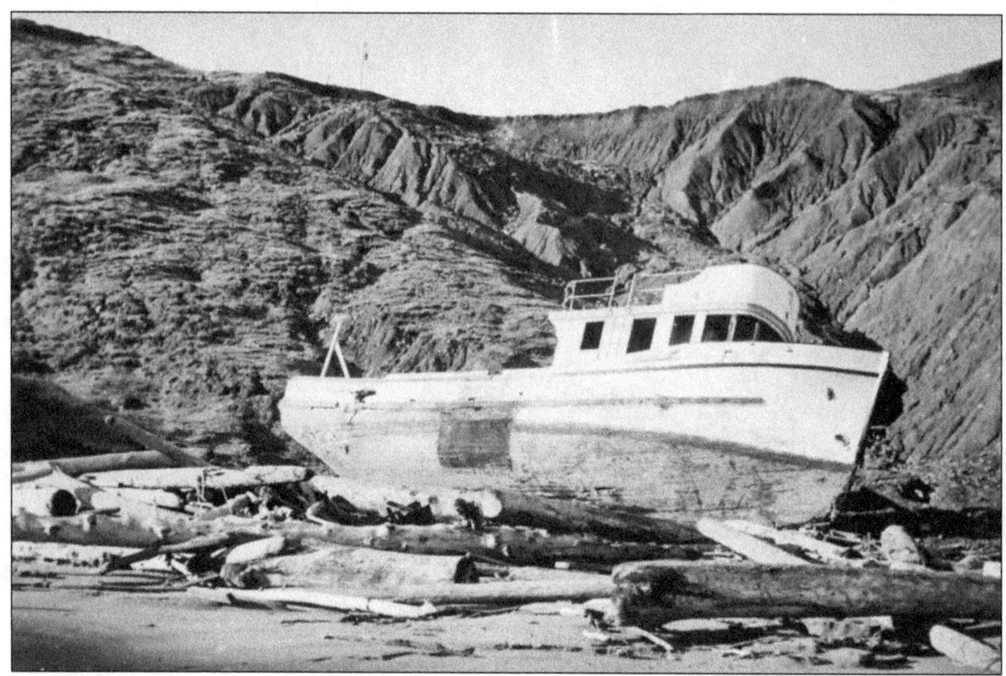

On February 15, 1956, the small fishing vessel (F/V) *Suzanne* ran into trouble while traveling in southern Oregon. The boat stranded on the beach south of Cape Blanco. Once it was discovered that the *Suzanne* was too badly damaged to be repaired, it was stripped of everything valuable, and the hull was abandoned to the elements. (Above, CHM 009-16.1223; below, Bandon Historical Society 107017.)

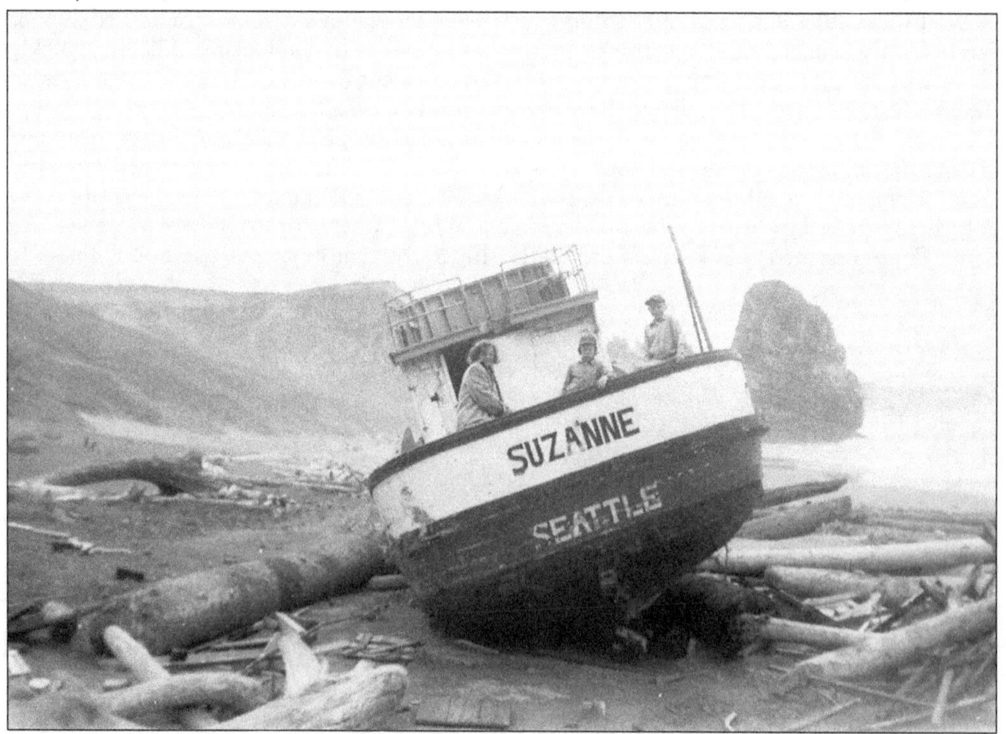

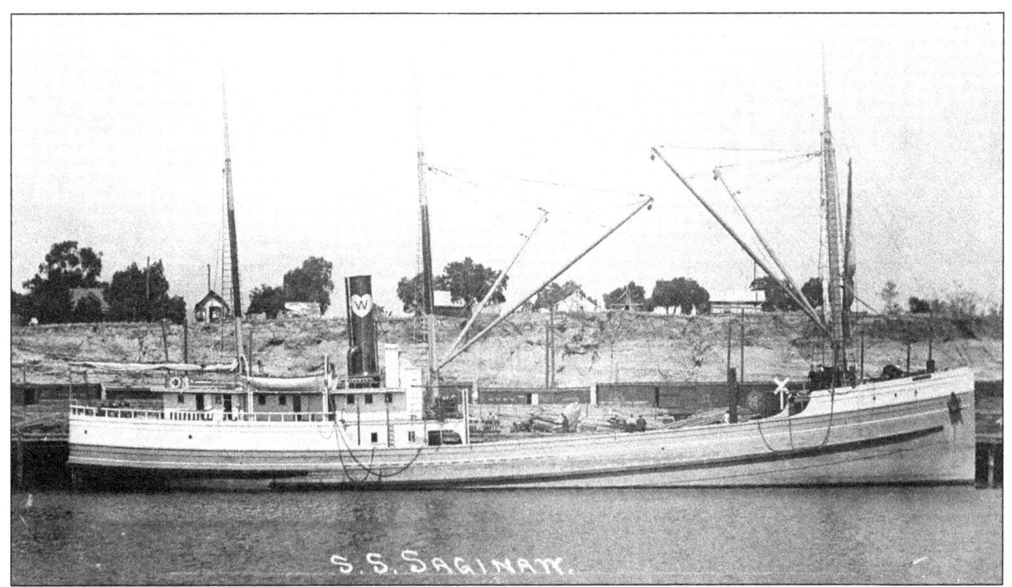

The steam stem-winder schooner *Saginaw* was built by the Mathew's Shipyard at Hoquiam, Washington in 1907. The 886-gross-ton vessel was 191 feet long with a 39-foot beam and a 14-foot depth. It had an 800,000-board-foot lumber capacity and carried a 26-person crew. (CHM 009-16.2508.)

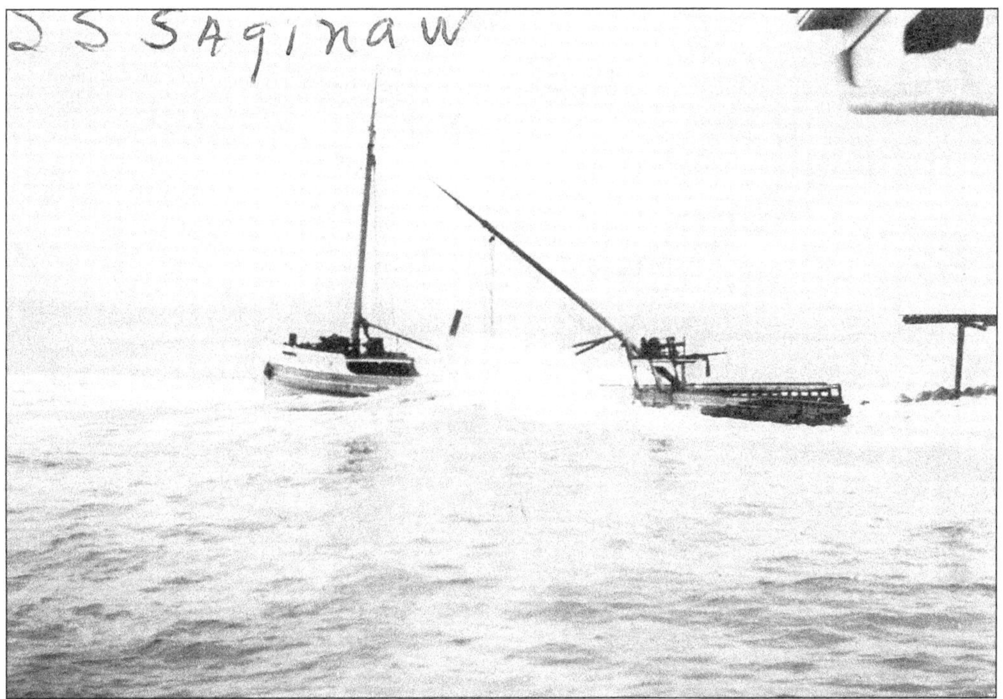

The *Saginaw* had trouble on two occasions in Curry County. On November 9, 1907, the steamer *Quinault*, commanded by Capt. J.L. Christensen, was towing the newly constructed *Saginaw* to San Francisco to have its engine installed. The ships encountered fog near Cape Blanco. Due to a miscommunication, the *Quinault* reversed and collided with the *Saginaw*, causing minor damage. This photograph is from a later incident. (CHM 982-190.77.)

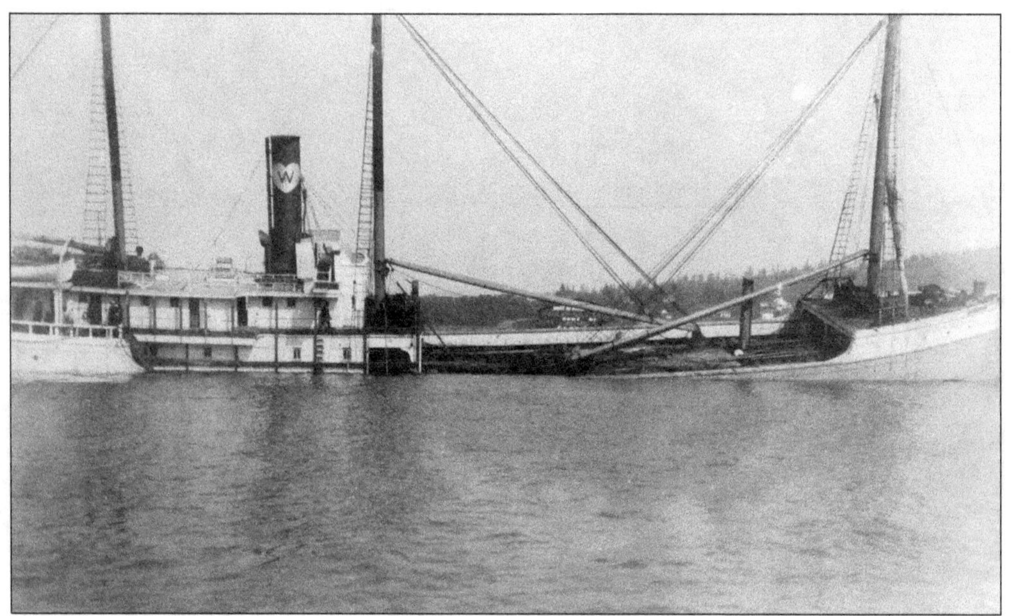

On August 11, 1911, the steam schooner *Saginaw* encountered a thick fog and strayed too close to Blanco Reef, where it struck a rock and began leaking. The ship, which was under the command of Captain Koffold, was transporting a cargo of general merchandise, cement, and 300 tons of asphalt on deck. (CHM 010-2.44.)

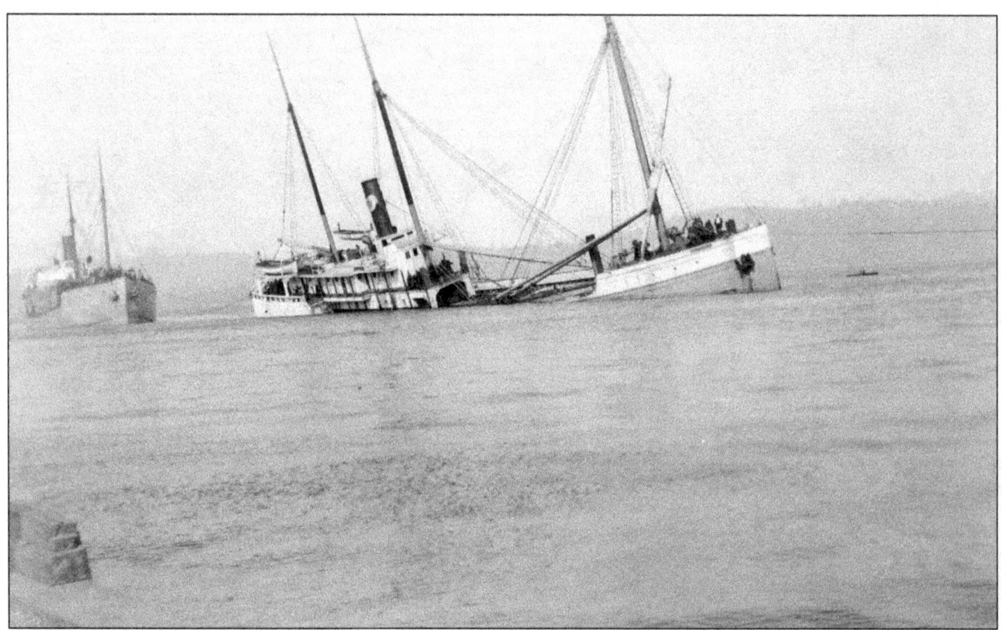

The steam schooner *Redondo* came to the *Saginaw*'s aid and succeeded in towing it as far as the entrance to the Coos Bay. The waterlogged *Saginaw* was riding too low in the water to cross the bar. The crew was forced to throw the deck load overboard to lighten the ship before it could cross. The tugboat *Gleaner* assisted the *Redondo* in towing the steamer *Saginaw* into the Coos Bay. (CHM 010-2.45.)

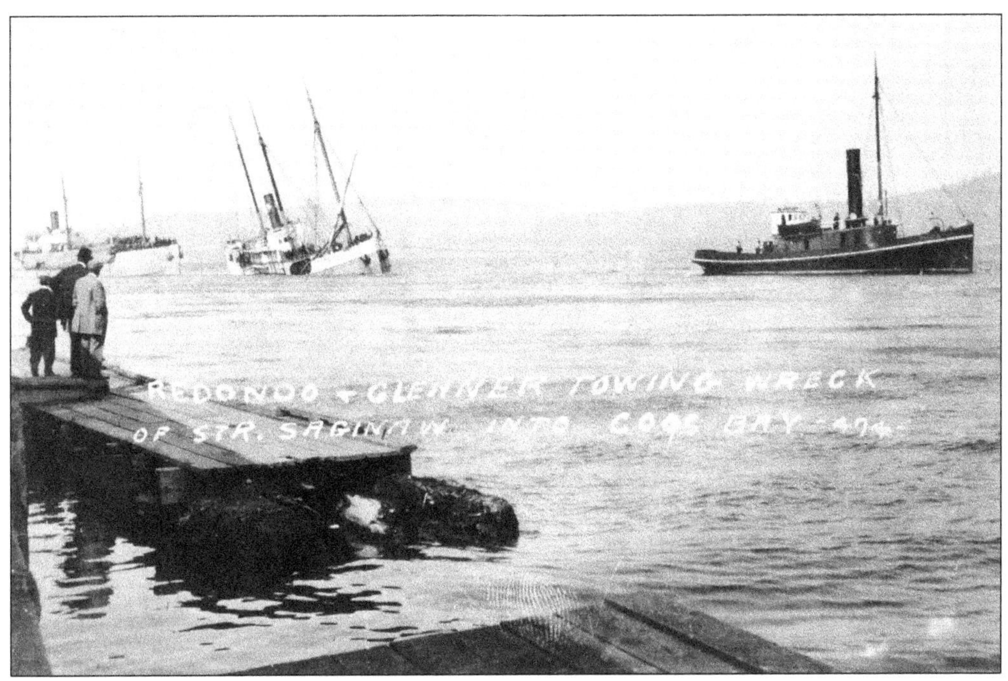

After the waterlogged steamer *Saginaw* had been towed into the Coos Bay, the wooden hulled vessel was intentionally beached across the bay from Marshfield (now the city of Coos Bay). The water was pumped out by the Marshfield Fire Department's steam fire engine. The *Saginaw* was patched and transported to Portland for permanent repairs. None of the ship's crew of 27 were injured during the incident. (Above, CHM 007-25.167; below, CHM 007-25.46.)

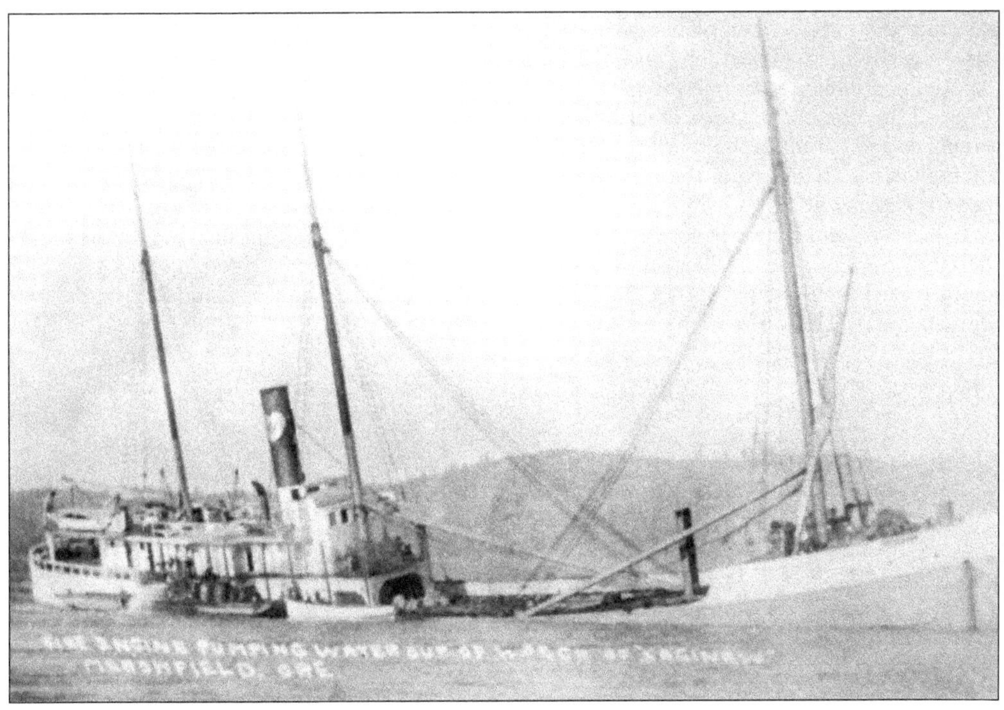

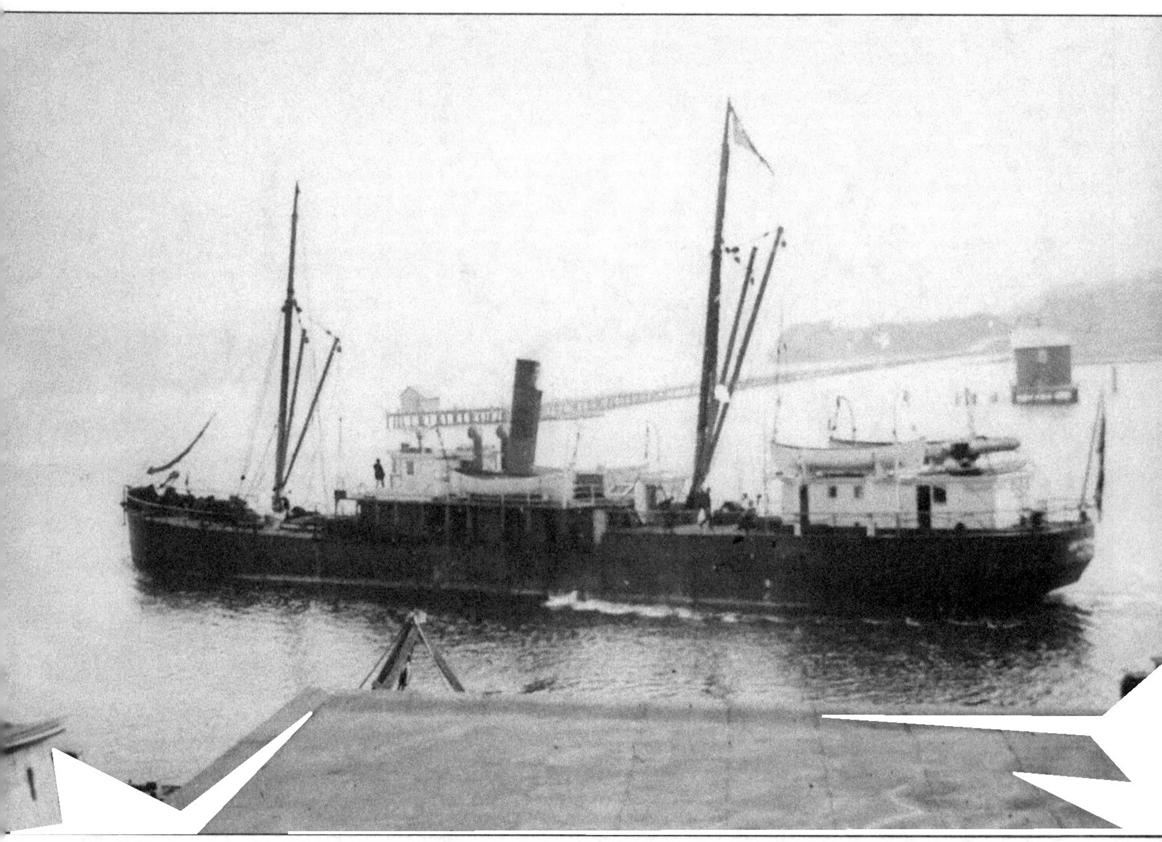

The steamer *South Portland* was built in England by Dobson & Charles in 1883 as the *Dawn*. It was later sold to American owners and renamed the *Caroline Miller* then the *South Portland*. It was 909 gross tons, 180 feet long with a 29-foot beam and a 19-foot depth. On October 18, 1903, the *South Portland* departed Astoria with a cargo of grain. The following day, the steel hulled vessel struck Blanco Reef in a thick fog and began taking on water. After the collision, there was chaos and confusion onboard the ship. Capt. J.B. McIntyre left in the first lifeboat without leaving anyone in charge of the evacuation. With the engine still running, the *South Portland* traveled another 40 miles before sinking. Of the 39 passengers and crew on board, 18 lost their lives. Captain McIntyre was found criminally negligent for abandoning ship before "seeing to the safety of passengers and crew." The ship's name board drifted north to Cape Lookout and was displayed at the Boy Scouts of America's Camp Meriwether. The ship is shown here prior to the accident. (CHM 007-25.378.)

Two

Port Orford

Port Orford is one of the oldest incorporated towns in the state of Oregon. It is home to "the most unique fishing dock in Oregon" (according to their webpage). Port Orford is not a bar port. Ships do not have to cross the mouth of a river to get to the harbor. Instead, it is located right along the coastline. It is the only open water port on the Oregon coast. Historically, the location of the harbor provided some shelter from storms but only on one side. The other side is exposed to the sea, so ships at dock could get damaged during storms or by strong winds coming from that direction.

Although Port Orford was founded in 1856, the port district was not formally established until 1911. However, the harbor has been in use since the 1850s. Initially, their main export was lumber. They were known for their local Port Orford Cedar. In modern times, they no longer ship lumber. The port is mainly used for commercial and recreational fishing.

Not having a natural harbor was sometimes problematic for early settlers. Local leaders often had difficulty securing funding for port improvements. Over the years, they built numerous docks, breakwaters, and jetties. But these were always temporary. Inevitably, a strong storm would come along and wash away the harbor improvements. Eventually, they developed an unusual setup. They constructed a "high dock." Everyday, boats are lowered to and raised from the ocean using giant cranes capable of lifting up to 25,000 pounds. When not in use, they are stored on homemade trailers, or "dollies." In other words, the boats are dry-docked. Port Orford is one of only six dolly ports in the world.

According to Patrick Masterson, author of *Port Orford: A History*, there have been more than 30 major maritime mishaps near Port Orford; however, his list excluded small boats and local fishing vessels.

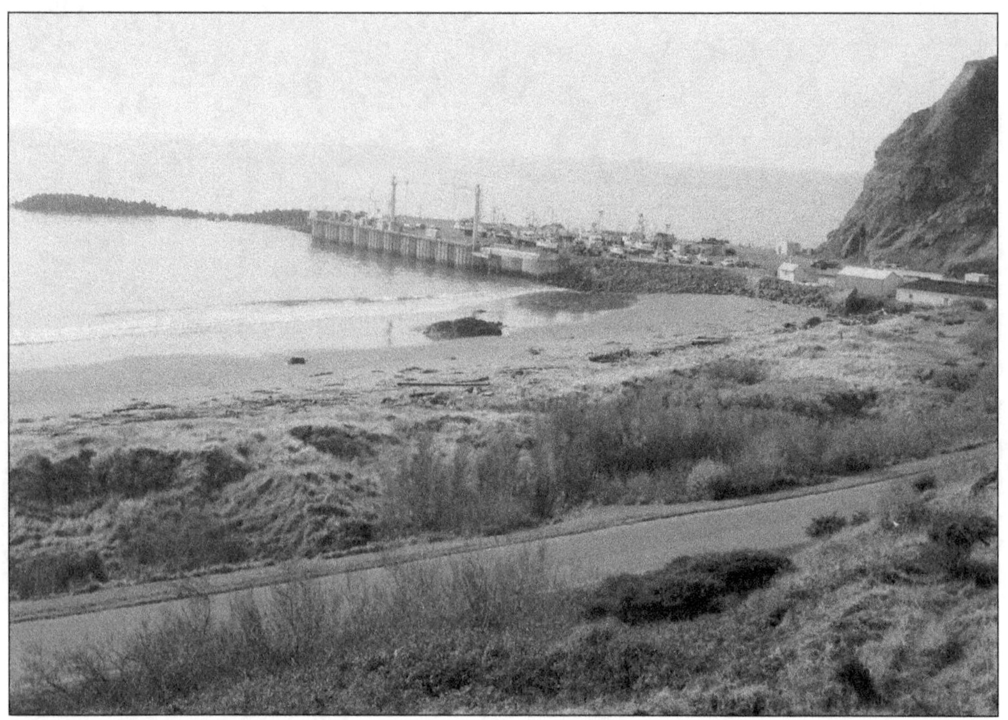

This photograph provides a wide view of the Port Orford dock, which is elevated high above the water. It is mostly used by small fishing boats. They are moved into and out of the water using one of two large cranes. Instead of traditional boat slips, they are moored on trailers (or dollies), which are used to transport the boats to their parking spots. (Author's collection.)

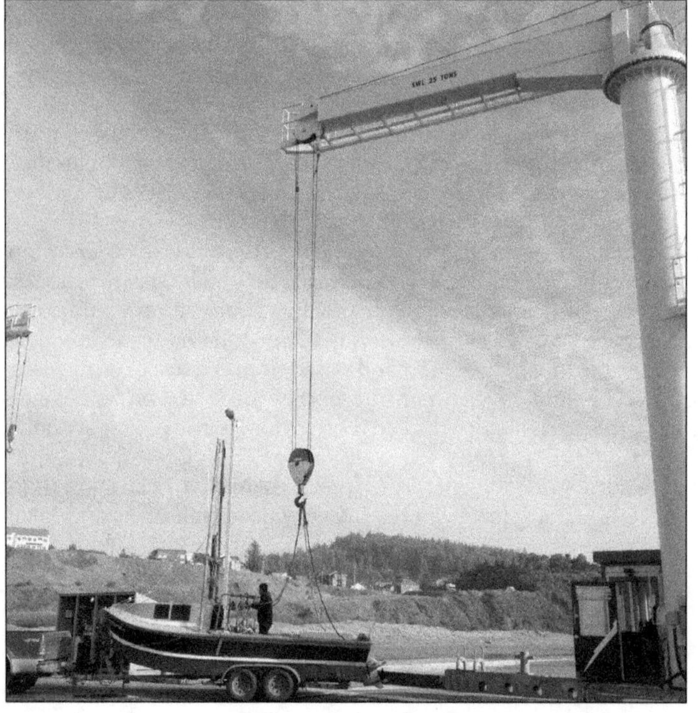

The next few photographs demonstrate how a ship is launched from the Port Orford dock. In the image here, a fisherman is preparing his boat. He begins by attaching ropes to the vessel. He will then attach the ropes to the large hook on the crane. (Author's collection.)

In the photograph at right, the crane has begun lifting the boat off of its trailer. Below, it has been moved over the side of the dock. At this point, the crane operator waited patiently while the fisherman moved his truck and trailer out of the way and then climbed on board the boat, which was then slowly lowered down to the level of the water. (Both, author's collection.)

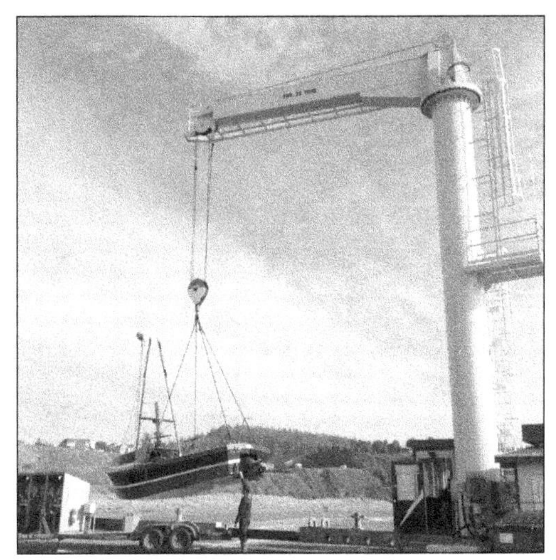

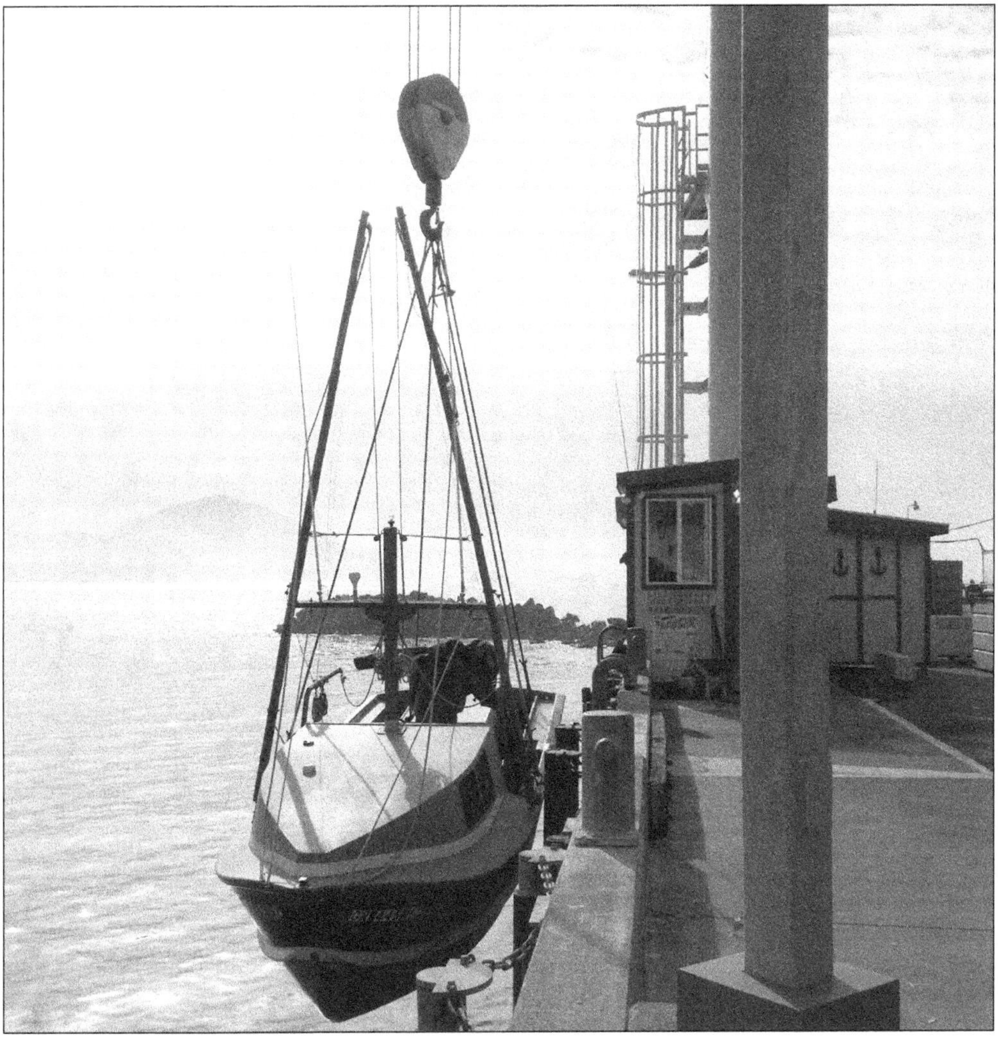

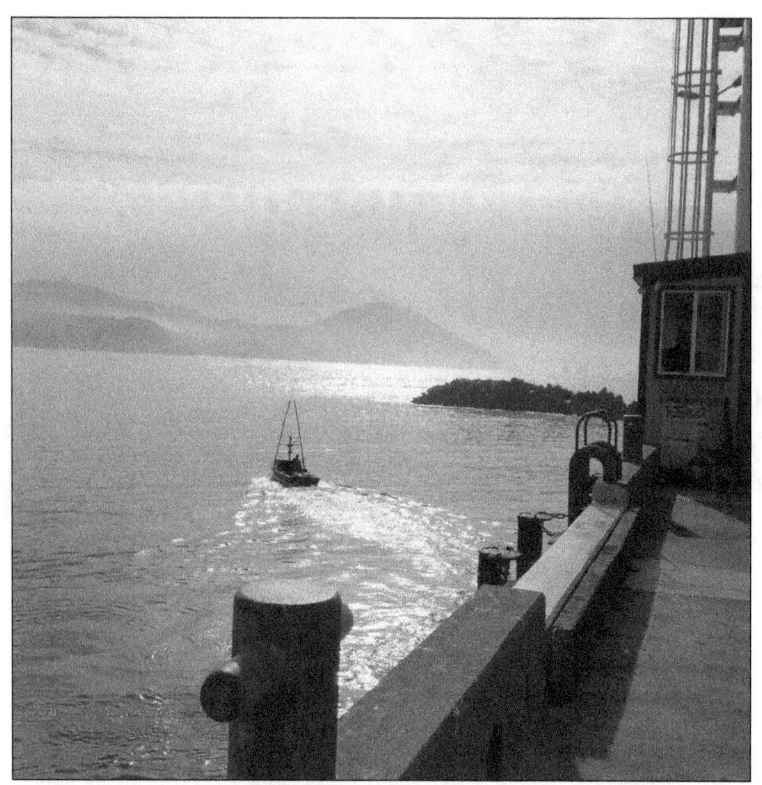

Now that it has been safely launched, the fishing boat departs the port. (Author's collection.)

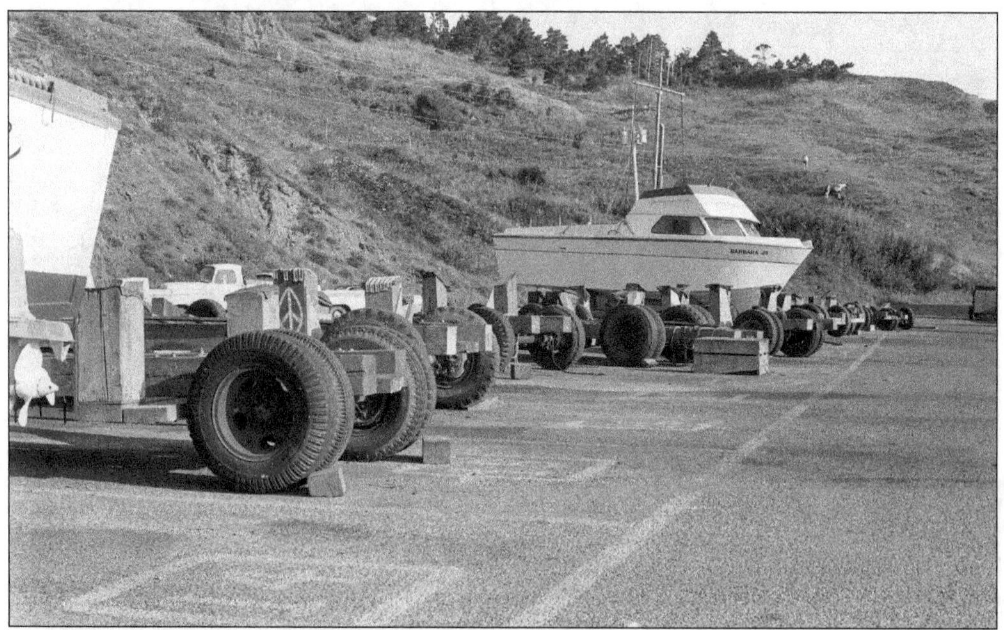

Here, several boats are moored at the Port Orford dock. Upon closer examination, the ropes that anchor the boats in place are visible. This prevents them from being moved around by the strong coastal winds. (Bandon Historical Society 49513.)

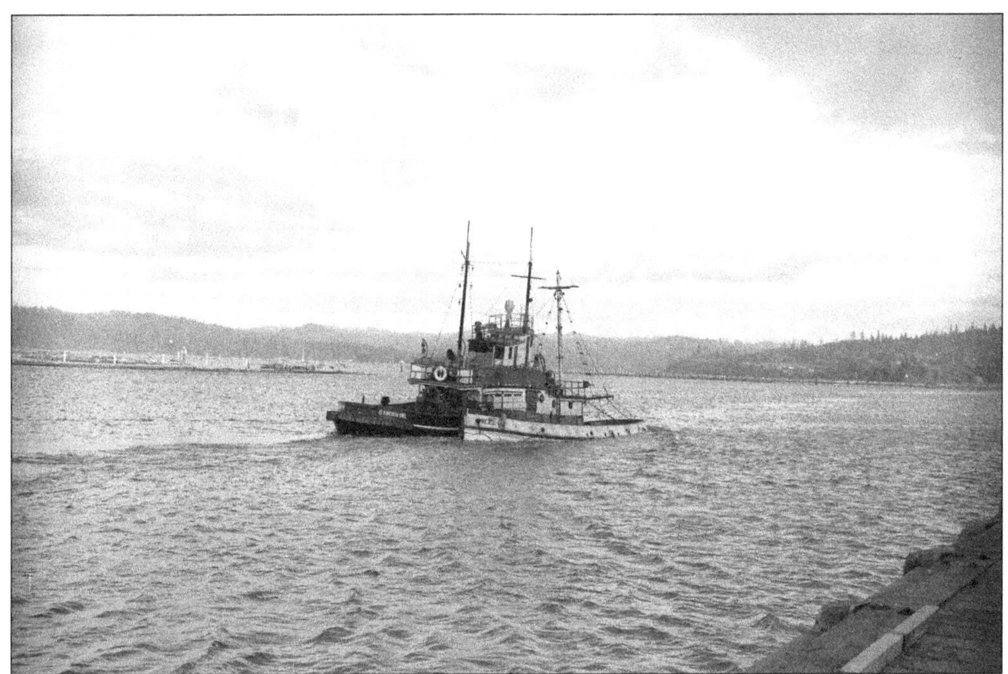

The F/V *Alice H.* was built at San Francisco in 1889 as the *Ida W.* The 61-gross-ton vessel was 63 feet long with an 18-foot beam and a 7-foot depth. On September 23, 1948, the *Alice H.* sprung a leak off of Cape Blanco during a storm. It managed to make it to Port Orford, where it was intentionally beached in order to avoid sinking. (CHM 995-1.4242.1.)

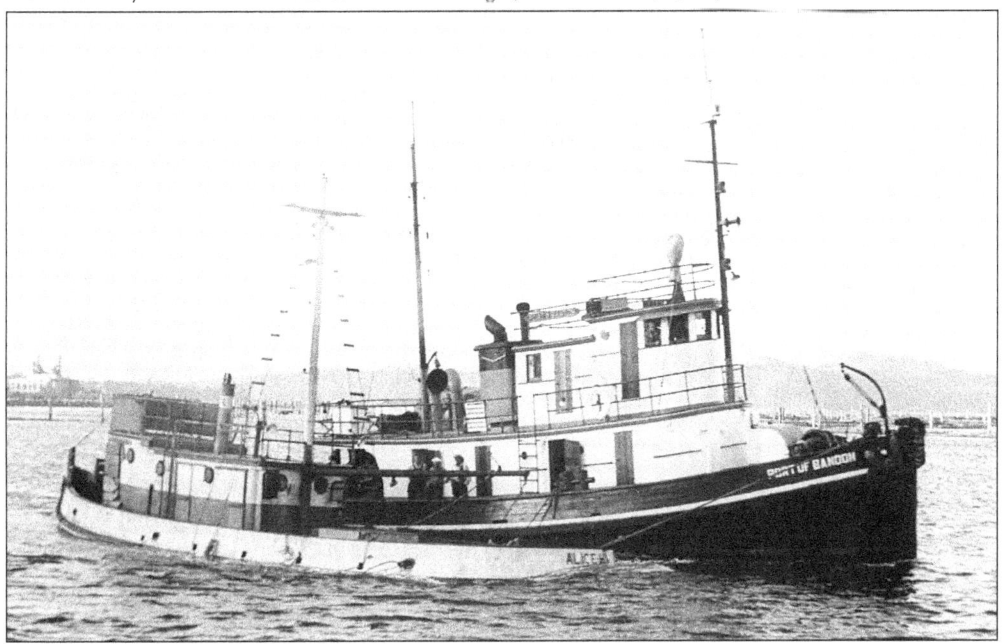

Initially, a local newspaper reported that the owners intended to have the damage repaired. The *Alice H.* was refloated using empty oil drums and towed to Coos Bay by the tug *Port of Bandon.* In this photograph, the *Alice H.* is being towed a few days after the accident. The boat is mostly submerged. (CHM 009-16.945.)

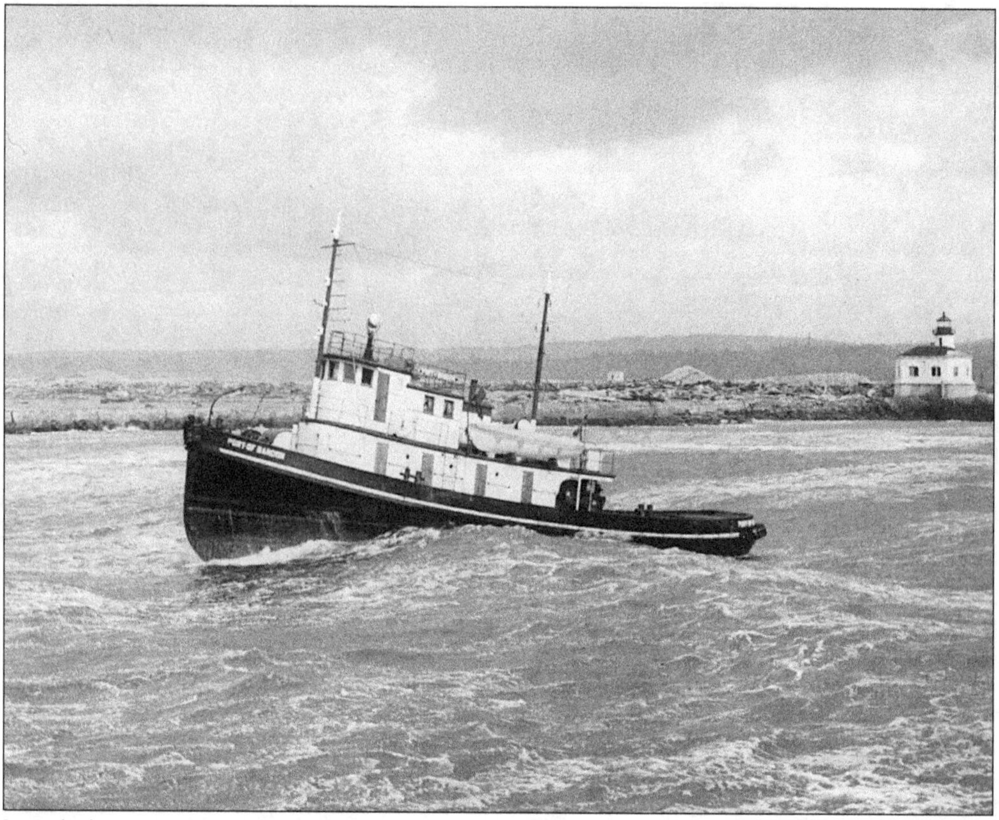

It took the tug's crew 24 hours to tow the disabled fishing boat from Port Orford to the Central Dock on Coos Bay. They used 90 oil drums to provide the *Alice H.* with buoyancy for the trip. The tug *Port of Bandon* often assisted ships in the area. It is shown here on the Coquille River with the lighthouse in the background. (Bandon Historical Society 10372.)

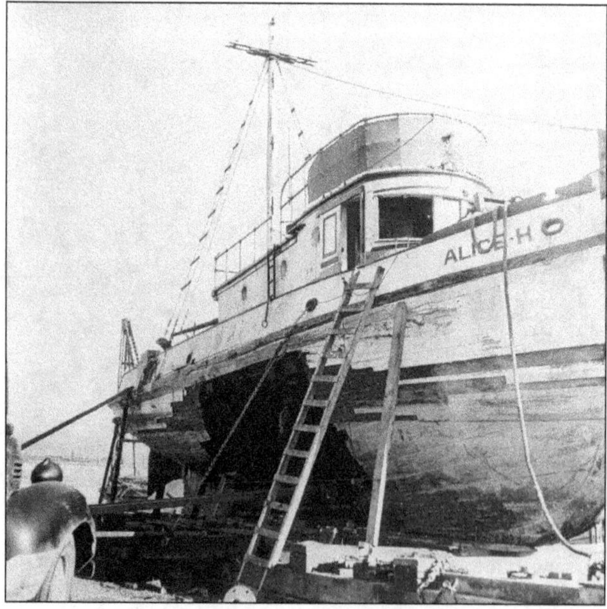

On October 14, 1948, the *Coos Bay Times* reported that the *Alice H.* was "too badly damaged in its recent storm-beaching at Port Orford to be repaired. The great hole in the *Alice H.* was made as workmen removed the engines from the craft before taking the hull away for disposal." The *Alice H.* is shown here at dry dock. (CHM 009-16.946.)

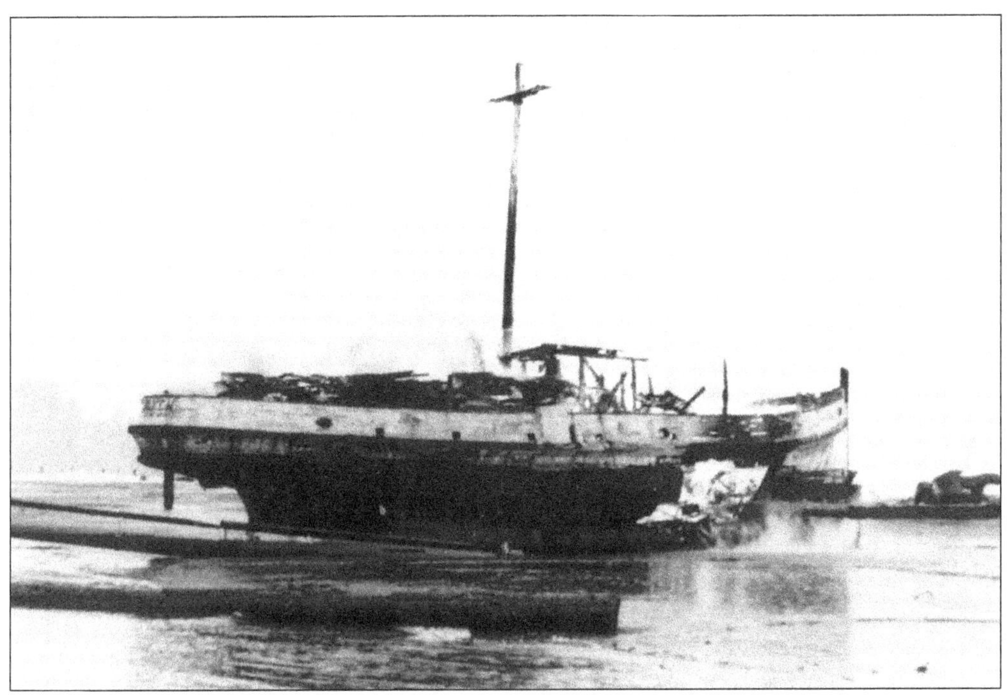

After the engine of the *Alice H.* was removed, the hull of the boat was scrapped. Once everything of value was removed from the fishing vessel, the hull was burned. The *Alice H.* is shown here with the hull fully engulfed in flames. (Above, CHM 009-16.142a; below, CHM 009-16.1142.)

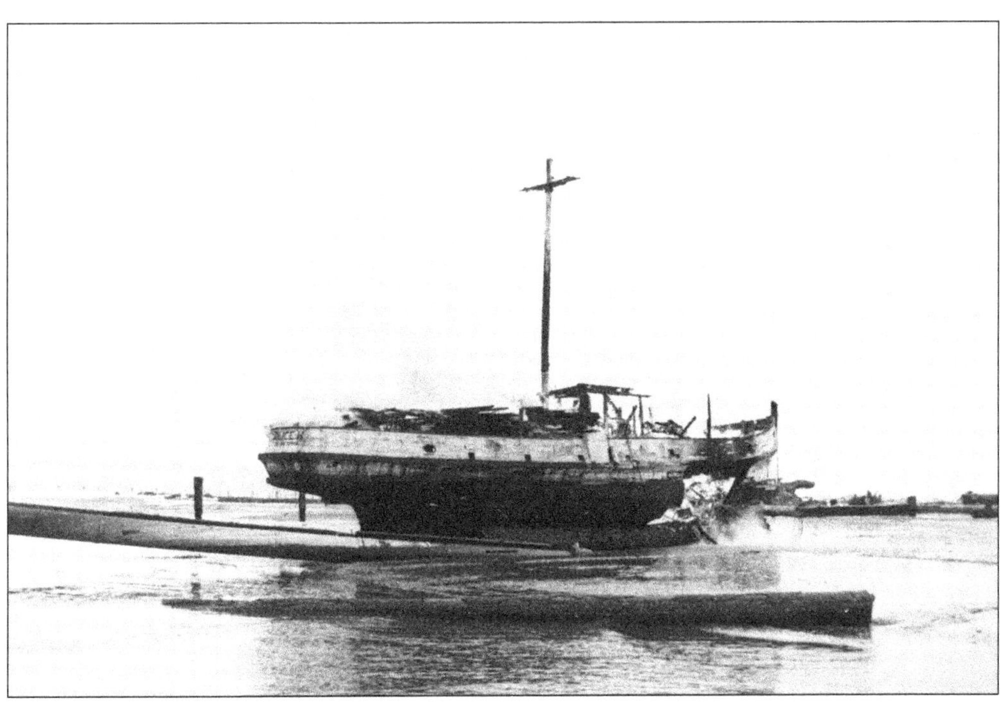

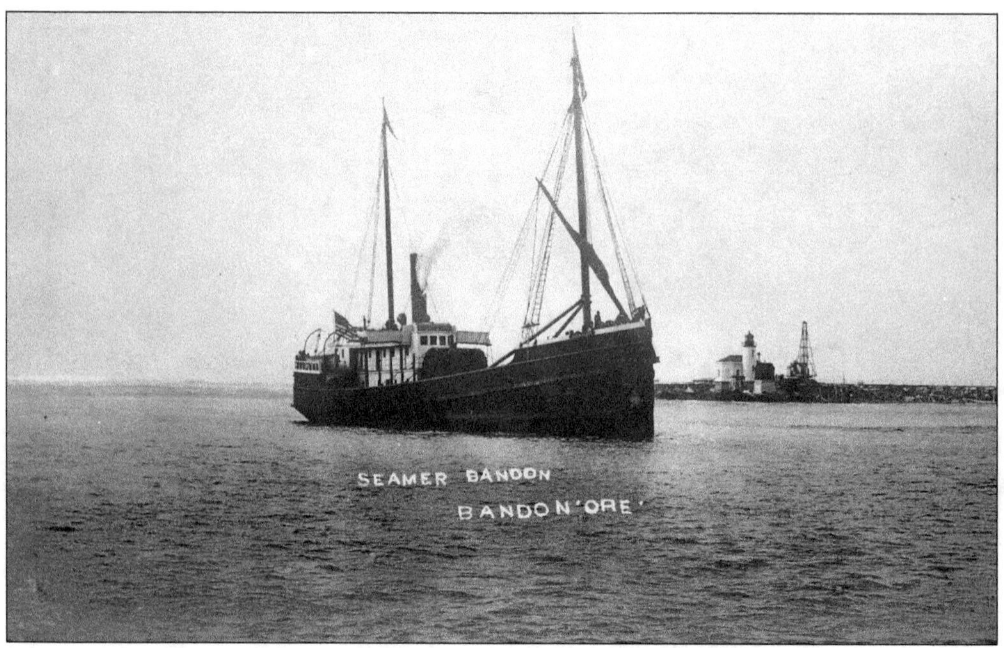

The steam schooner *Bandon* had a very eventful career. It was built by the Kruse & Banks Shipyard in North Bend for A.F. Estabrook in 1907. The wooden-hulled vessel was 642 gross tons, 172 feet long with a 39-foot breadth, and an 11-foot depth. It had a lumber capacity of 992,000 board feet. It is shown here at Bandon with the Coquille River Lighthouse in the background. Although the records are full of discrepancies, the American steam-winder schooner *Bandon*'s colorful career included at least six shipwrecks and numerous other marine mishaps. Two of the accidents occurred in Curry County. (Above, CHM 992-8-1488; below, 009-16.375.)

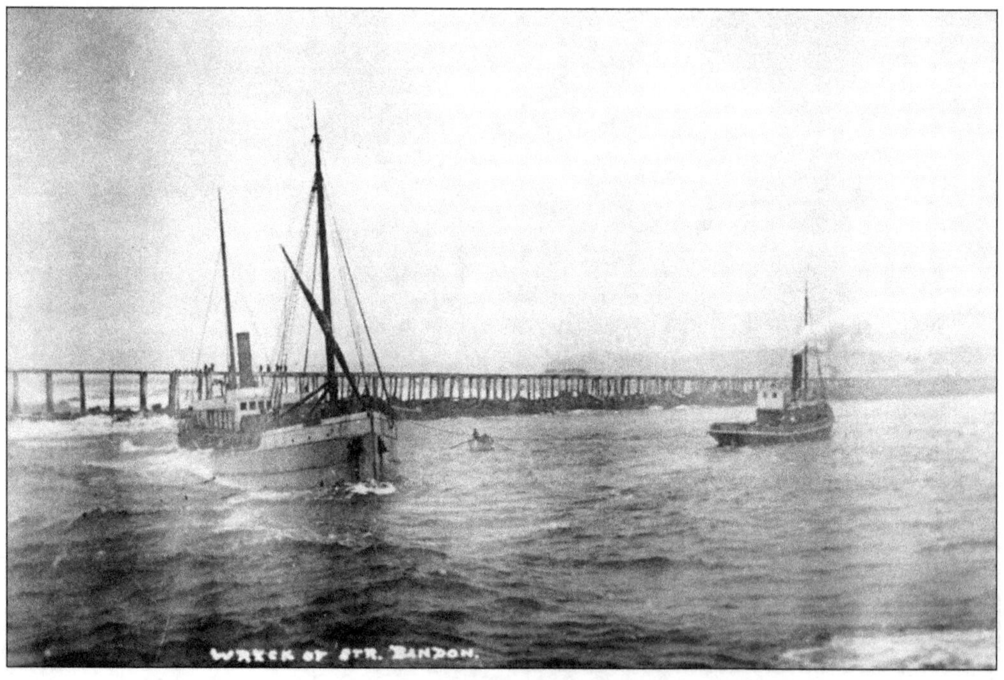

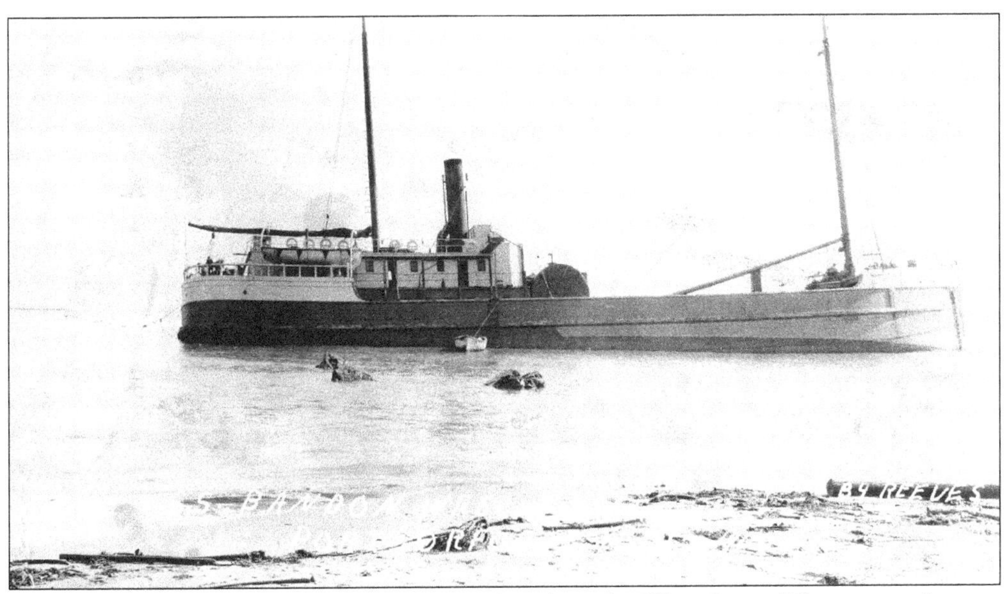

On September 1, 1916, foul weather was predicted on the West Coast. The steam schooner *Bandon*, under the command of Captain Hermanson, attempted to leave Port Orford for the open sea in order to avoid being caught at the exposed port during the storm. Unfortunately, a line got tangled in one of the ship's propellers, which caused the crew to lose control of the ship. In the above photograph, a small boat can be seen tied up beside the steamer, which is grounded close to shore. The photograph below shows a battered old life ring that was used on the steamer *Bandon*. (Above, Bandon Historical Society 25010; below, CHM 959-70.)

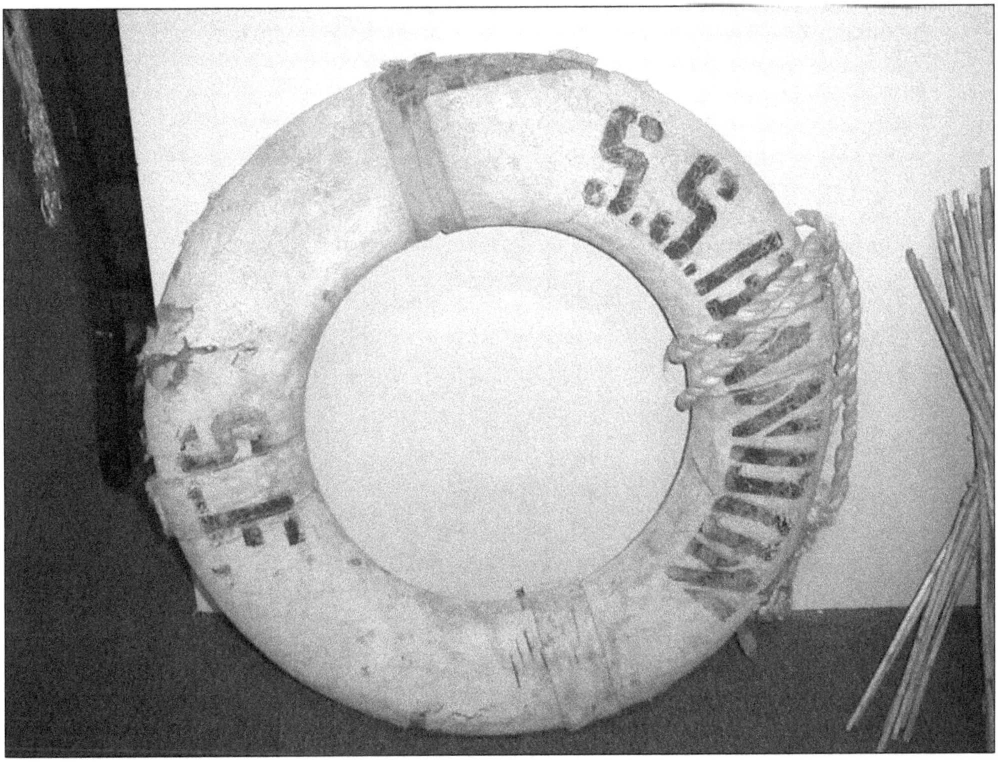

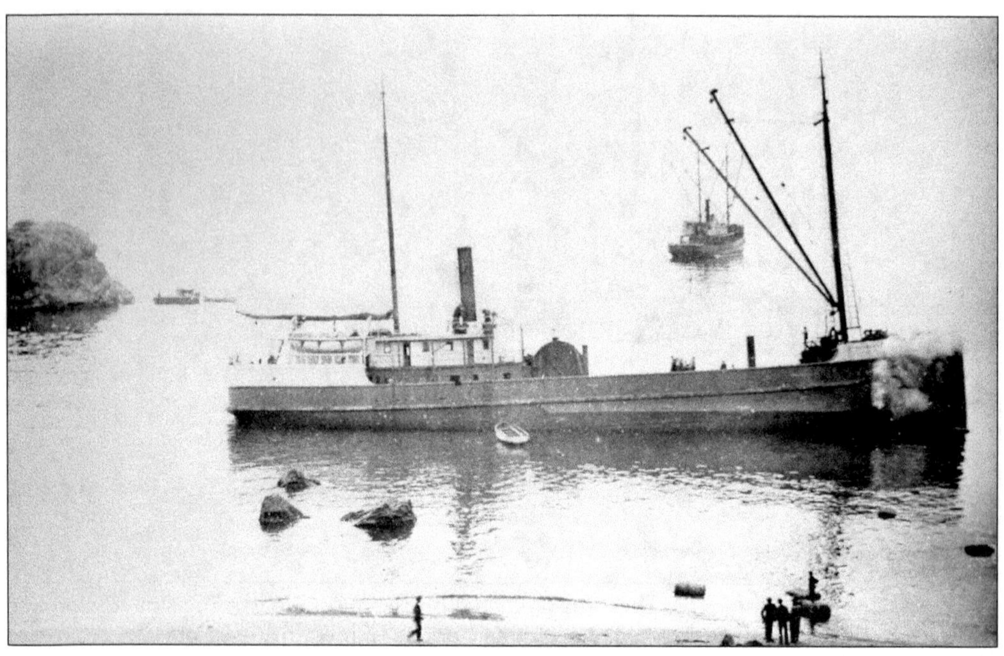

After a line tangled in the ship's propellers, the steamer *Bandon* drifted onto the beach at Port Orford on September 1, 1916. The above photograph was taken shortly after the ship grounded. Several people can be seen on the beach, and another ship is visible a short distance away. It was likely standing by to see if it could render assistance. The ship was refloated on September 17th and repaired. (Above, CHM 009-16.391; below, CHM 009-16.918.)

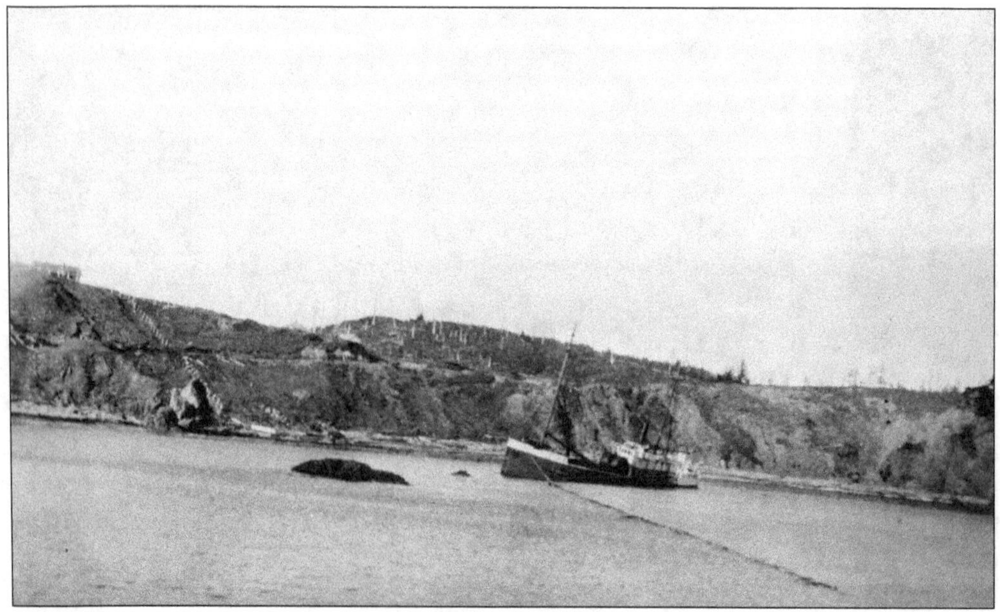

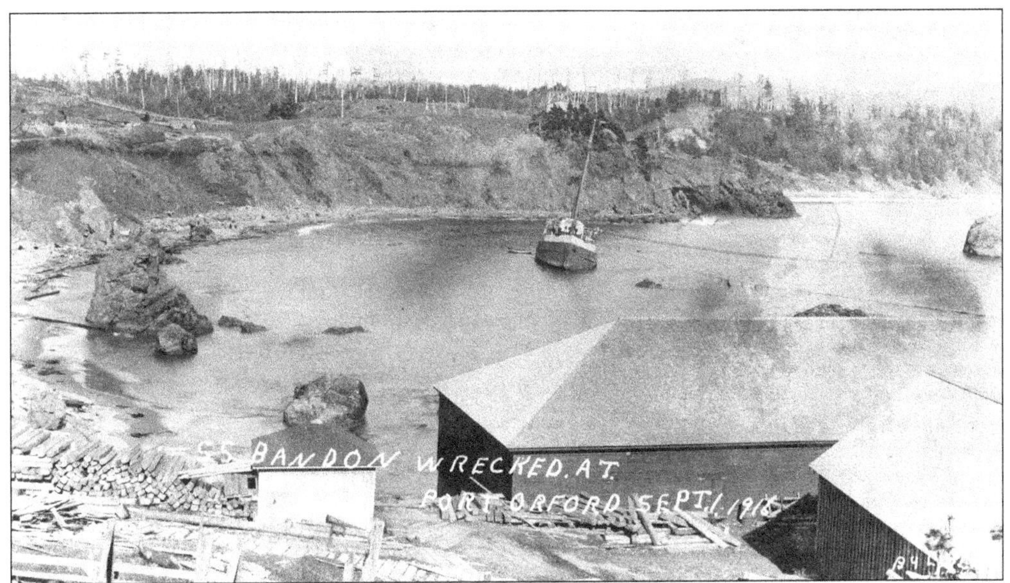

The above photograph was taken while standing on the hillside and looking down at the *Bandon* shipwreck on the beach. According to one source, the steamer *Bandon* grounded a second time at Port Orford on August 30, 1917. However, it is possible that this is a discrepancy and they were referring to the incident in 1916. The cup in the photograph below was used on the steamer *Bandon*. It is on display at the Bandon Historical Society Museum. (Above, Bandon Historical Society 25007; below, Bandon Historical Society.)

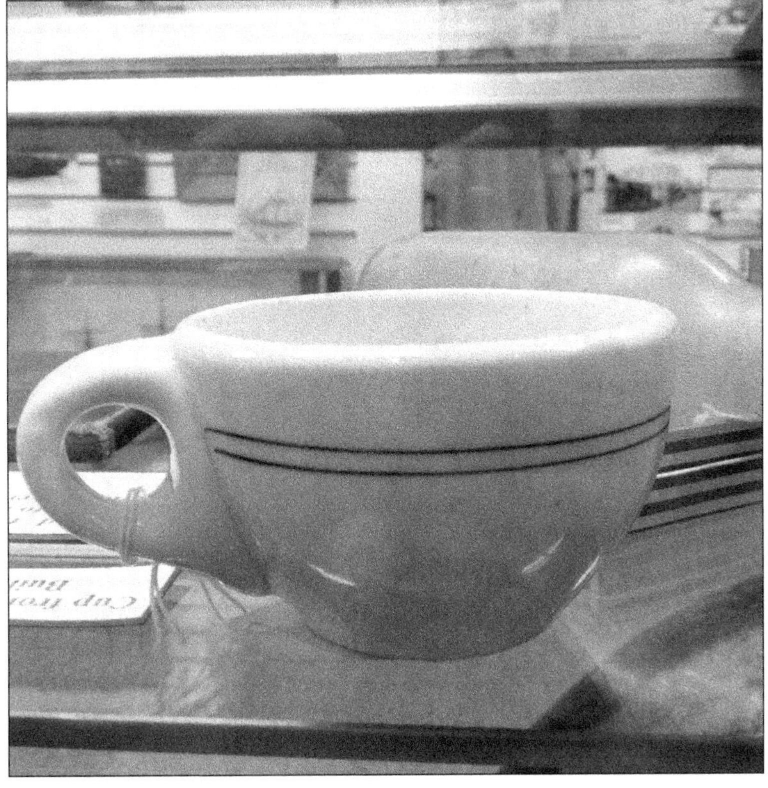

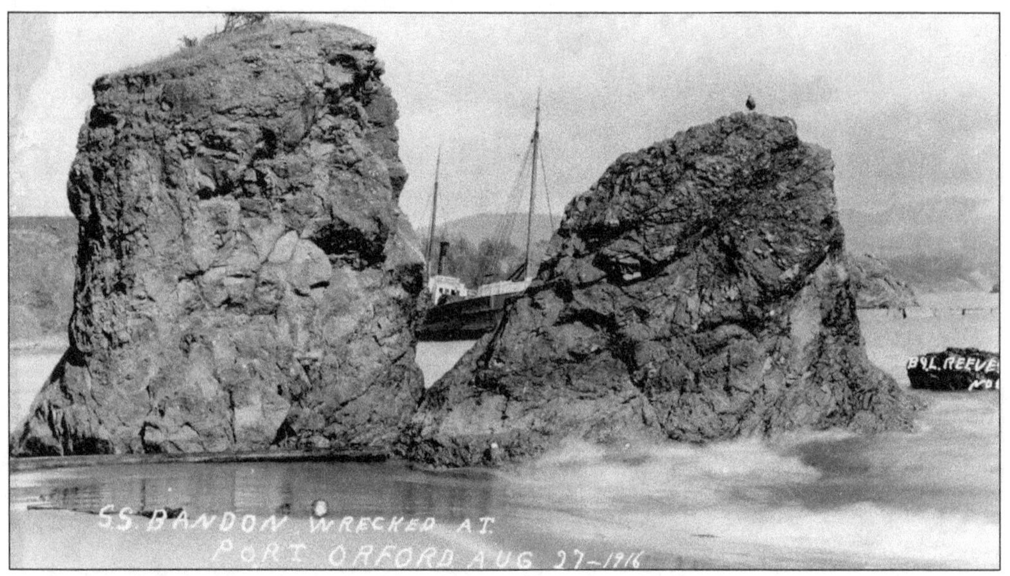

In this creative photograph, the *Bandon* shipwreck can be seen between two large rocks on the beach at Port Orford in September 1916. In addition to the two accidents in Curry County, the Bandon also wrecked several times in Coos County. (Bandon Historical Society 25031.)

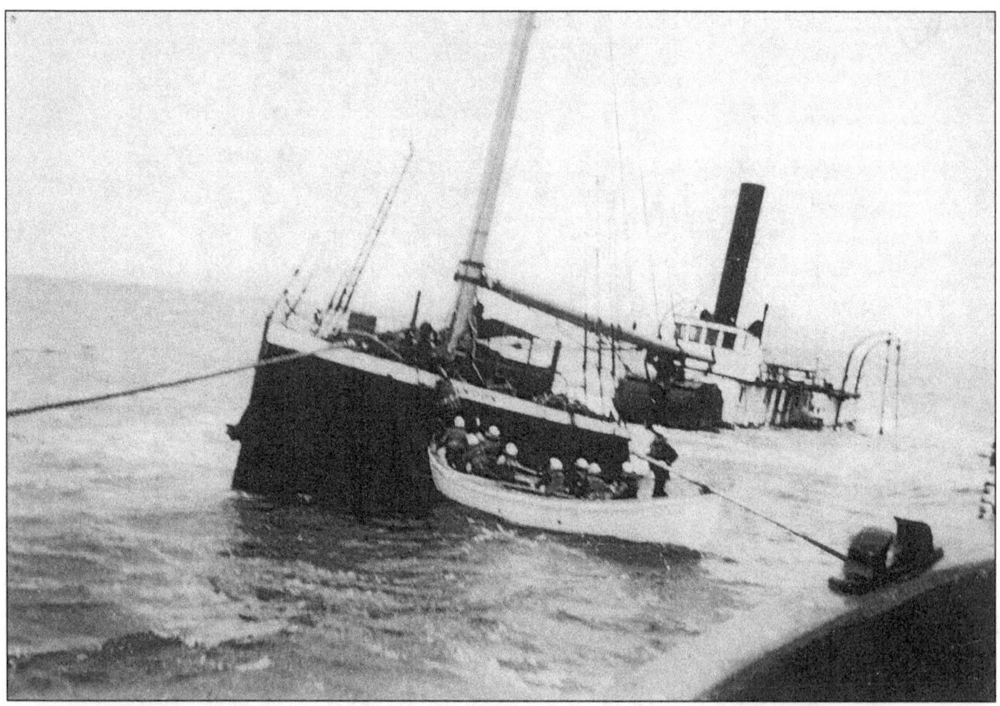

In February 1941, the steamer *Bandon* departed the Coquille River while transporting a cargo of 450,000 board feet of lumber to San Francisco. On February 9th, the ship encountered a severe storm near the Oregon-California state line. The wind battered the wooden hulled vessel and it began to leak. (Bandon Historical Society 14635.)

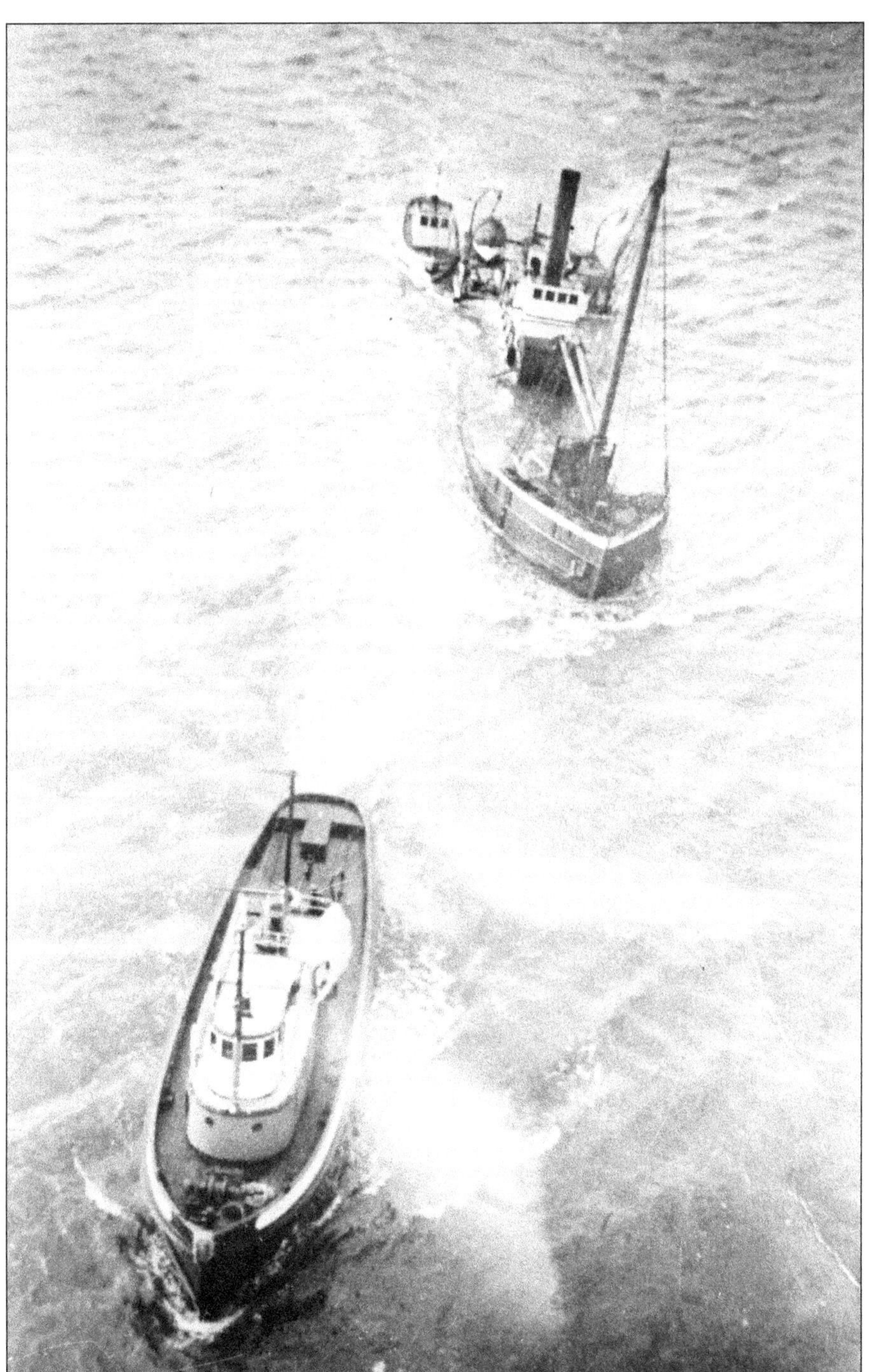

After the steamer *Bandon* became waterlogged during a storm on February 9, 1941, the crew was forced to jettison the deck load of 200,000 board feet of lumber in order to reduce the ship's weight. Although this prevented the ship from sinking, the bilge pumps were overwhelmed, and the vessel became water logged. The crew of 25 escaped in a lifeboat. The tanker *Solano* later picked them up before transferring them onto the Coast Guard cutter *Shawnee*. Here, the *Shawnee* is attempting to tow the waterlogged *Bandon* to port to be repaired. (CHM 009-16.69.)

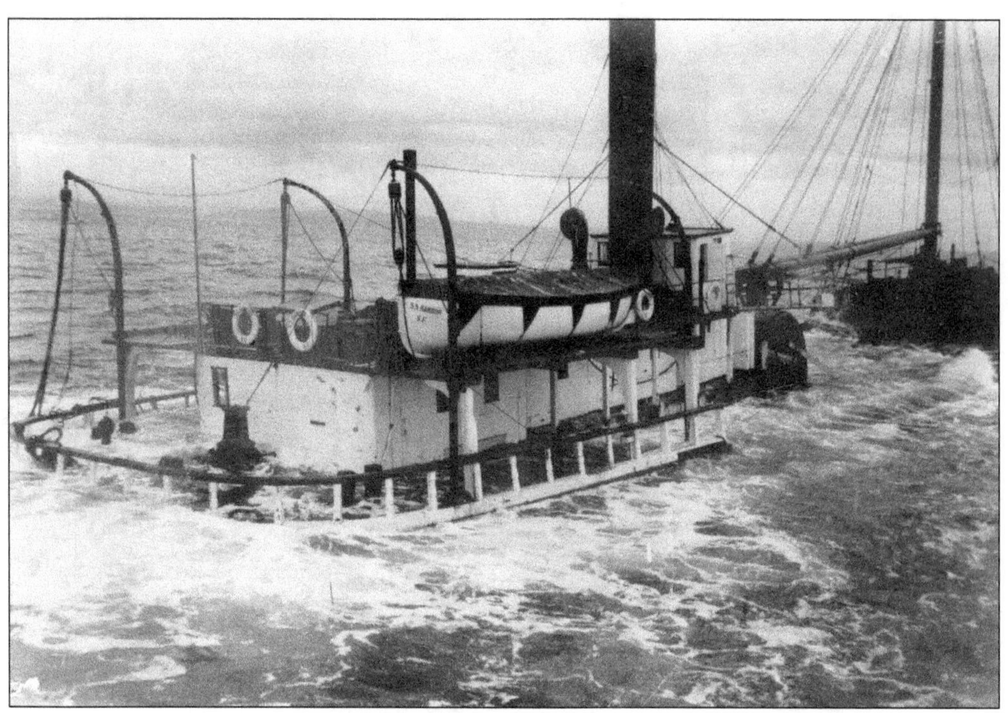

The above photograph is a closer view of the flooded steamer *Bandon* off the coast of Oregon in 1941. The majority of the ship is submerged. The entire deck is beneath the water with only a portion of the wooden railing visible. The deckhouse, funnel, and rigging are still visible. Ironically, one of the ship's lifeboats is still stowed above the waterline. The Coast Guard cutter *Shawnee* towed the disabled *Bandon* up the coast to Coos Bay where the tug *Port of Bandon* helped to transport the waterlogged ship across the Coos Bay bar. Once at dock, the ship was unloaded and pumped out. The Moore Mill and Lumber Company owned the *Bandon*. They decided it would be too expensive to repair the 34-year-old ship. (Above, CHM 006-44.128; below, 009-16.380.)

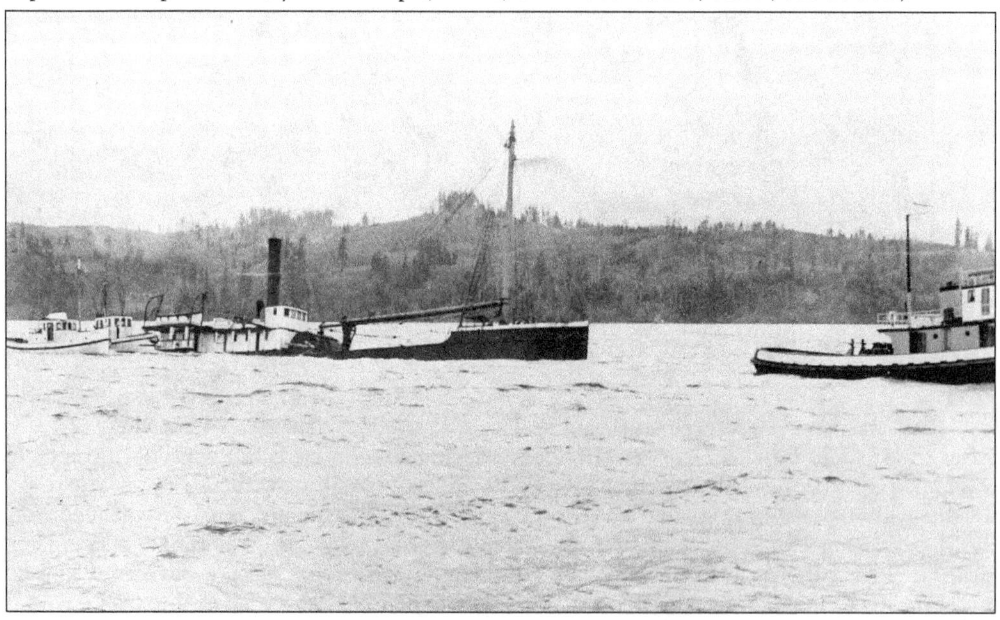

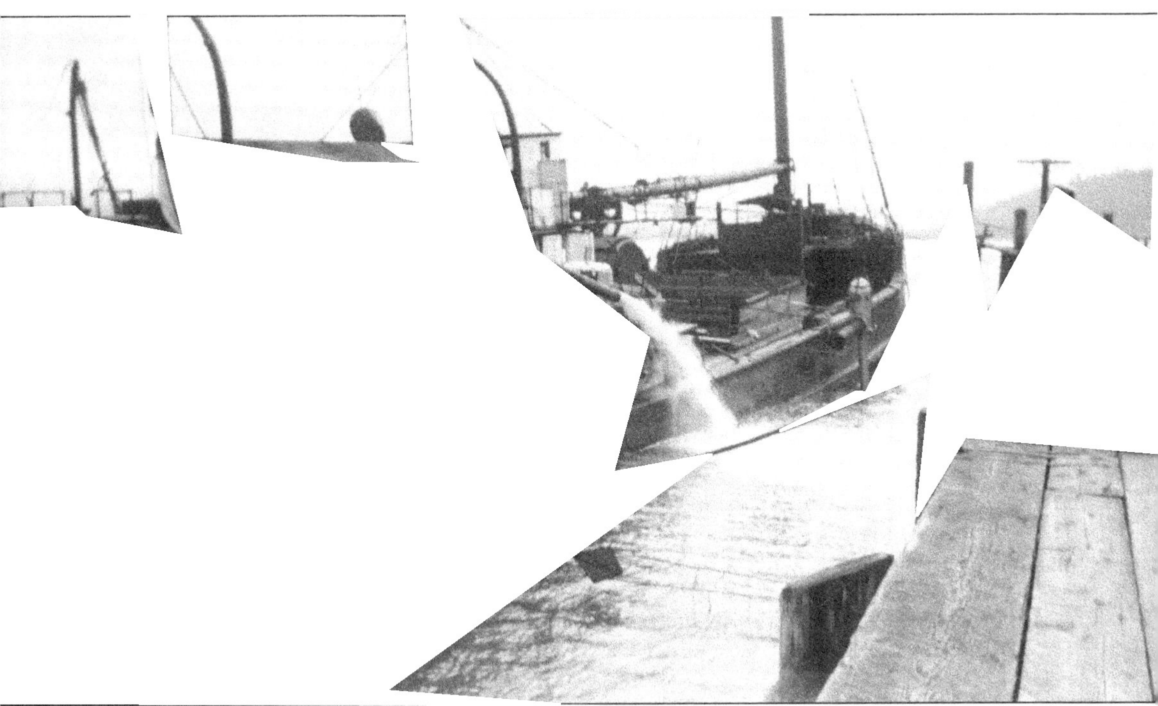

The *Bandon* remained tied up at a dock on the Coos Bay for several months before it was towed up the Isthmus Slough and abandoned. Around 1944, the old steamer was sold to Mexican owners, repaired, and renamed the *Atrevedo*. They intended to use the ship to transport salt in the Gulf of California. Unfortunately, the boilers failed to pass inspection, and the ship was abandoned again. The ship's bad luck continued. A year later, Capt. Sam Thompson purchased the *Bandon* and towed it back onto the Coos Bay. A short while later, the ship was scorched by a dock fire. The *Bandon* was then towed to a Portland dock for repairs. The ship foundered at the dock and was abandoned a third time. Several years later, the *Bandon* was towed to Columbia City, Oregon. It was then intentionally sunk in order to incorporate the hull into the breakwater. The battered old ship's adventures were finally over. The *Bandon* is shown here at dock after its 1941 accident, with the water being pumped out. (CHM 006-44.170.)

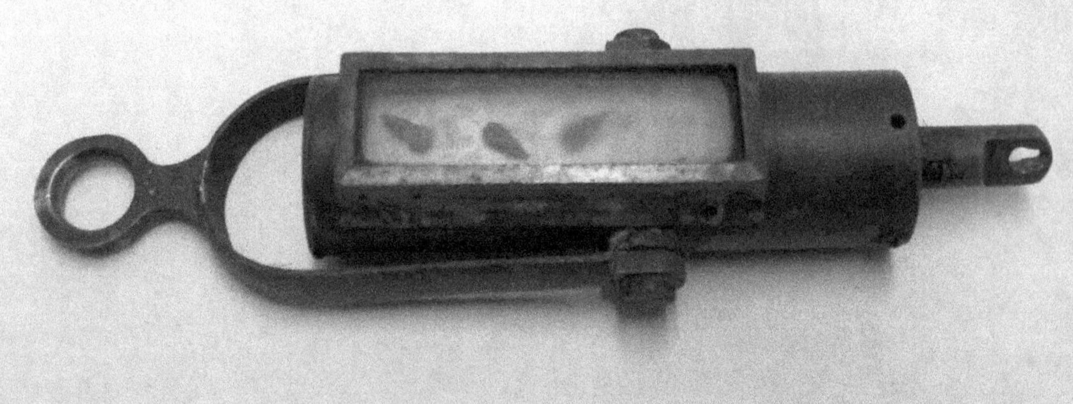

This object is part of a taffrail log that was used on the steamer *Bandon*. A taffrail log was a nautical instrument used to calculate a ship's speed. The taffrail is the aftermost railing around the stern of a ship. The log was mounted to the rail using a clamping mechanism. The device was dragged from the stern of a ship in order to determine the vessel's speed through the water. It consisted of three parts: a rotator (also known as the "fish" or propeller), a log line, and a recording device (or register). There were a variety of types and styles of taffrail logs. This one is a Bliss "American" taffrail log, which was manufactured by John Bliss & Company. They were made between 1885 and 1893. The first logs consisted of a piece of wood attached to a line with knots tied in it. When tossed over the stern, the number of knots that ran out indicated the speed in nautical miles per hour, or knots. (CHM 964-27.)

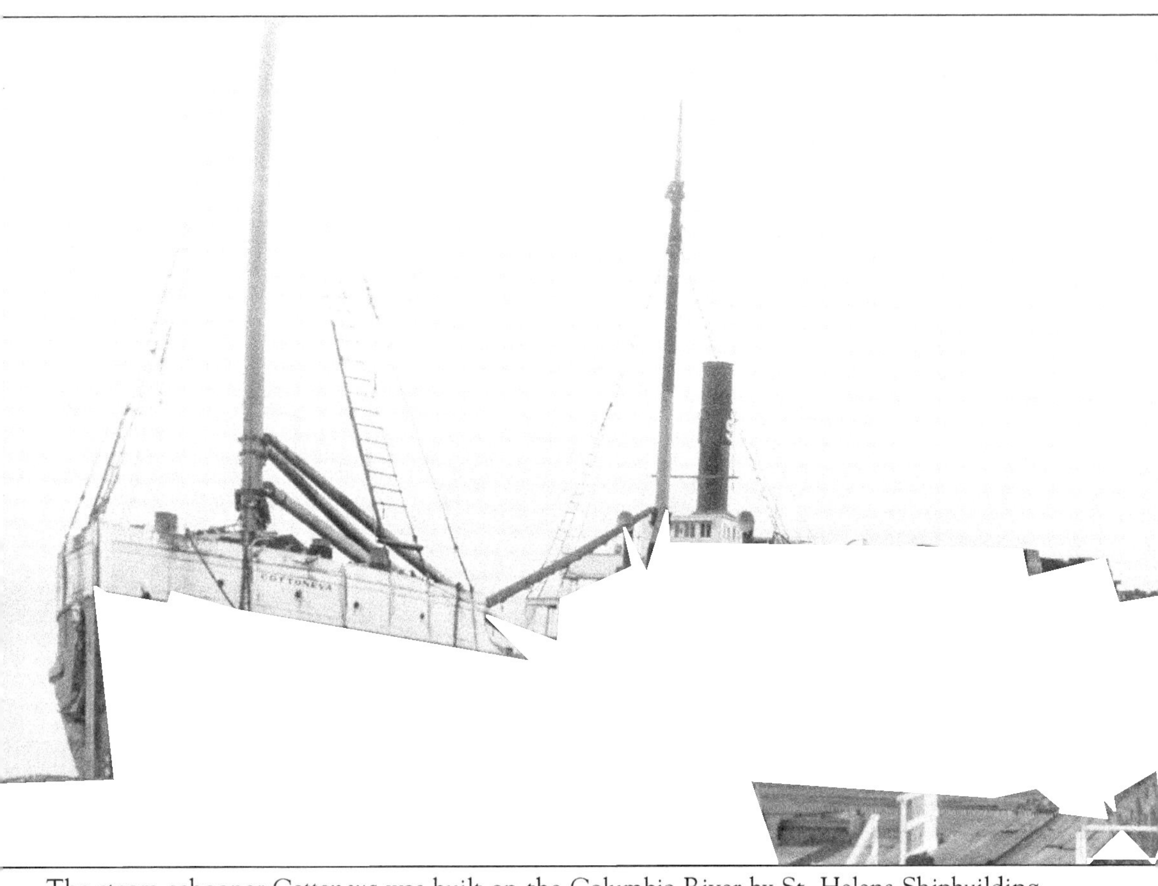

The steam schooner *Cottoneva* was built on the Columbia River by St. Helens Shipbuilding Company in 1917 as the *Frank D. Stout*. The wooden-hulled ship was 190 feet long and 43 feet wide with a 15-foot depth. It was powered by a 600-IHP triple-expansion engine. The ship could transport up to 20 passengers and 29 crewmen and had a capacity of one million board feet of lumber. The 1,113-gross-ton vessel was built for the Brookings Commercial Company of San Francisco but was later sold several times. The name was changed in the 1930s when E.H. Stahlbahm owned it. Regardless of its owner, the ship continued to run in the coastal lumber trade. (CHM 009-16.1090a.)

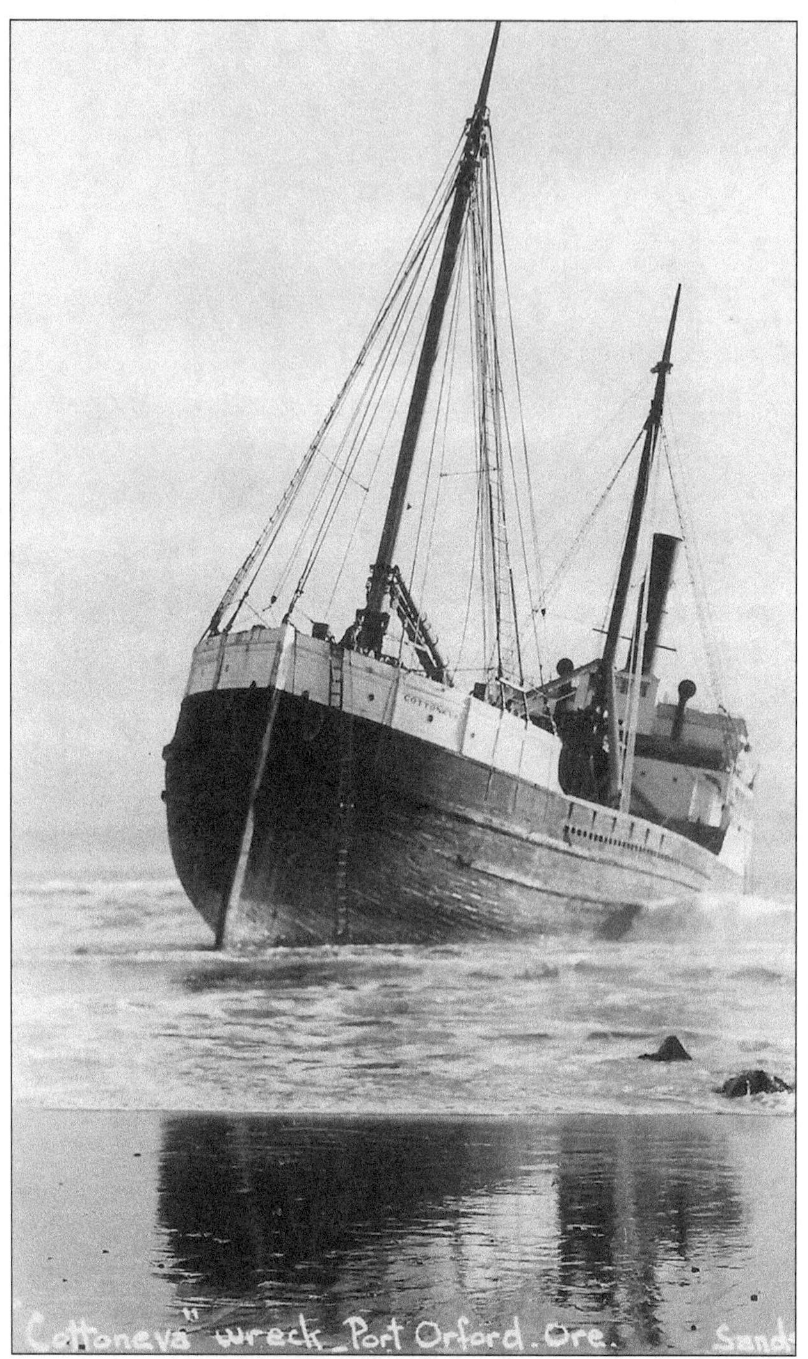

In 1937, Charles R. Ayers purchased the steam schooner *Cottoneva* at a foreclosure sale. He put the steamer to use on the Steeltree Line. He did not own the ship for long. On February 10, 1937, the *Cottoneva* stranded on the beach near Port Orford during a storm. It was reported that the heavy southerly gale contained winds as strong as 75 miles per hour. Capt. E. Stahlbaum and his crew of 26 were rescued by the Port Orford lifesaving crew, who were led by CPO Nils Nilson. They used a breeches buoy device to get the men off of the grounded ship. This photograph shows the ship at low tide. The majority of the hull is out of the water. (Alan Mitchell.)

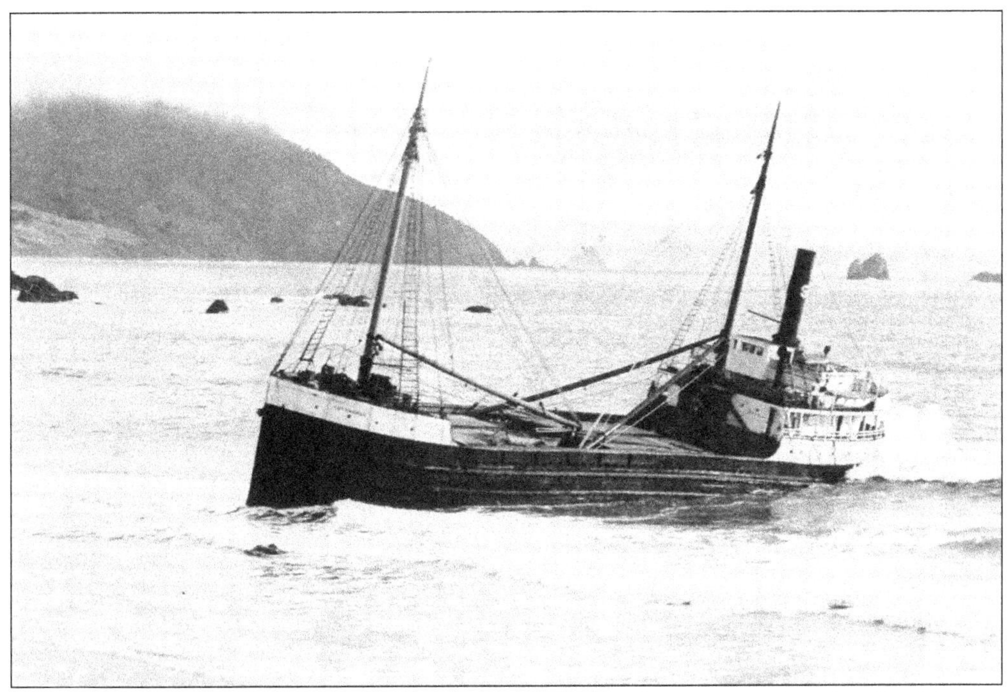

The *Cottoneva* travelled to Port Orford in February 1937 to pick up a cargo of lumber. On February 10th, a storm began brewing with predictions of incredibly strong winds. At this point, they had already loaded around 200,000 feet of lumber. As the storm approached, the crew attempted to take the ship out to sea and away from the danger. Unfortunately, with the partial load, the weight was unevenly distributed. With the bow riding high, the ship proved too unmanageable. There are discrepancies concerning what happened next. Some say the ship struck a submerged object, and Capt. E. Stahlbaum was forced to beach the ship to save the crew. Others say that the winds were simply too strong. Either way, the *Cottoneva* ended up on the beach. (Above, CHM 009-16.1157; below, 009-16.362.)

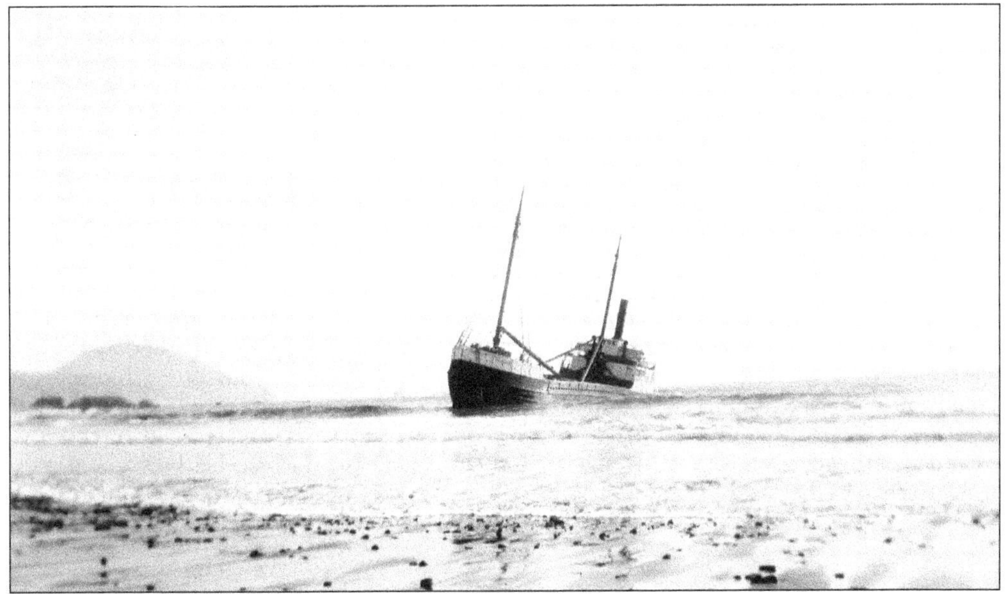

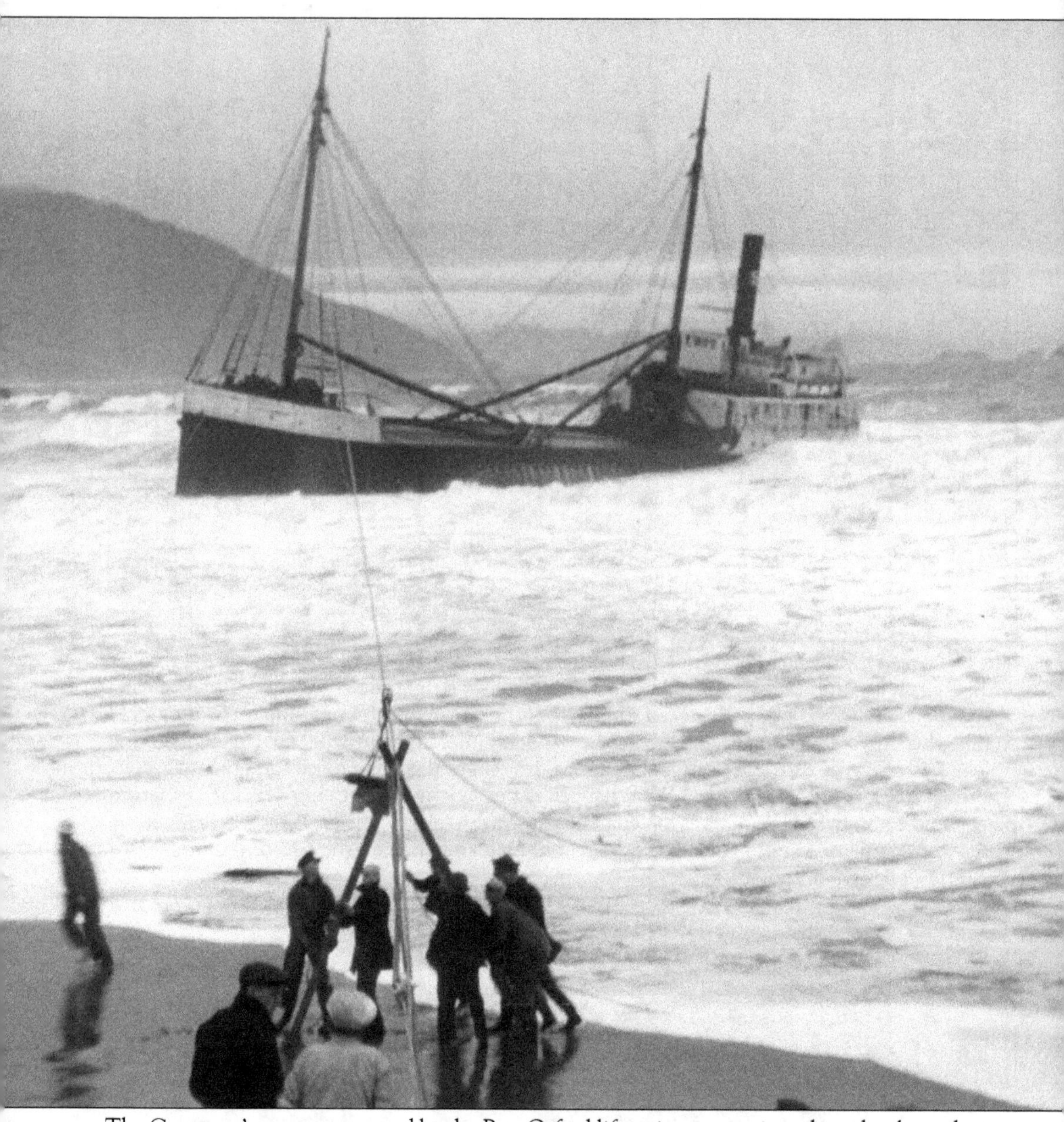

The *Cottoneva*'s crew was rescued by the Port Orford lifesaving crew using a breeches buoy device. The ship grounded in front of what is now the Battle Rock Wayfinding Point. In an article by the Point Orford Heritage Society, the location was described as an "excellent spot for spectators . . . who watched both rescue and salvage operations." In this photograph, the lifesaving crew is assembling the breeches buoy device. They have already attached a line to the ship. This is done by firing a rope from a small cannon, called a Lyle gun. Someone on the other end then attaches the rope to the ship. On the beach, the equipment that has been set up to anchor the other end of the rope can be seen. To the left of the wooden base, the breeches buoy has already been attached to the rope. (Alan Mitchell.)

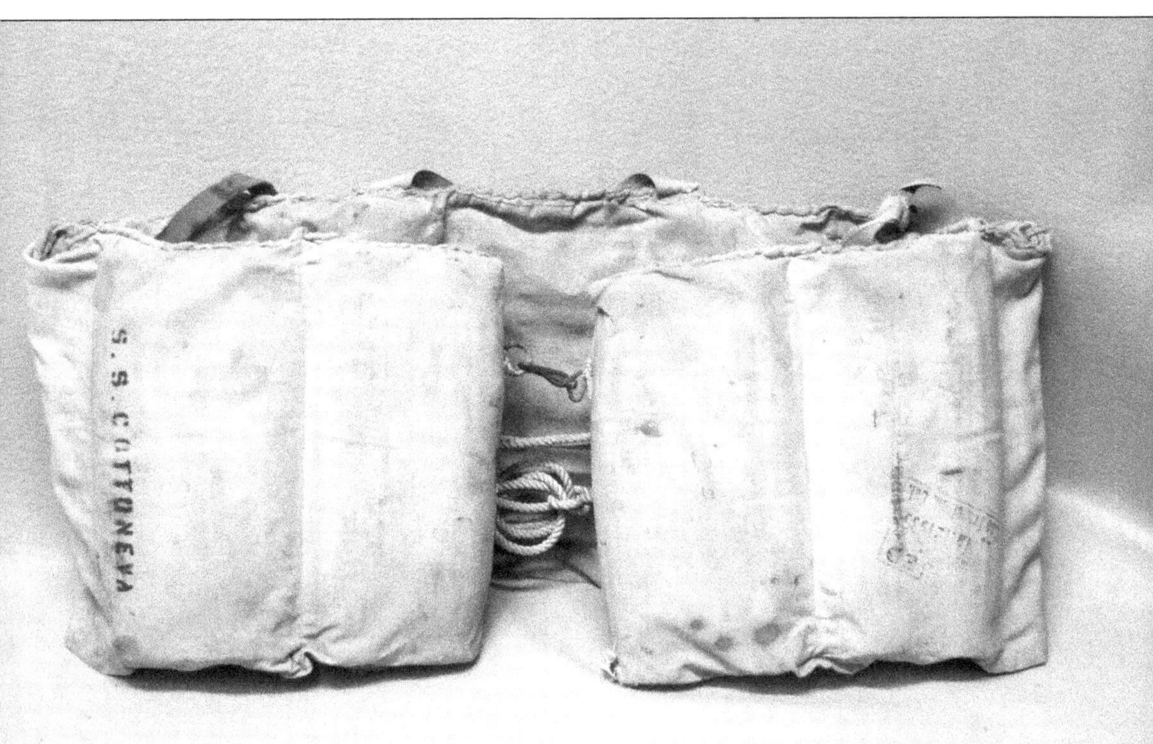

The *Cottoneva* came ashore on the beach just east of Battle Rock. When the ship struck the shore, its "back was broken," making it a total loss. This life jacket came from the wrecked steam schooner. The name of the ship has been stamped along the side. The *Cottoneva* shipwreck could be reached by foot at low tide. There were discussions about taking bids to salvage materials and cargo from the shipwreck, but there were disagreements regarding shore rights to the wreck. In mid-March, the ship's underwriters signed over the rights to Orris Knapp, a local landowner. He then salvaged the lumber, machinery, and other equipment from the wreck. Orris and Louie Knapp used some of the salvaged lumber to build a barn at their Elk River Ranch. (CHM 981-278.)

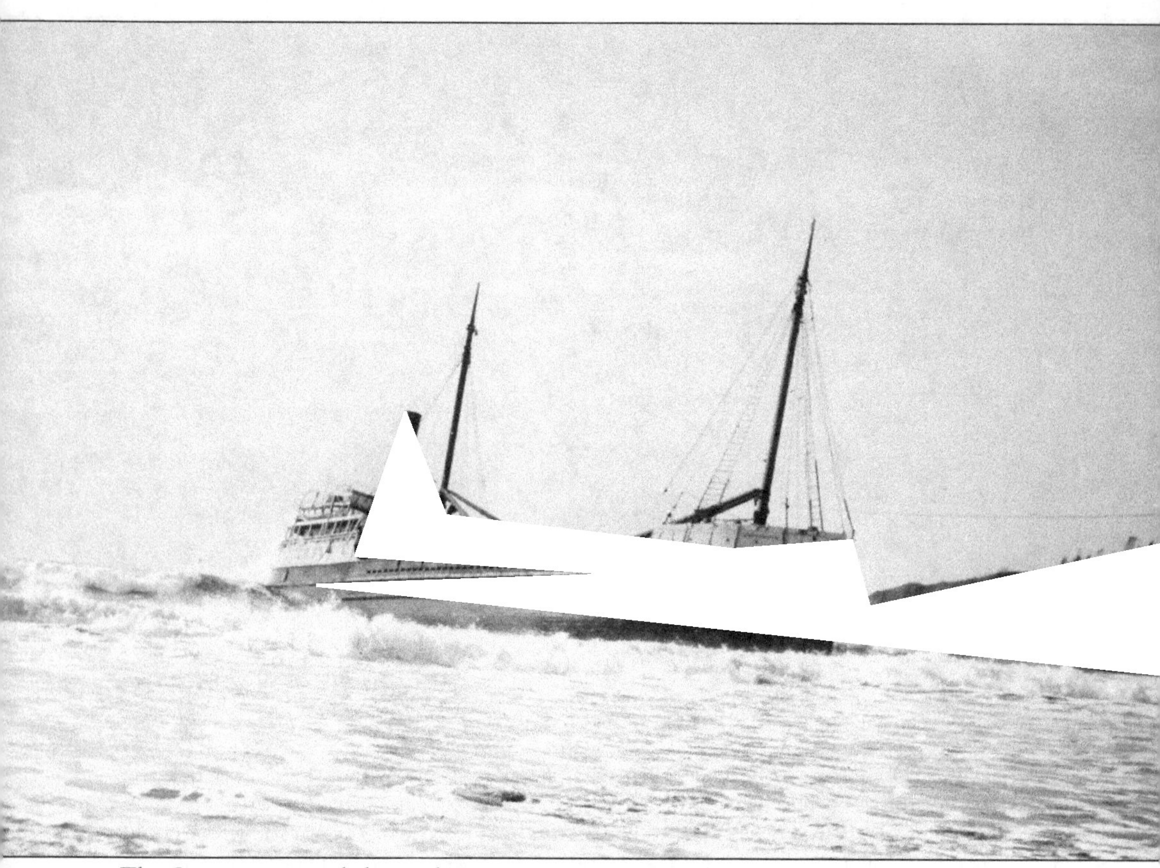

The *Cottoneva* grounded near the current visitor center which is located a short distance from the Battle Rock Wayfairing Point. The easily accessible point made it easy for curious spectators and visiting tourists to watch both the rescue of the crew by the Port Orford Life-Saving Station crew and the later salvage efforts. Since the wreck lay so close to shore, many locals speculated that it would take several years for the waves to break up the wooden hull. An article in the *Reporter* joked that "a group of Port Orford citizens . . . [thought] that the city might convert it into a city jail, now much needed. The jail would be equipped with a salt water pool which would be useful in the treatment of drunks." (CHM 009-16.1157a.)

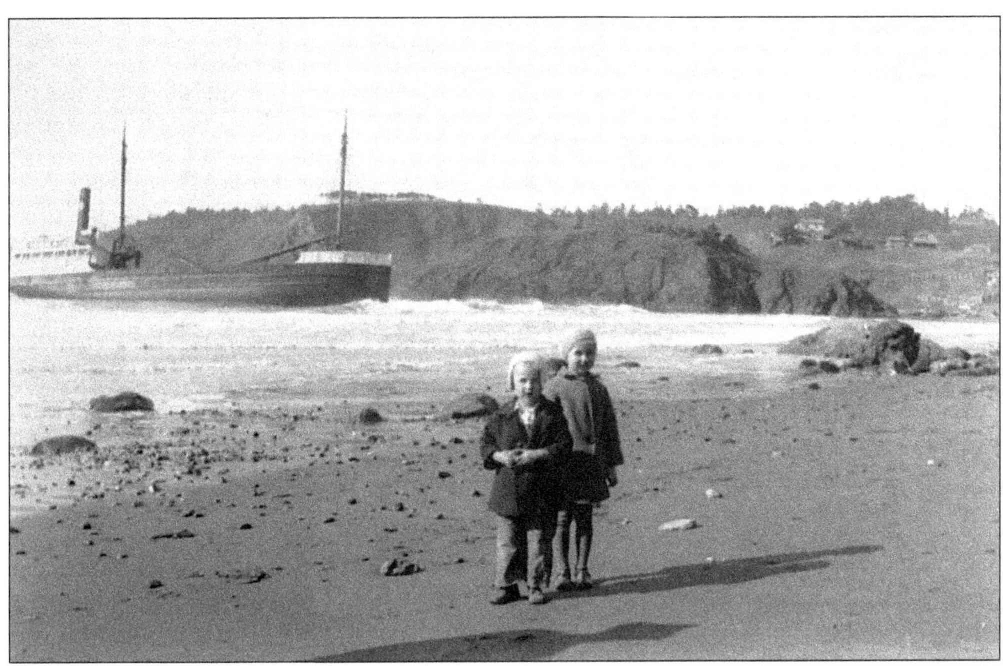

Above, two children pose on the beach in front of the wreck of the *Cottoneva.* They have been identified as Ronny and Lucy Haga. Hundreds of people visited Port Orford over the next few months to view the shipwreck. The hull was located high enough on the beach that it could be approached by foot at low tide. By March 18th, the ship's underwriters had turned possession of the wreck over to Orris Knapp. He intended to turn the hull into a tourist attraction that summer. Unfortunately, the wreck began breaking up during a storm before he could act on his plans. The photograph below provides a bird's-eye view of the wreck of the wooden hulled steamer breaking up. (Above, Bandon Historical Society 30693; below, CHM 009-16.1157b.)

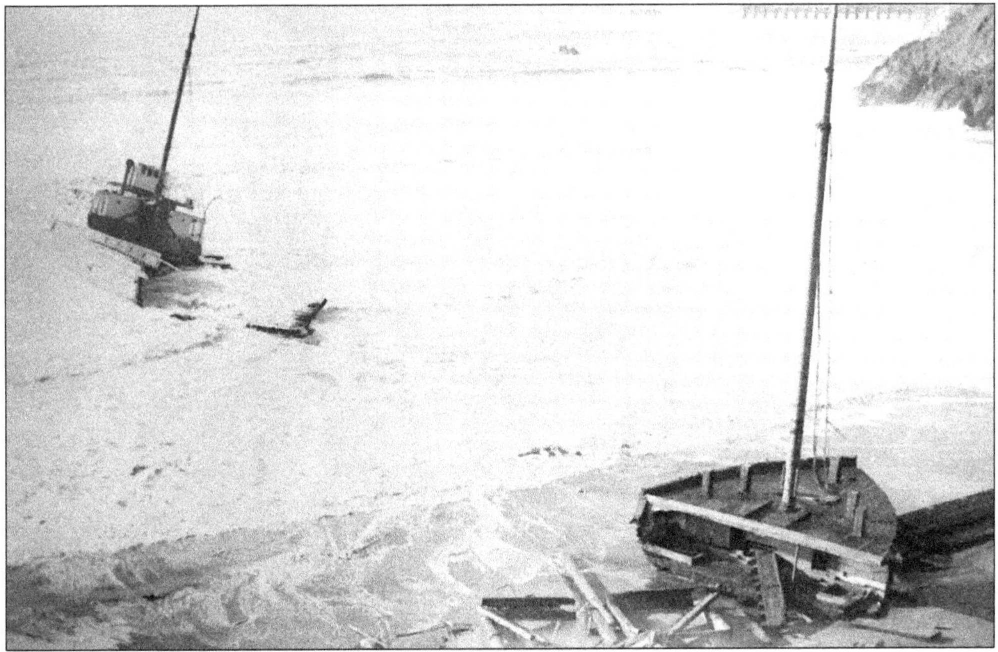

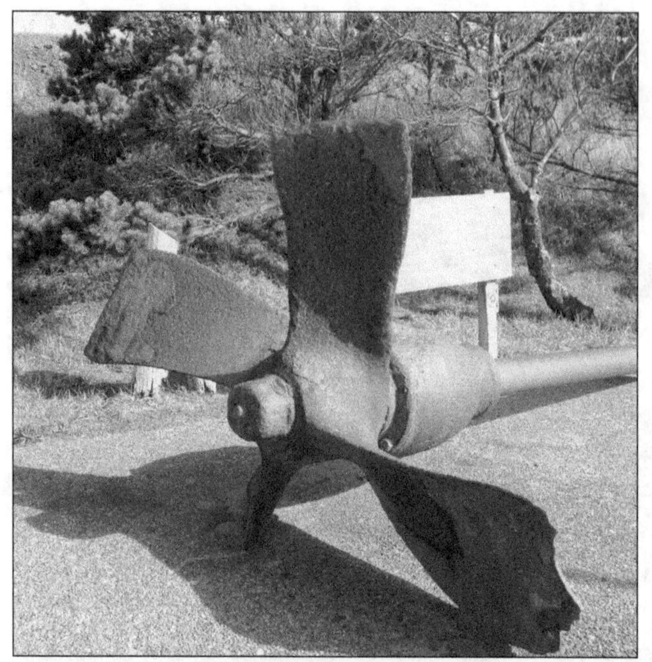

The propeller from the *Cottoneva* shipwreck has been on display outside of the Port Orford Visitor Center for several years. The informational sign beside it provides the basic details about the shipwreck. It is interesting to note that the metal propeller is the only part of the wooden steam ship that still remains. On one final note, after surviving the wreck of the *Cottoneva* in 1937, E. Stahlbaum was unfortunate enough to be on board another ship when in wrecked in Curry County. Four years later, he was the first mate on the *Willapa* when it wrecked 20 miles south of Port Orford on December 2, 1941. (Both, author's collection.)

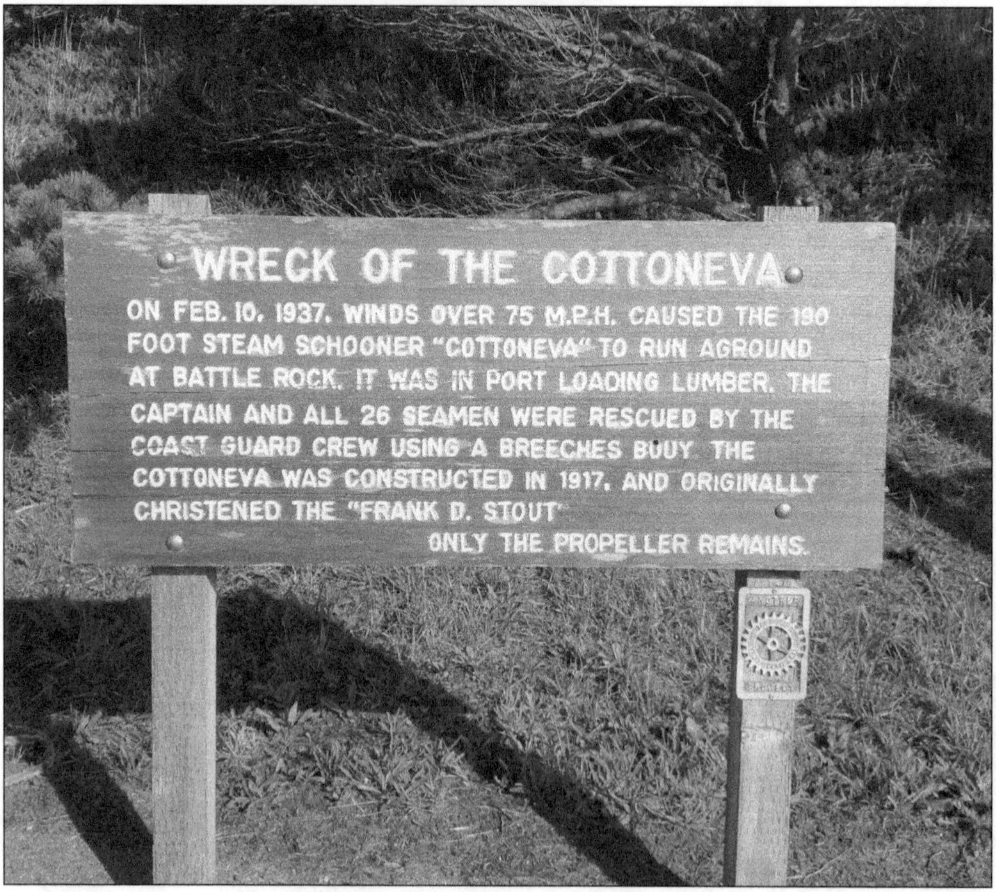

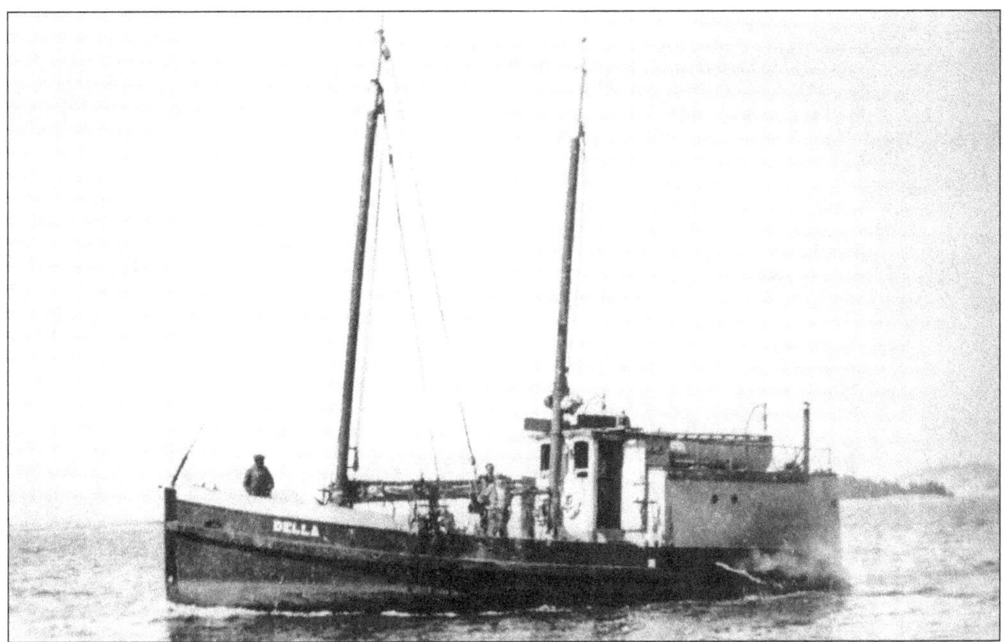

The two-masted gas schooner *Della* was built from lumber salvaged from the *Pioneer*, which wrecked on the northern Oregon coast on December 17, 1900. The *Della* was built at Woods, Oregon in 1901. The 30-gross-ton ship was 45 feet long with a 14-foot beam and a 4-foot depth. The People's Company owned it. This photograph shows *Della* prior to the accident. (CHM 007-25.372.)

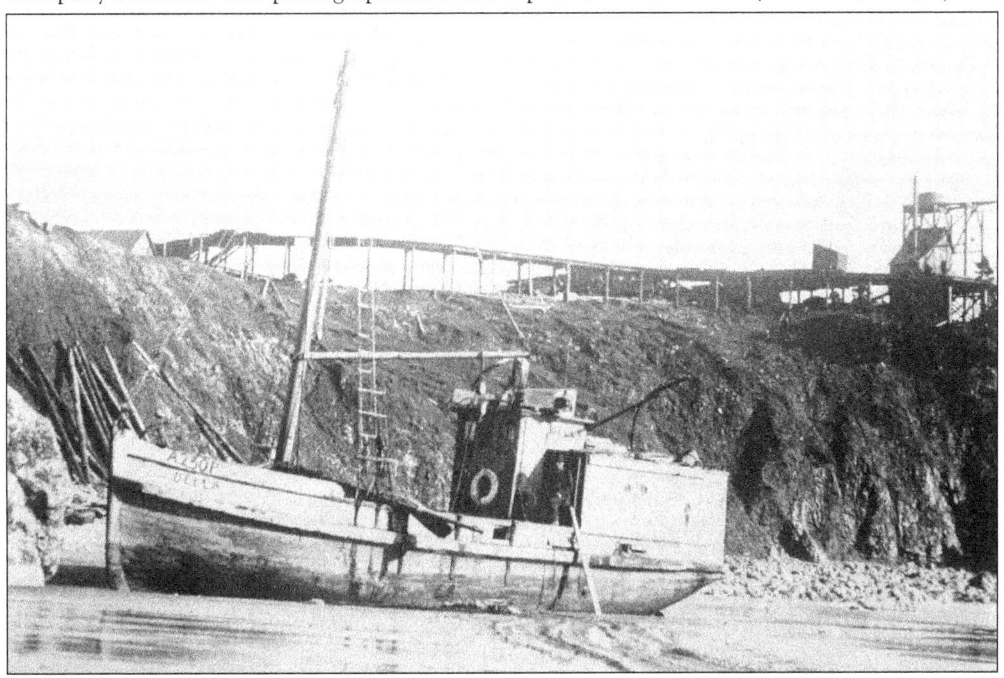

On December 9, 1918, the *Della* was anchored at Port Orford during a storm. After being battered by the weather for 12 hours, an anchor chain parted. The crew of four was asleep when it happened. By the time they realized there was a problem, it was too late. The vessel washed up on the beach. Although the ship was totaled, the crew made it safely ashore. (CHM 009-16.1806.)

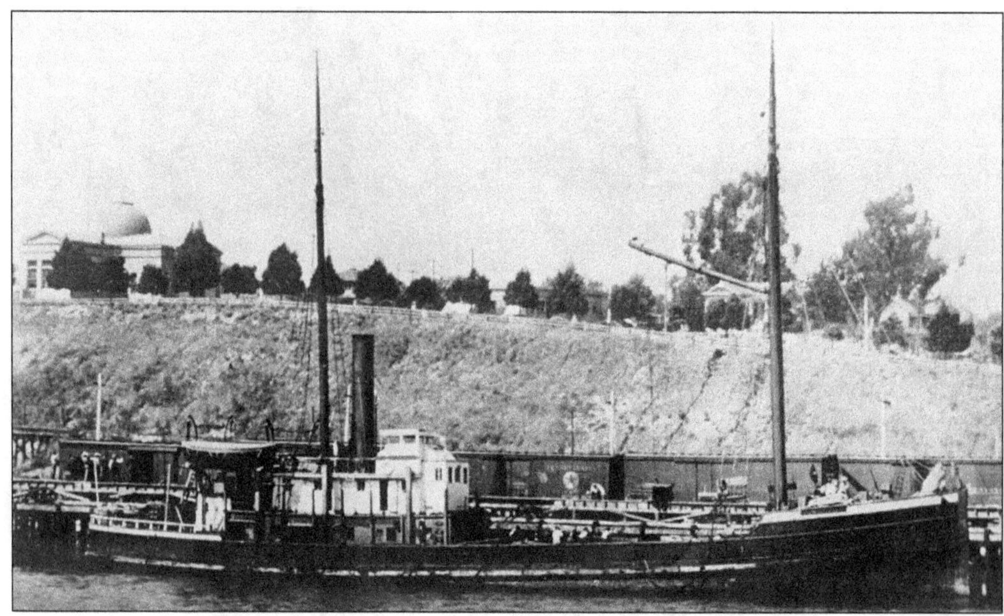

The *Fulton* was a steam stem-winder schooner. In was built in 1898 at Fairhaven, California by Hans D. Bendixsen. The 605-ton ship was 153 feet long with a 34-foot beam and an 11-foot depth. A 265-IHP engine powered it. The *Fulton* is shown here at dock. It usually employed an 18-person crew. (CHM 009-16.2261.)

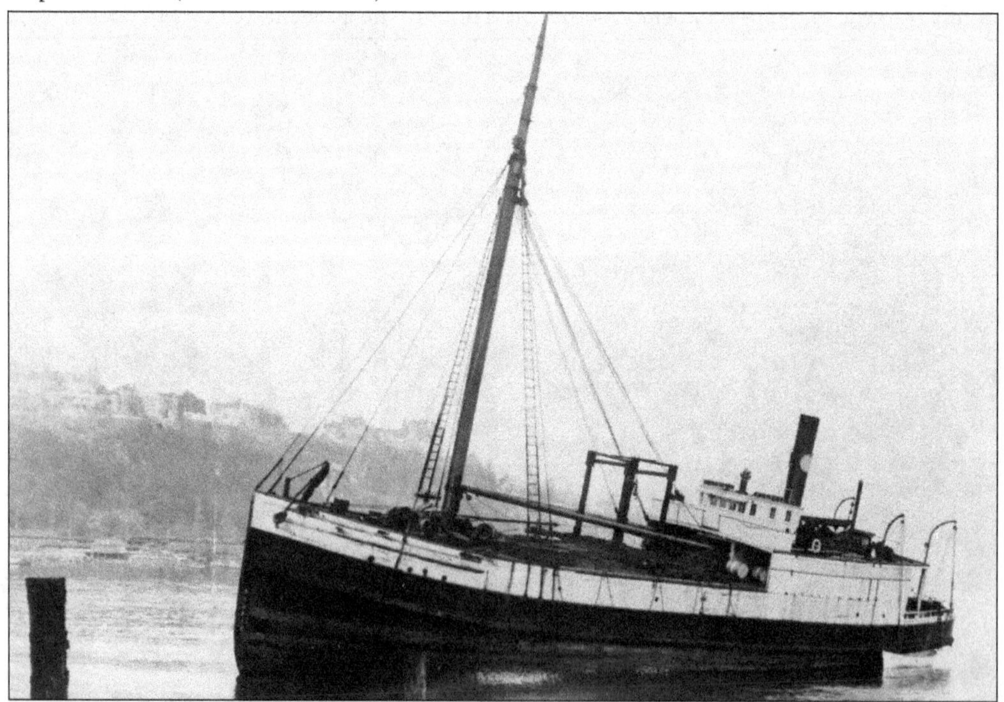

On February 12, 1904, the steamer *Fulton* was driven ashore near Port Orford during a storm. A boat was lowered from the ship in order to take a line to shore, but it capsized, causing the second mate to drown. The rest of the crew made it safely ashore on a raft. Several months later, the *Fulton* was refloated and repaired. (CHM 009-16.9420.)

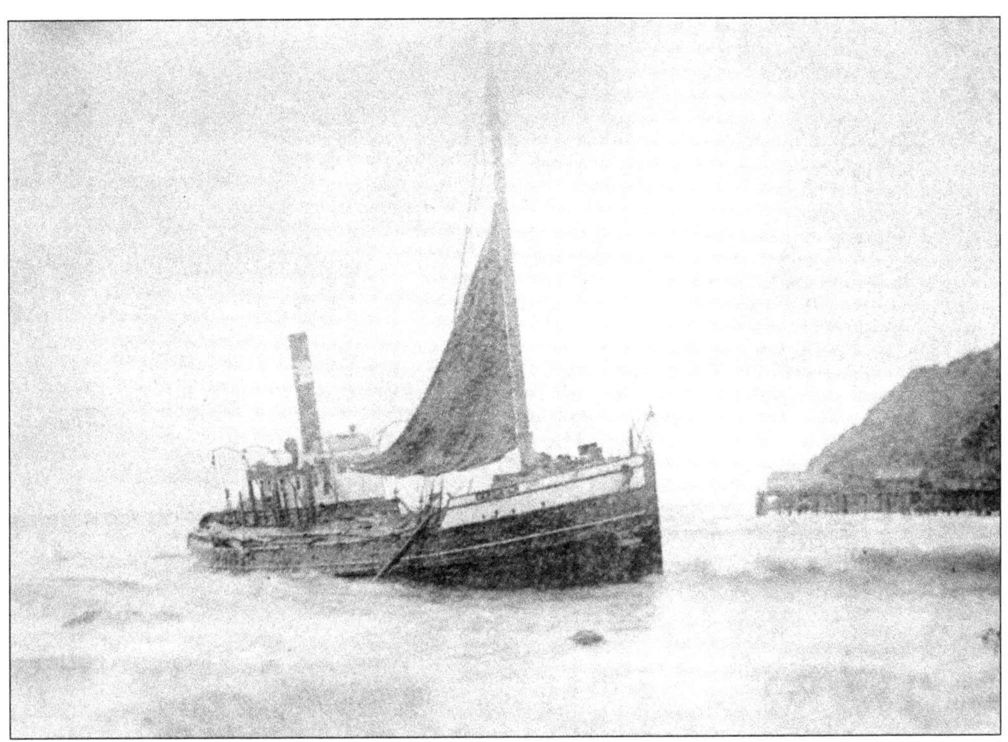

The *Fulton* operated on the West Coast for another 24 years under several owners. It grounded on one other occasion—this time on the British Columbia coast—but survived the incident. As of 1928, the *Fulton* was converted into a floating cannery at Willapa Harbor, Washington. It was later abandoned in Raymond, Washington. (CHM 007-25.376.)

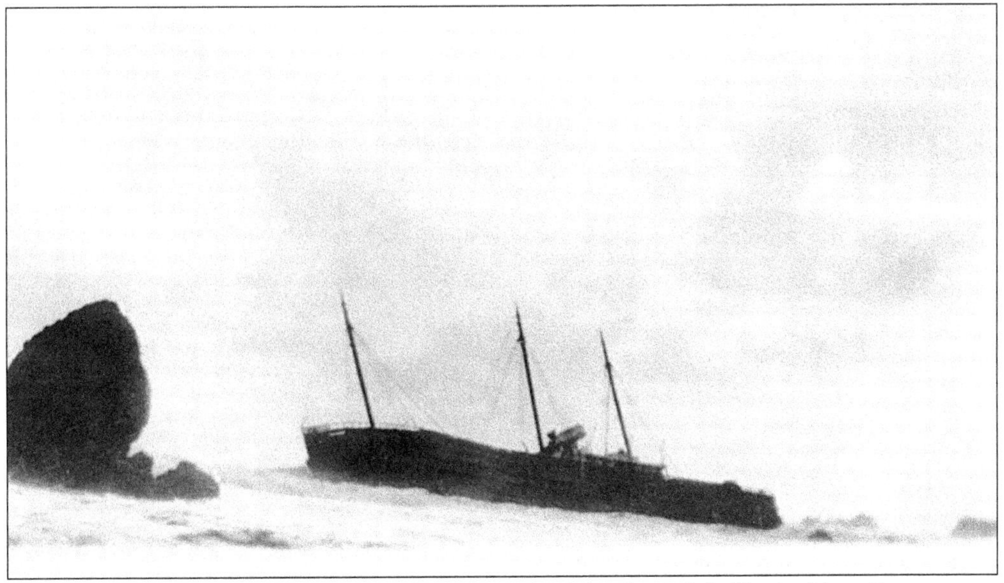

The steam schooner *Joan of Arc* (*Joan de Arc*) was built by the Rolph Shipbuilding Company in Rolph, California in 1918. The wooden hulled vessel was 2,360 gross tons and 245 feet long with a 45-foot breadth and a 28-foot depth. It was owned by the Rolph Navigation Company. This photograph, depicting all three masts, is rare. (Bandon Historical Society 14621.)

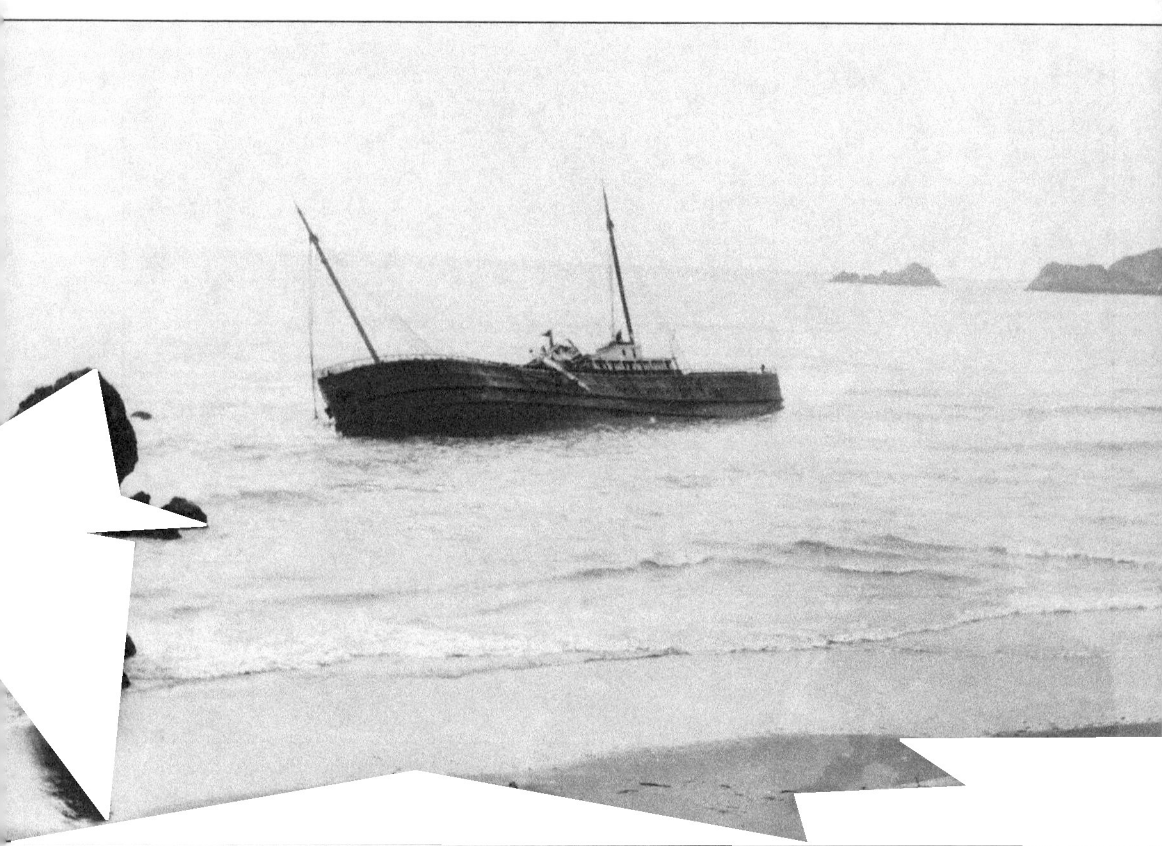

On November 16, 1920, the *Joan of Arc* struck a Rogue River reef during a storm. The ship had been en route from Portland to San Pedro with a cargo of lumber. Capt. Hans Michelson attempted to take the ship out to sea, but the fires in the boilers in the leaking ship went out. The *City of Topeka* arrived and rescued the *Joan of Arc*'s 28 passengers and crew. Above, one of the masts has fallen. Since this is one of the best know photographs of the wreck, many falsely believed that the ship had only two masts. Although the vessel was initially refloated, it ended up drifting onto the beach, where it became a total loss. (CHM 009-16.348.)

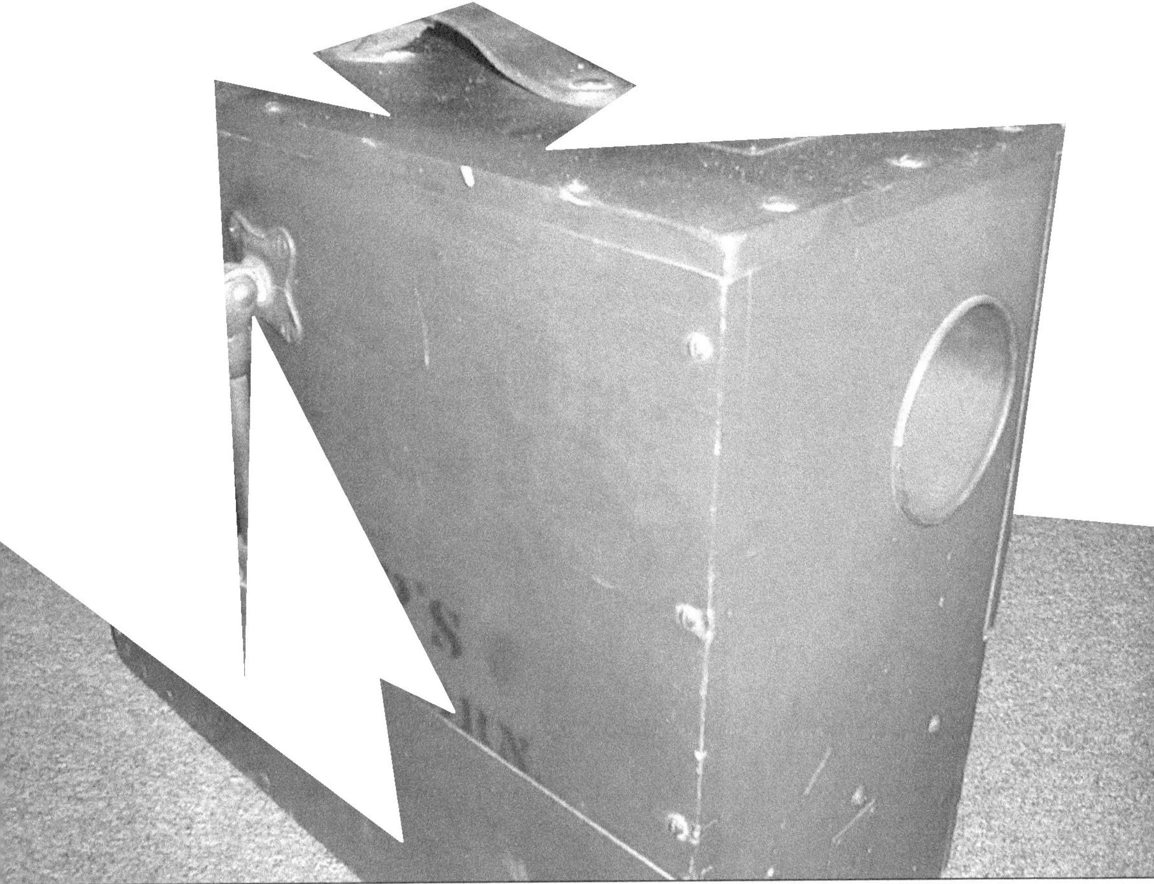

Fortunately, there was no loss of life during the shipwreck of the steam schooner *Joan of Arc*. Most of the gear and cargo was salvaged from the ship. The hull was later broken up by winter storms. This foghorn was one of the items salvaged. It was manufactured by L.D. Lothrop in Gloucester, Massachusetts, and donated to the Coos History Museum by Robert Forty. (CHM 970-20.)

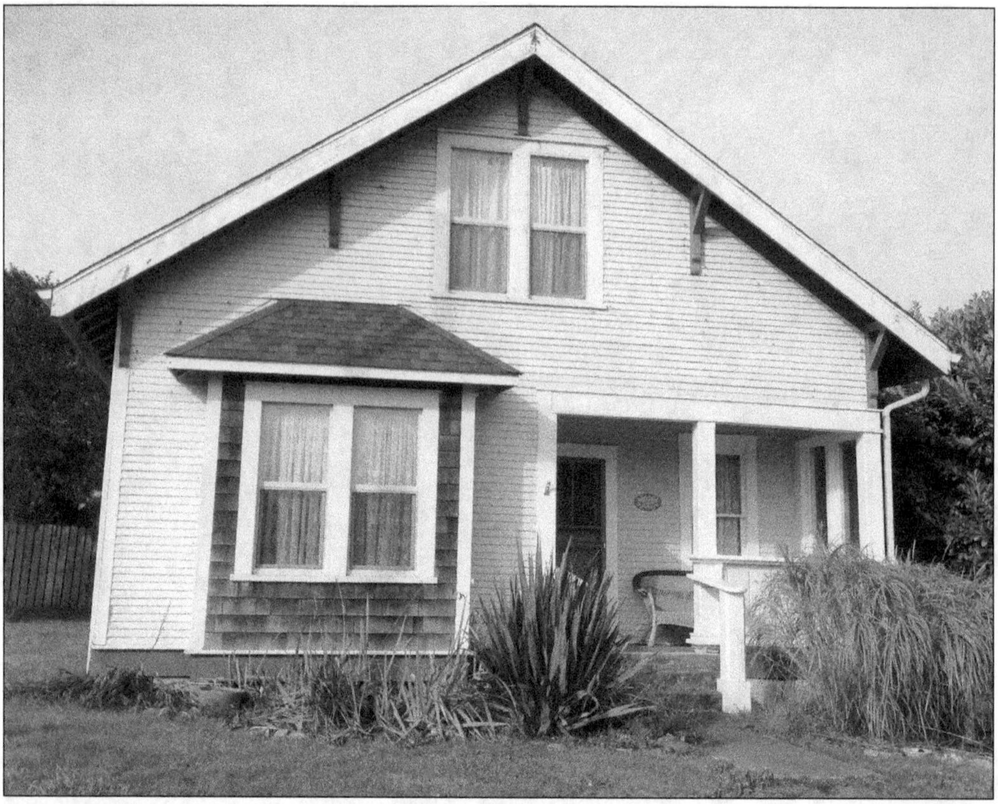

Robert "Bob" Forty salvaged lumber from the wreck of the *Joan of Arc* and used it to build this house in 1921. For many years, he and his family lived there. It was known locally as the "Forty House." Since then, it has been a restaurant and a bed and breakfast. It has been a vacation rental since 2002, appropriately named after the ship *Joan of Arc*. (Both, author's collection.)

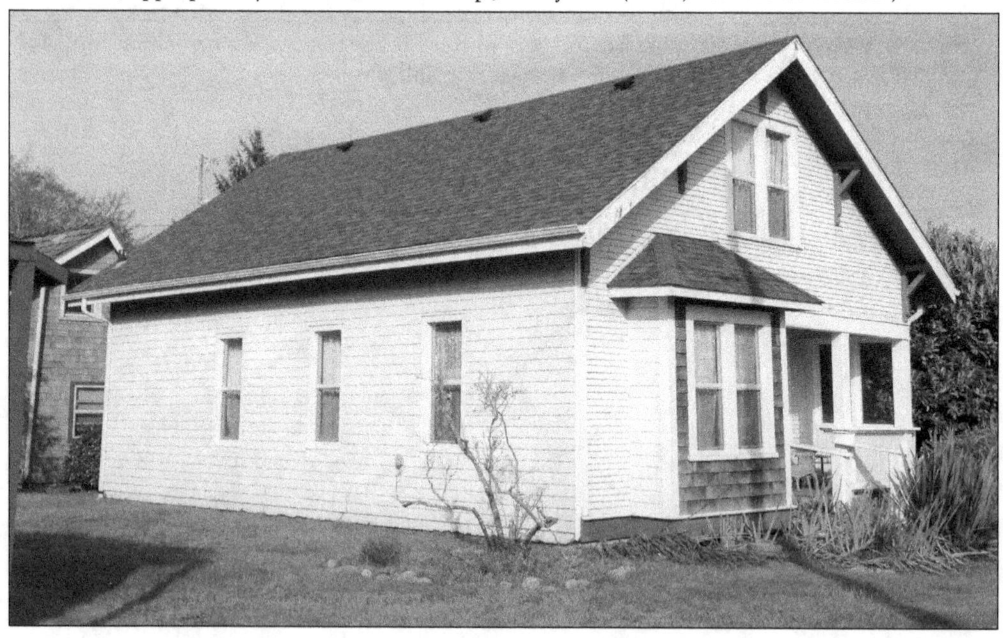

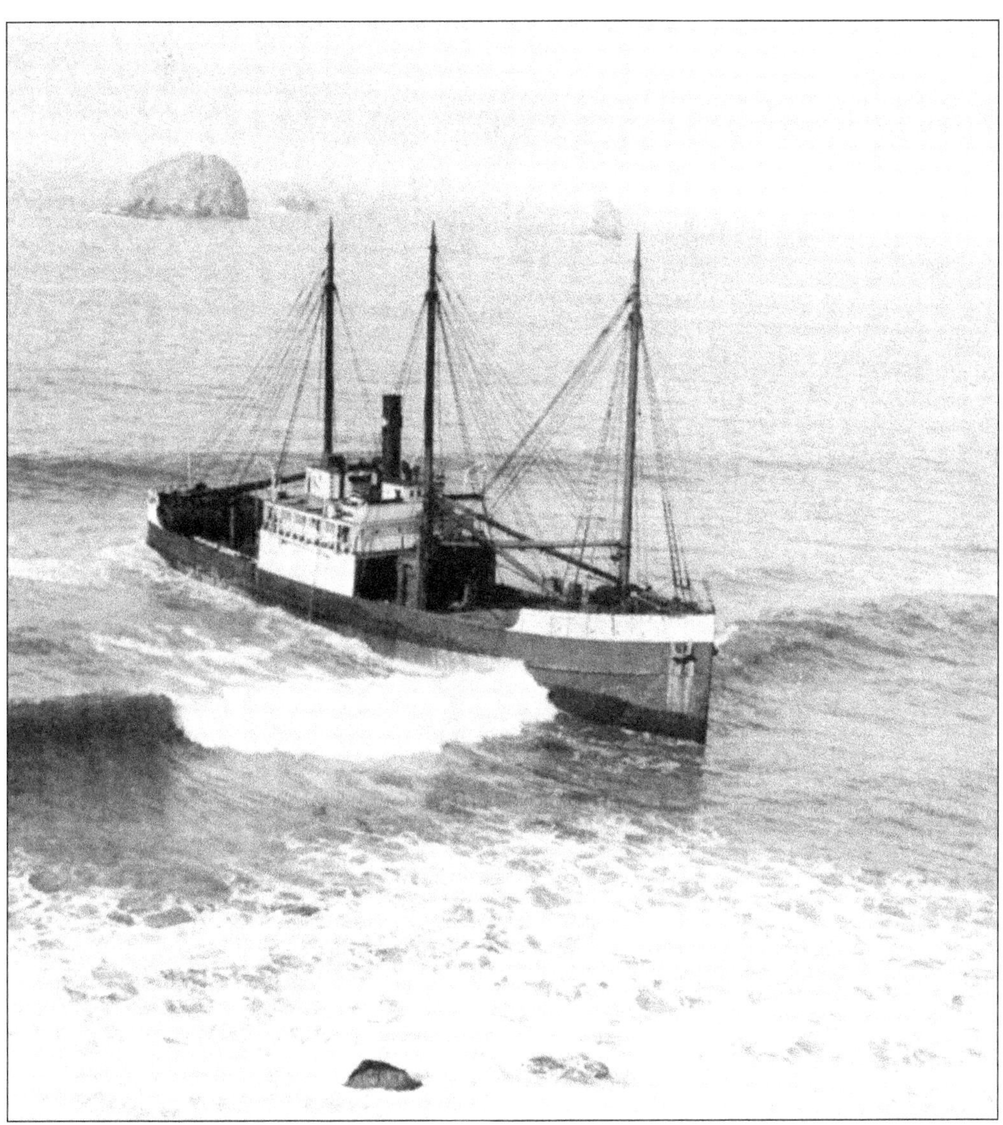

The 1,266-gross-ton steam schooner *Phyllis* was built by the Aberdeen Shipbuilding Company for W.R. Chamberlin and Company at Aberdeen, Washington, in 1917. The wooden-hulled vessel was 215 feet long with a 42-foot beam and a 17-foot depth. The lumber carrier was powered by an 800-IHP triple-expansion engine. On March 9, 1936, the steamer *Phyllis* struck a submerged object off the coast of Curry County. With the ship taking on water, Capt. Victor Jacobson intentionally beached it a mile north of Humbug Mountain (south of Port Orford). The crew of 22 took to their lifeboats and were later picked up by the Port Orford Coast Guard. (Bandon Historical Society 53503.)

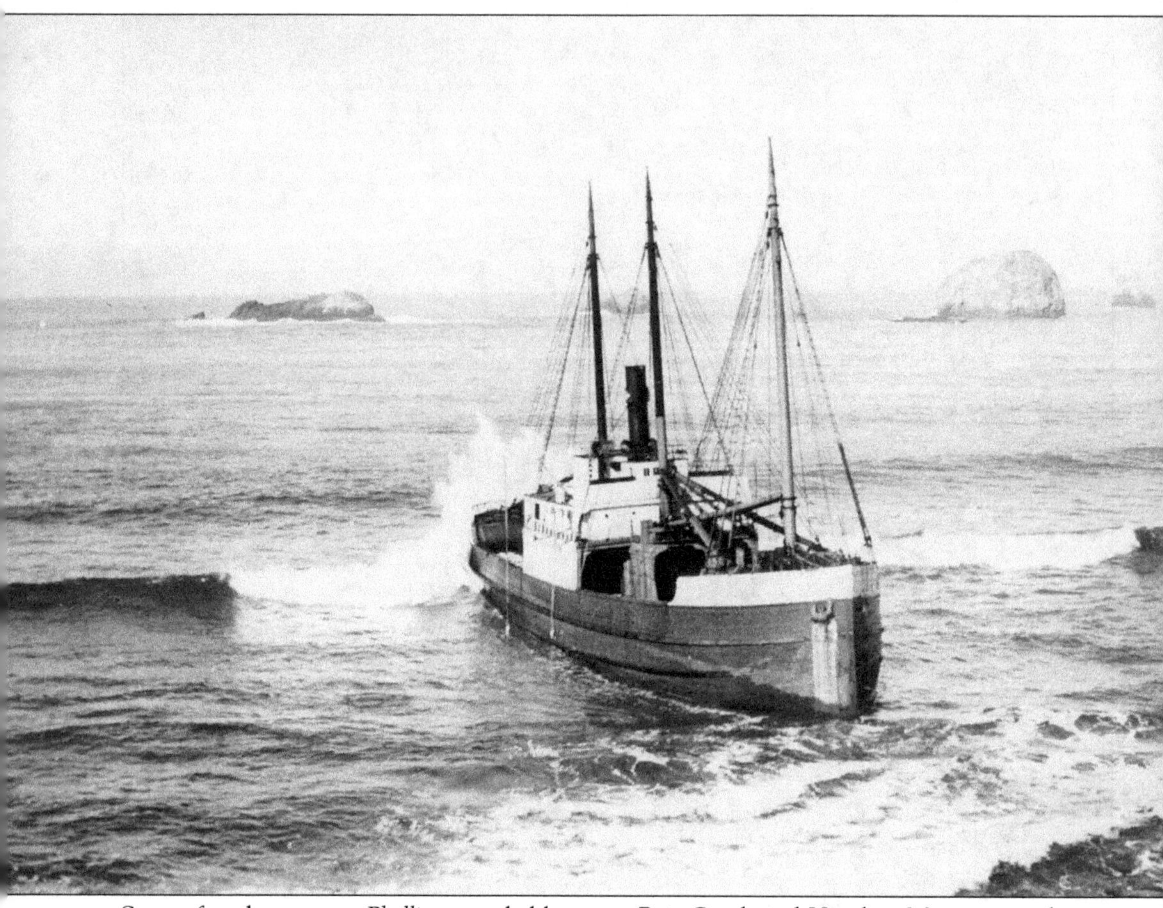

Soon after the steamer *Phyllis* grounded between Reiz Creek and Humbug Mountain, it began to break up in the rough surf. The ship was carrying 800 tons of general cargo. Tom Hatcher and Charley Davis built a cart road to the wreck site where John Marsh, Jack Kronenburg, and Fred Caughell salvaged the cargo, which included sugar, oil, canned goods, grain, and five-gallon containers of malted milk mix. Among the salvaged cargo was a large amount of canned food. The cans were intact, but many of the labels washed off before they were salvaged. The cans were sold cheaply as "mystery meals." (CHM 007-25.531.)

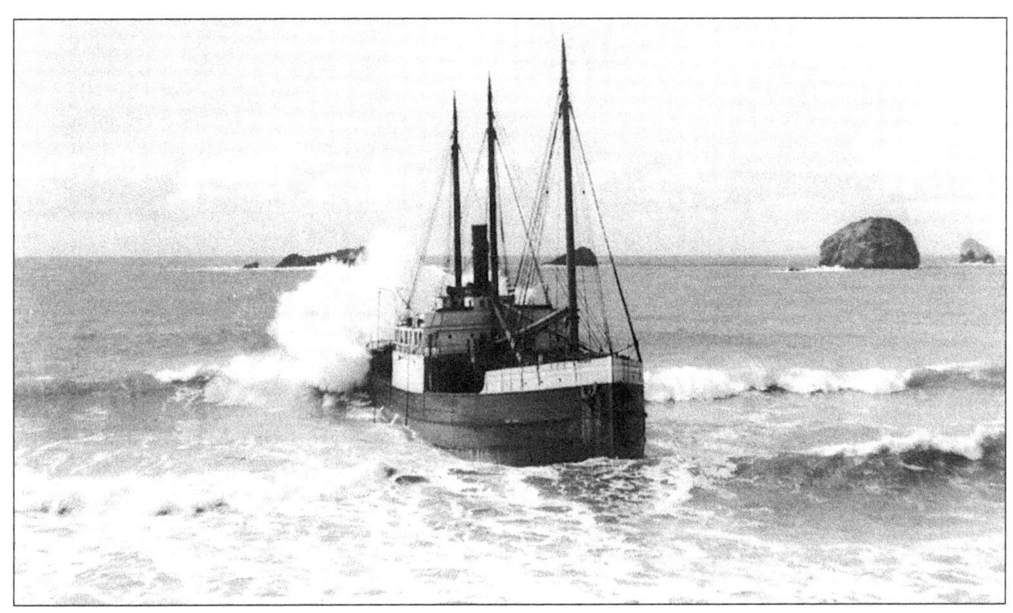

Above, a large wave breaks against the hull of the grounded steam schooner *Phyllis* near Port Orford in March 1936. The below photograph was taken some time later after the weather had calmed down. There are men standing on the deck of the disabled ship. A breeches buoy device can be seen rigged up on the right. A line runs between the ship and the shore. (Above, Alan Mitchell; below, CHM 009-16.1595a.)

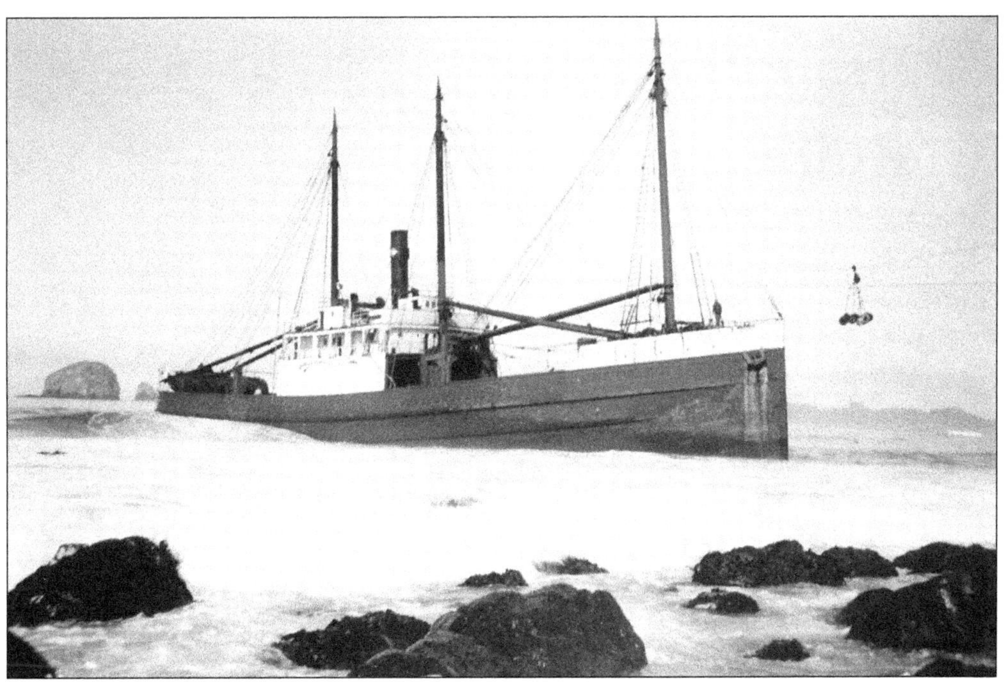

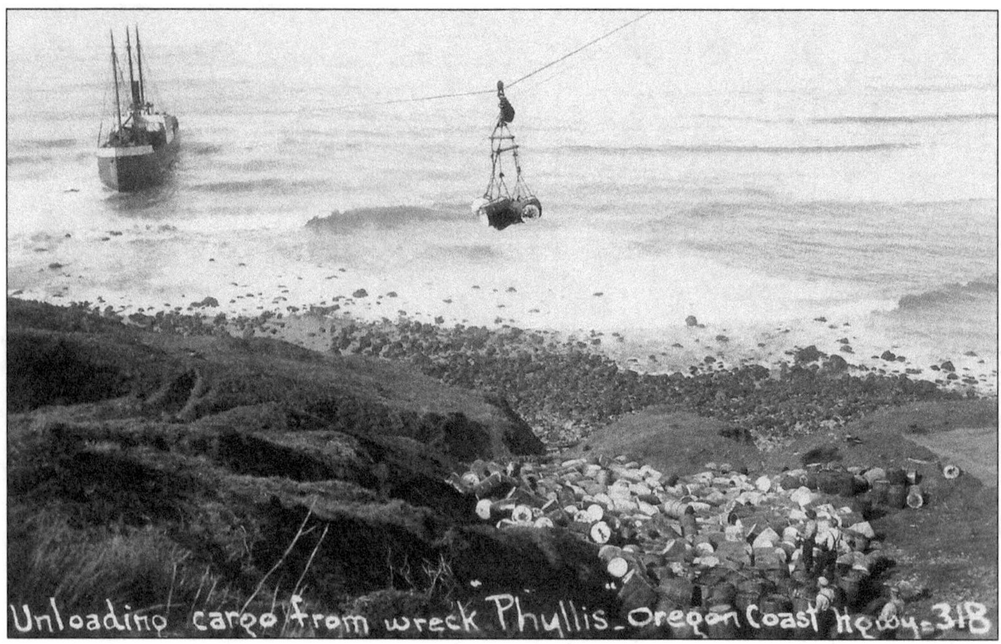

On March 9, 1936, the *Phyllis* grounded after striking a submerged rock off the beach near Humbug Mountain during stormy and foggy conditions. Henry Axtel purchased the hull of the shipwreck. He intended to turn it into a tourist site. As part of his plan, he cut the ship into two pieces. Unfortunately, another storm struck the coast and the pieces began to break up. (Both, Alan Mitchell.)

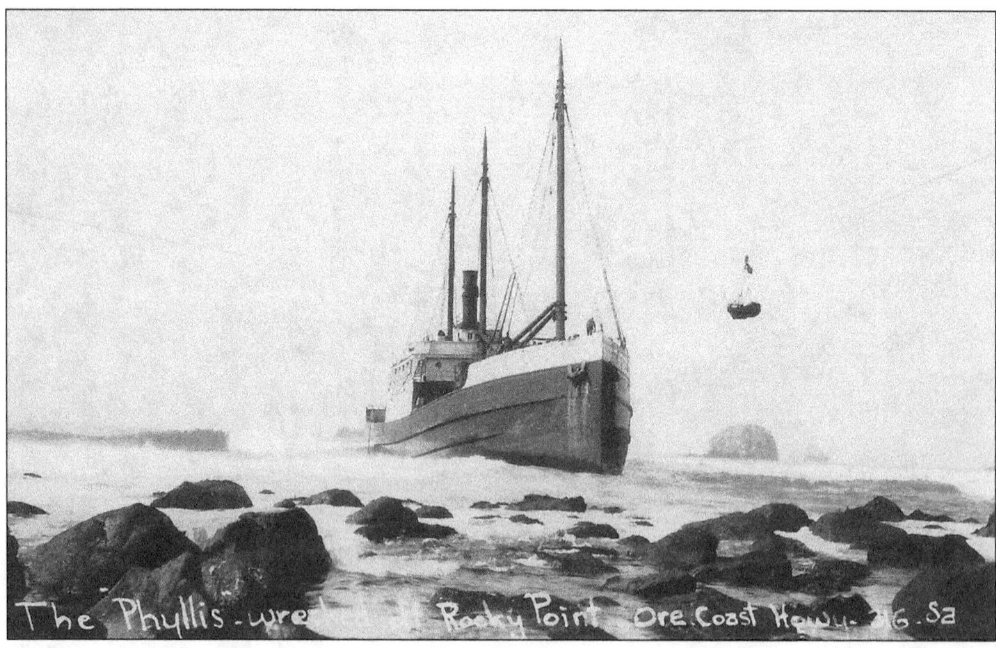

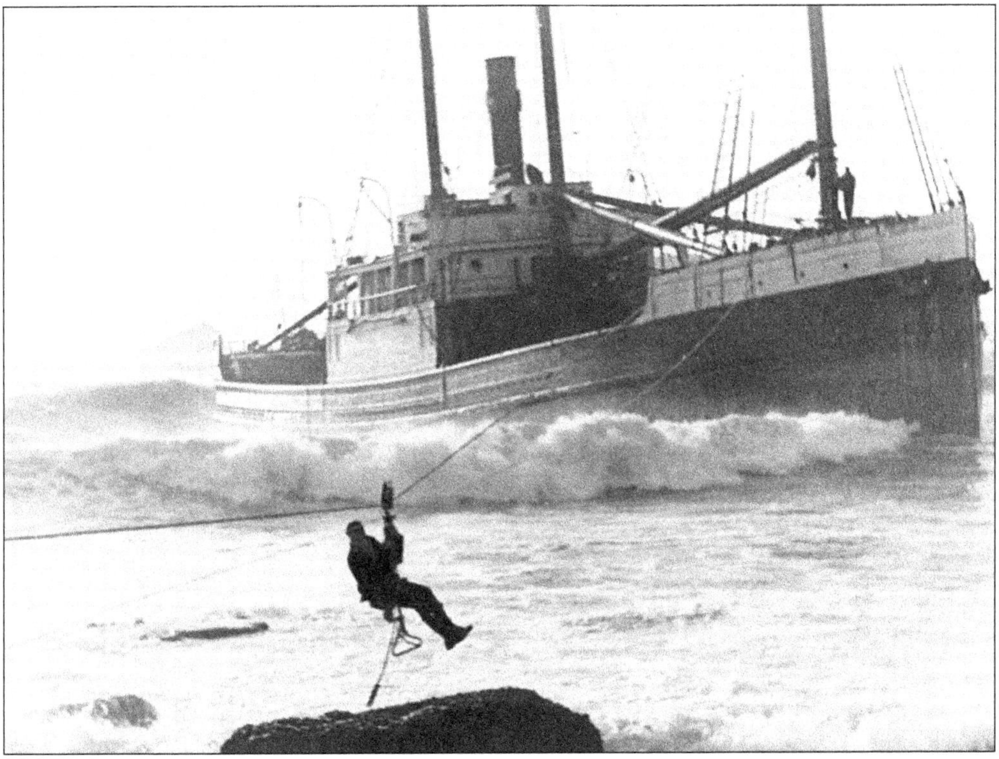

Above, a rope extends between the grounded steam schooner *Phyllis* and the shore while a man demonstrates how to use a breeches buoy device. The ship's cargo was salvaged using a "high-line" spanning the mile and a quarter from the wreck to the shore. Although the cargo was successfully salvaged, the hull of the ship became a total loss. (CHM 970-146.)

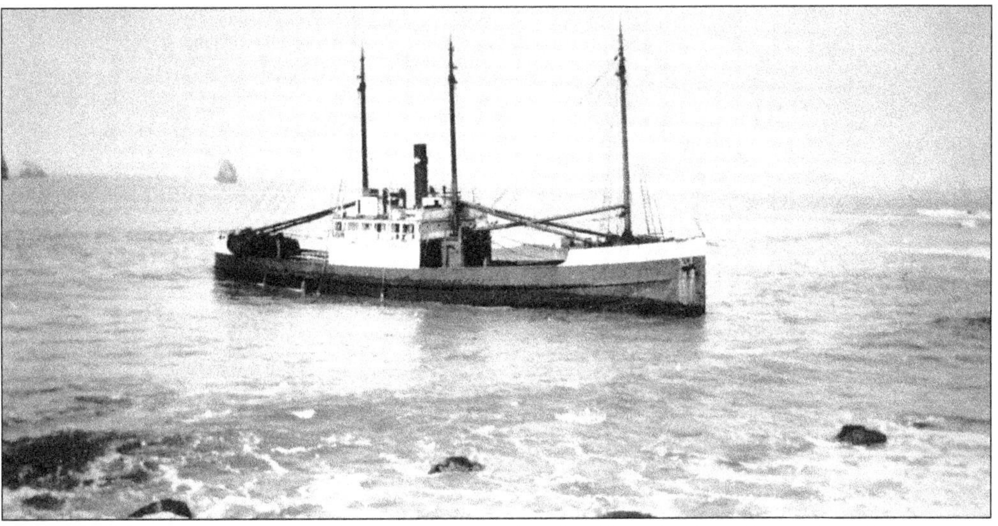

The wooden steam schooner *Phyllis* was owned by the Chamberline Steamship Company at the time of its loss. This photograph shows the wreck off the coast during calm conditions. A number of submerged rocks are visible. It is easy to imagine how hard they would be to spot during stormy conditions and how easy it would be for a passing ship to accidentally strike one. (CHM 009-16.1595.)

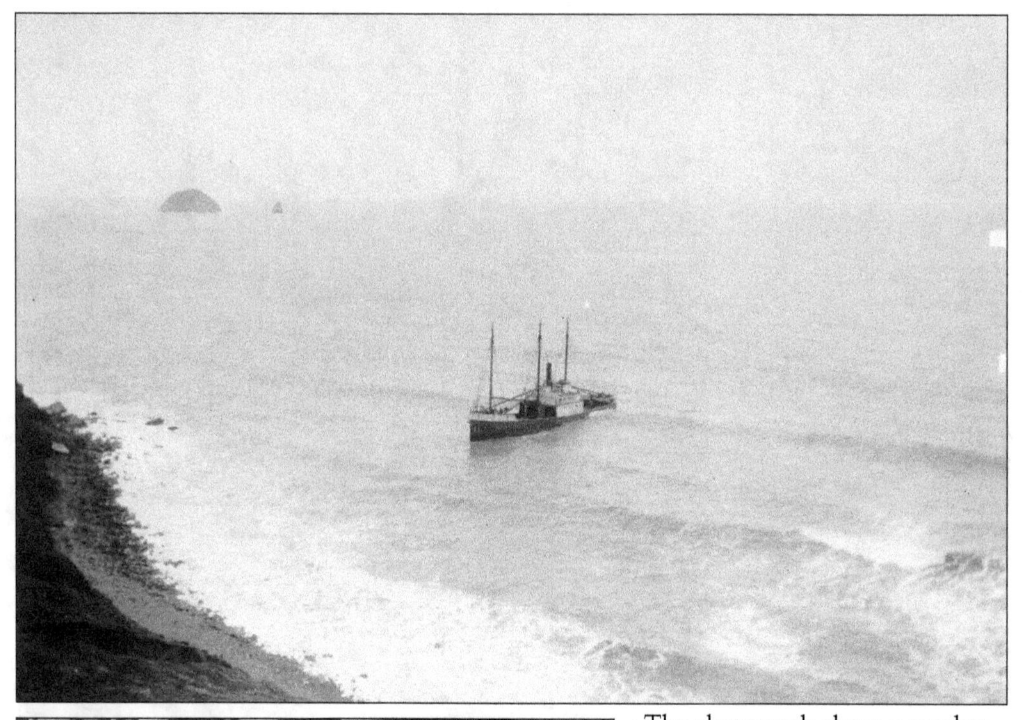

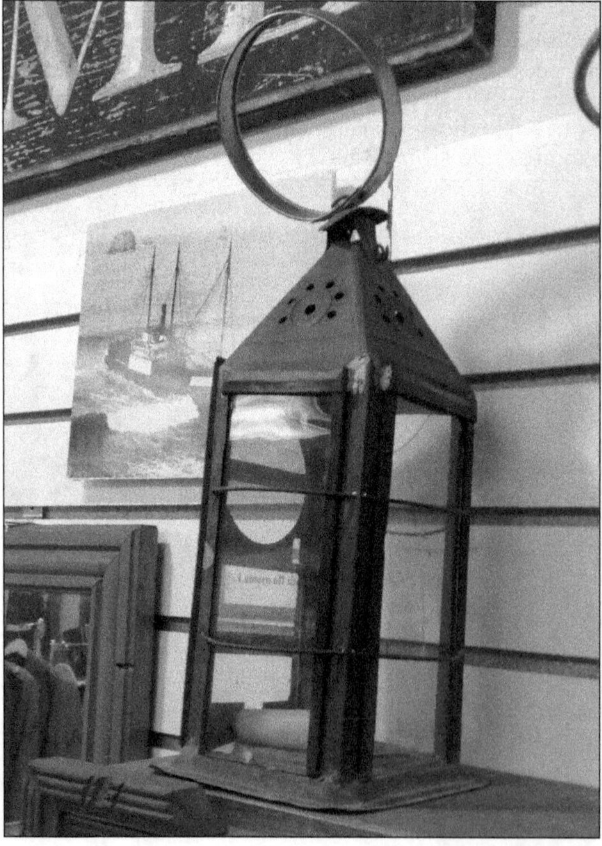

The photograph above was taken from the hillside looking down at the grounded ship in the surf. It demonstrates just how close to shore the *Phyllis* rested. This lantern was also salvaged from the shipwreck. It is currently on display at the Bandon Historical Society Museum. (Above, Bandon Historical Society 48091; left, Bandon Historical Society.)

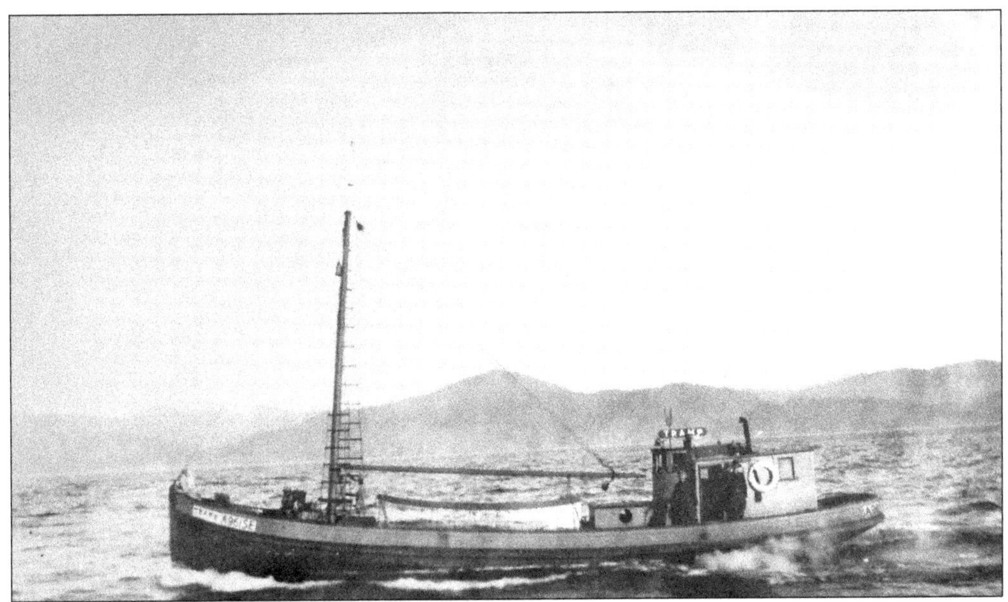

The gas schooner *Tramp* was built by John Swing at Empire City (on the Coos Bay) in 1911. The 56-foot vessel was originally named the *Pilot*. It is shown here near Empire City in 1911. On December 3, 1923, the *Tramp* departed the Rogue River on its way to Coos Bay, under the command of Captain Knight. Shortly after its departure, a fierce coastal storm developed. (CHM 992-8-1862.)

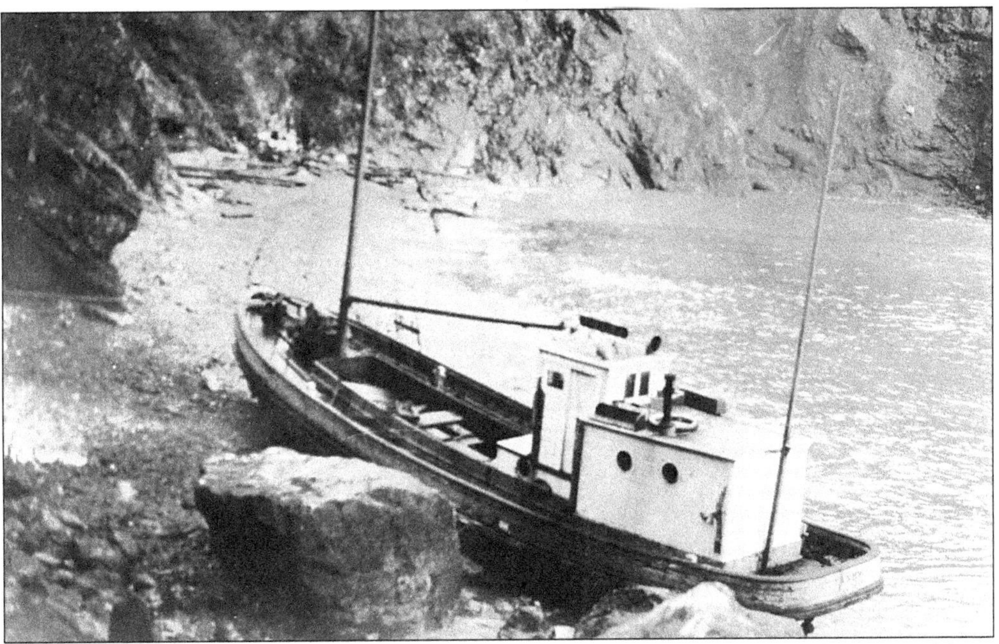

Initially, it was feared that the *Tramp* had been lost at sea. However, the ship and its crew of three had taken shelter in Nellie's Cove, a mile from Port Orford. It is tucked away behind a headland where there is less wind. Unfortunately, there is not much room for vessels to maneuver between the rocks at the entrance to the cove. (Bandon Historical Society 31065.)

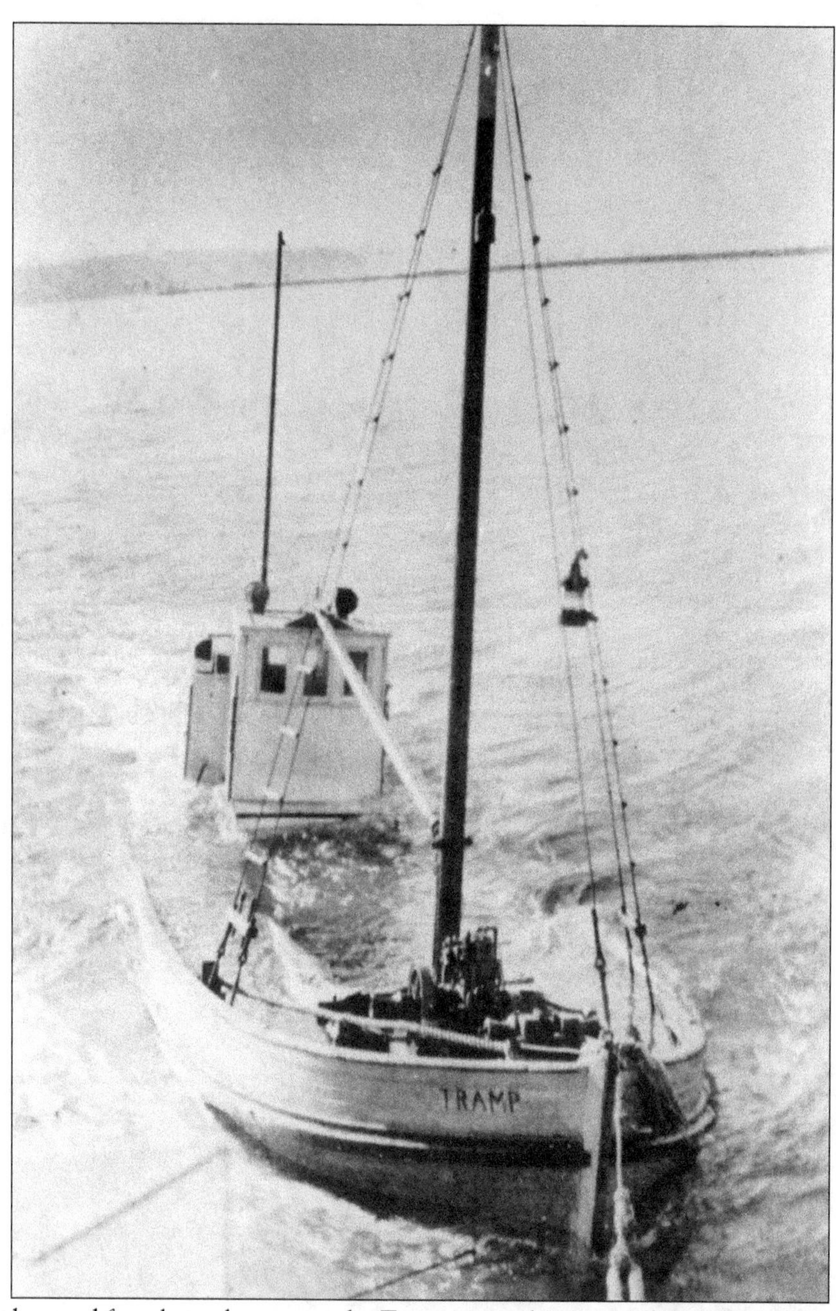

Although spared from being lost at sea, the *Tramp* went ashore in Nellie's Cove before the crew had time to moor it. Captain Knight later said that his vessel could have been tied up without any damage if the metal ring bolts had not been so badly rusted. Captain Knight and Engineer Norton made several attempts to refloat the *Tramp*. They succeeded twice, but both times it ended up back on the beach. Each time they had to re-caulk the damaged areas before they could make another attempt. Ed Prince was injured while attempting to repair the ship and taken to Bandon for treatment. After the third attempt, the *Tramp* remained afloat. On December 23rd, the steam schooner *Cleone* towed the waterlogged *Tramp* to Coos Bay for repairs, which were completed by Kruse & Banks Shipyard. (CHM 007-25.374.)

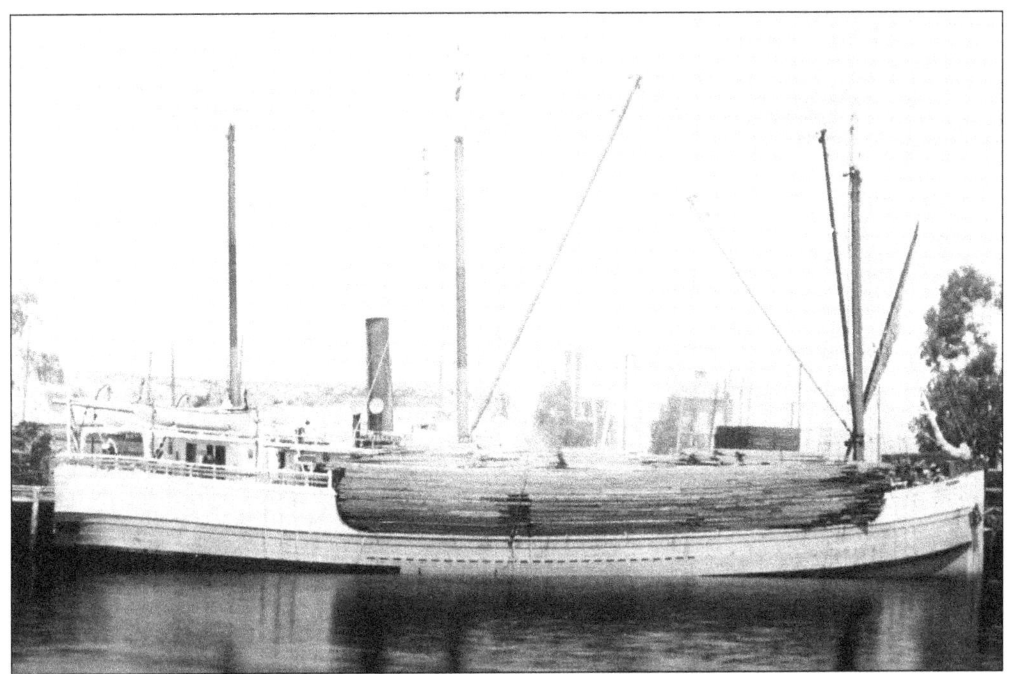

The steam schooner *Willapa* (also known as the *Willapa 2*) was constructed at the Kruse & Banks Shipyard in North Bend, Oregon, in 1917 as the *Florence Olson*. The 1,185-gross-ton lumber carrier encountered a storm while traveling from Marshfield to San Francisco on December 2, 1941. Overnight, the ship began to take on water before ultimately running aground south of Port Orford. Capt. Oscar Peterson was injured in the accident. The Coast Guard arrived and rescued all 24 hands from the ship before it broke up. The sea was too rough for the 36-foot motor lifeboat to make a landing at Port Orford. James Combs, a local fisherman, made a dozen trips across 800 yards of choppy water in a dory to bring them safely ashore. (Above, CHM 009-16.2399; below, CHM 009-16.118.)

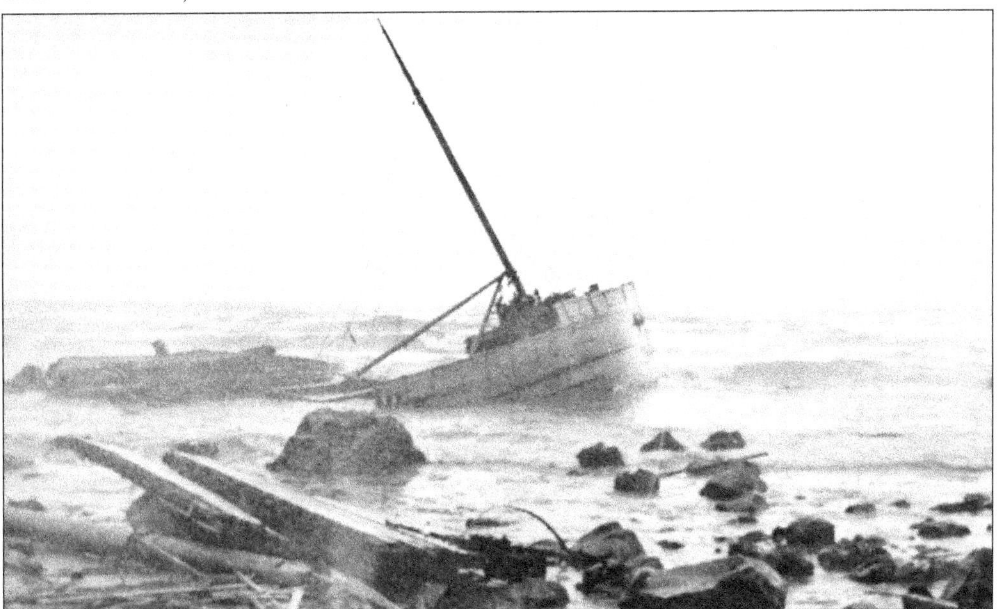

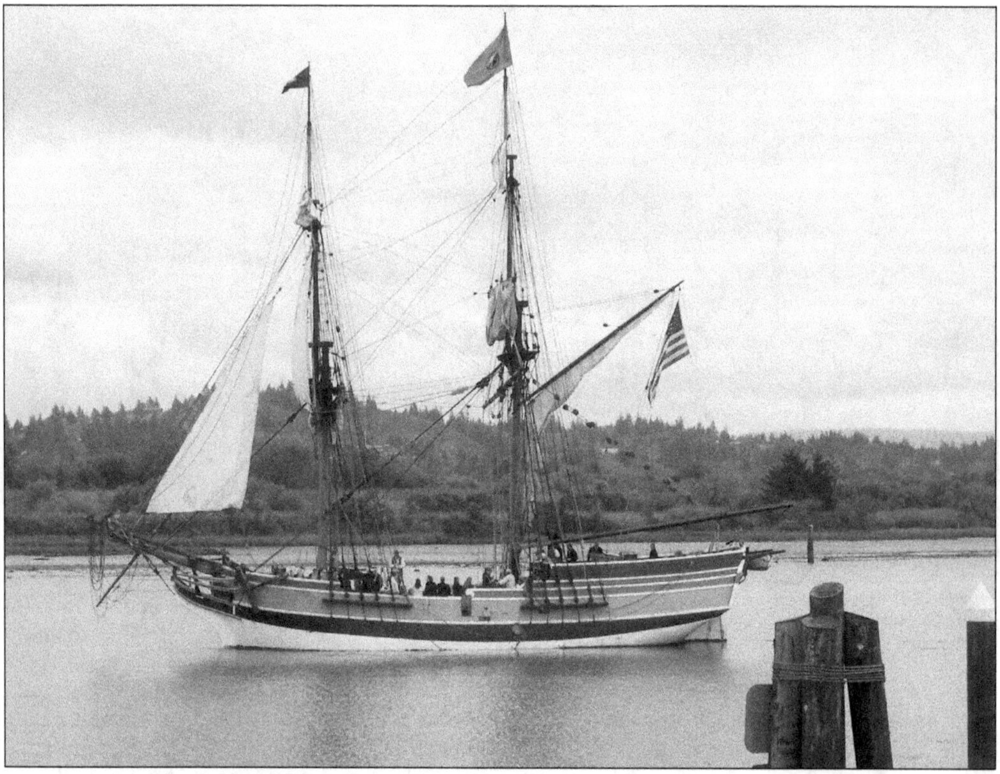

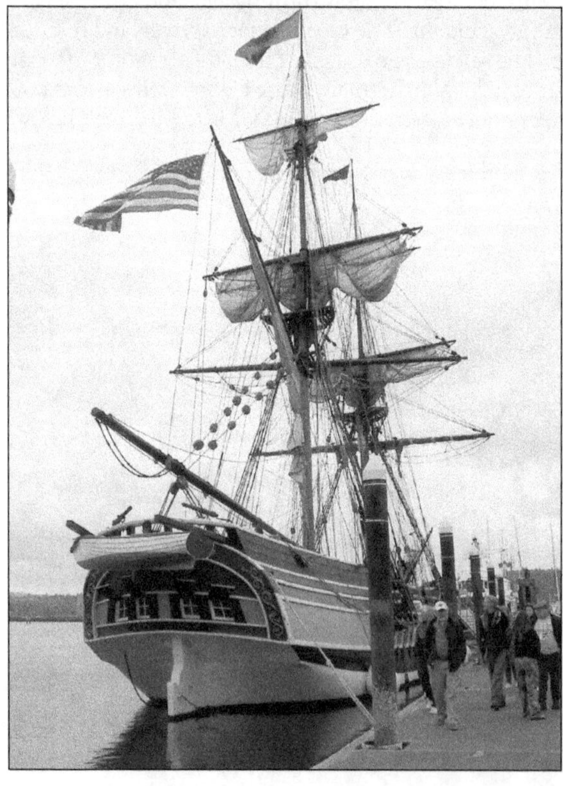

The *Lady Washington* is a full-scale replica of the original *Lady Washington*, which was the first American vessel to make landfall on the west coast of North America in 1788. The replica was constructed at Aberdeen, Washington, by the Grays Harbor Historical Seaport Authority. It was launched in 1989 as part of the Washington State Centennial celebration. The 99-gross-ton replica was constructed as a brig. It is 112 feet long with a 22-feet beam and an 11-foot depth. Over the years, the *Lady Washington* has become somewhat of a celebrity. The ship has appeared in numerous movies and television shows, including *Pirates of the Caribbean: The Curse of the Black Pearl*, *Star Trek: Generations*, and *Once Upon a Time*. The *Lady Washington* is shown here on the Coos Bay in 2006. (Both, author's collection.)

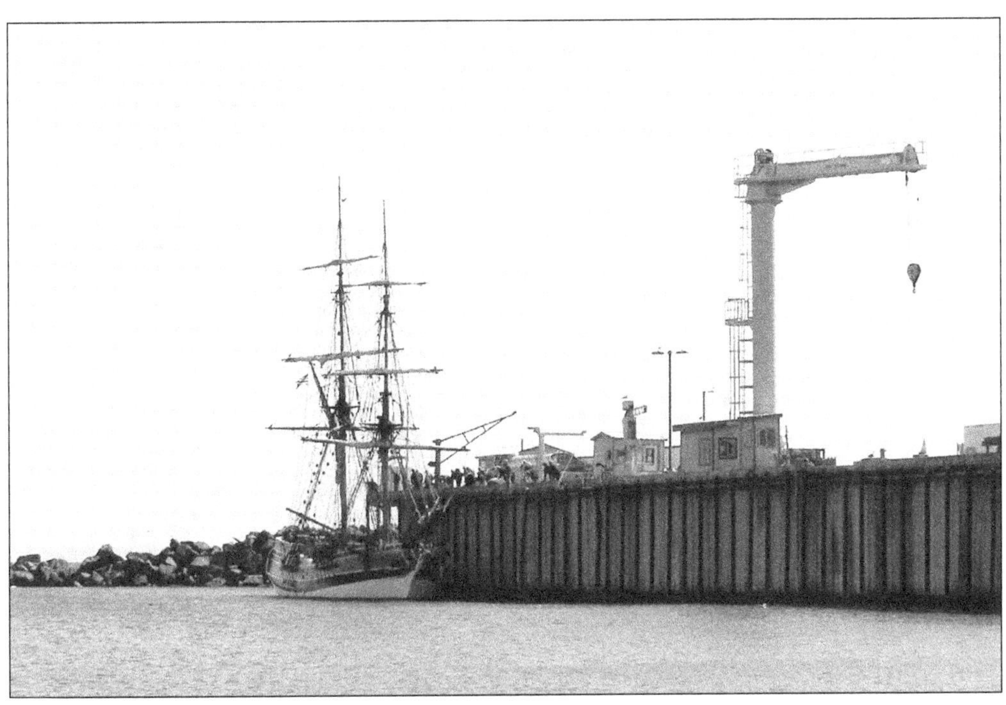

The *Lady Washington* is the Washington State Ship as well as the state's "Tall Ship Ambassador." The *Lady Washington* and the *Hawaiian Chieftain*, the ship's traveling companion, make regular trips up and down the West Coast. During their visits, the ships are open to the public for tours. They often host groups of school children where they teach them about maritime history, sailing ships, and the maritime life. When they visit the Coos Bay, people can pay to go on a sail down the bay to the McCullough Bridge. Once there, the ships turn to face each other and then engage in a mock cannon battle. It is lots of fun—both for the passengers and for the folks watching from the shore. The *Lady Washington* is shown here at Port Orford. (Both, Alan Mitchell.)

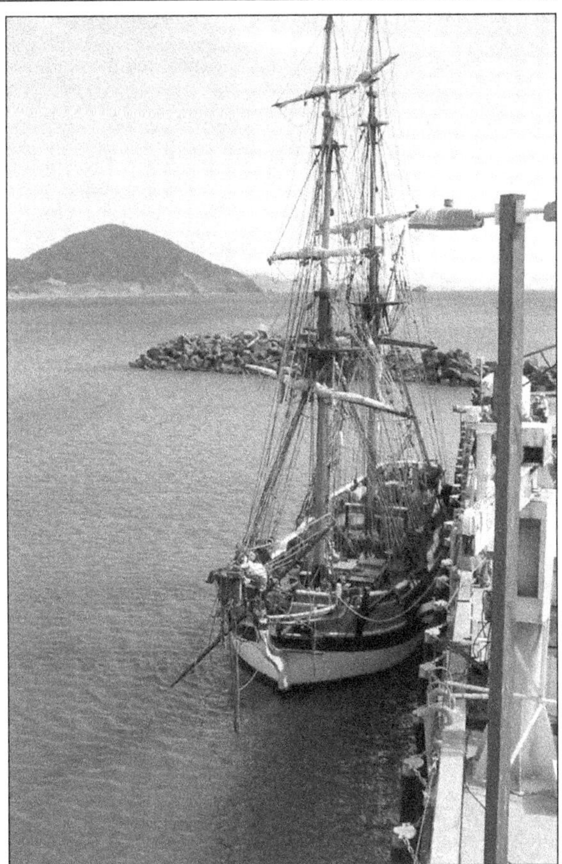

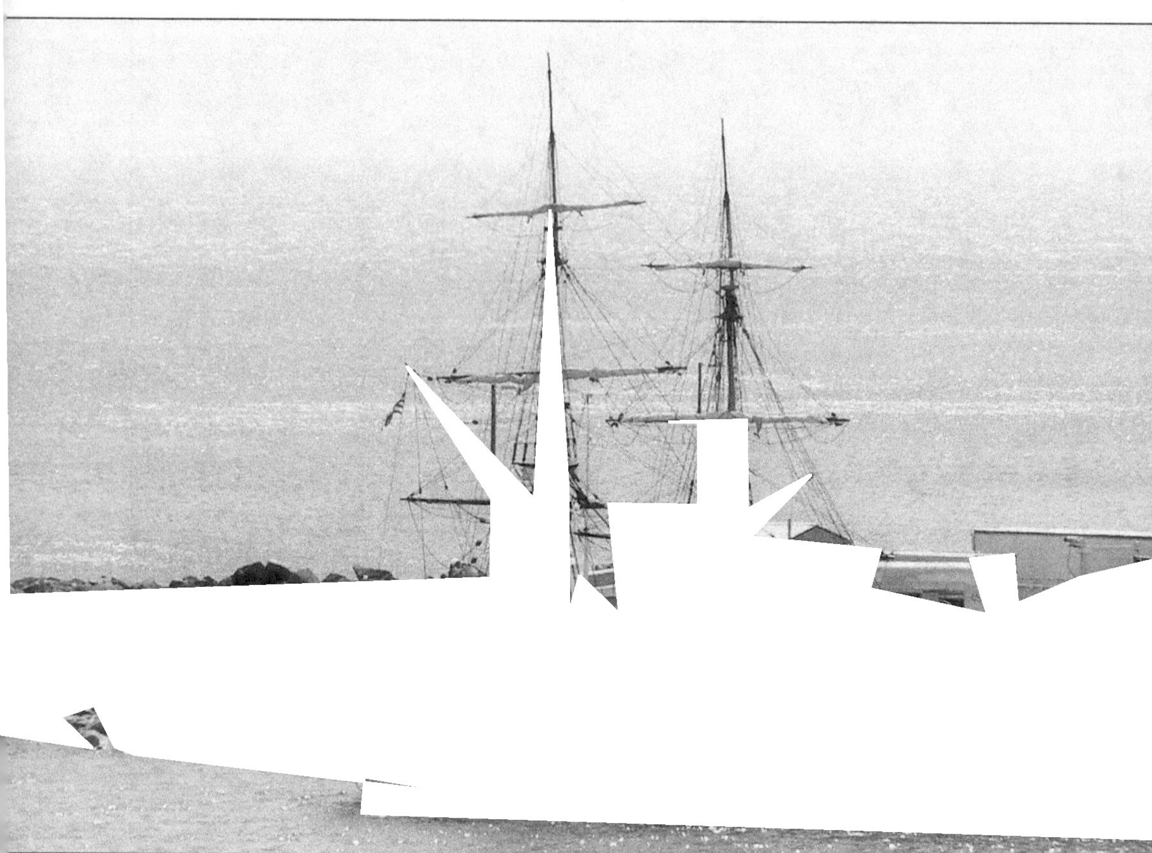

On May 13, 2008, the *Lady Washington* grounded in the Port Orford harbor. Although it is a replica of a two-masted sailing ship, it also has a diesel engine. The *Lady Washington* was traveling north after a tall ships festival at Crescent City. It had stopped at Port Orford to refuel on its way to Coos Bay. The crew was forced to wait over seven hours for the tide to come back in to refloat the ship. In the meantime, large groups of people visited the harbor to see the ship, take photographs, and visit with the crew. When the tide came in, the *Lady Washington* was pulled free with the assistance of the fishing vessel *Paiute*, which was owned by Orion Ashdown. The ship sustained minor damage during the incident. (Alan Mitchell.)

Three

Gold Beach and the Rogue River

Human habitation at Gold Beach (originally Ellensburg) dates back to 6600 BC. Numerous explorers visited the area over the years including a group from Spain in the 1540s, Hudson Bay trappers in 1827, and the Jedediah Smith expedition in June 1828.

In 1877, Robert Dennison "R.D." Hume established a hatchery on the Rogue River. Nicknamed the "pygmy monopolist," R.D. Hume also owned a cannery, several factories, hotels, local newspapers, a racetrack, and a sawmill. His businesses played a large role in making the early town successful. In 1895, R.D. Hume founded the town of Wedderburn, which was located north of the Rogue River. He owned all of the tidelands along the lower Rogue River. He also constructed small coastal ships.

The Gold Beach Port District was established in 1958. They have made numerous improvements over the years. In 1961, a rock jetty system was built on the Rogue River, which helped form and maintain a shipping channel with a reliable water depth. In the 1960s, the port exported an average of 70,000 tons of logs per year. In 1972, the rock jetty system was extended upriver with the intention of providing flood and high water protection for the port.

Fishing in the area has changed and diversified over the years. It has included salmon, shrimp, crab, and sea urchin. Most of the seafood was processed locally at the Cannery Building, which was erected in 1972. In 1994, the vacant building was converted into a multiuse facility, and it continues to function as one to this day. It includes a seafood processing facility, coffee shop, restaurant, and office spaces with an ocean view.

In modern times, the Rogue River is known for its year-round fishing and its jet boat rides, which extend far upriver.

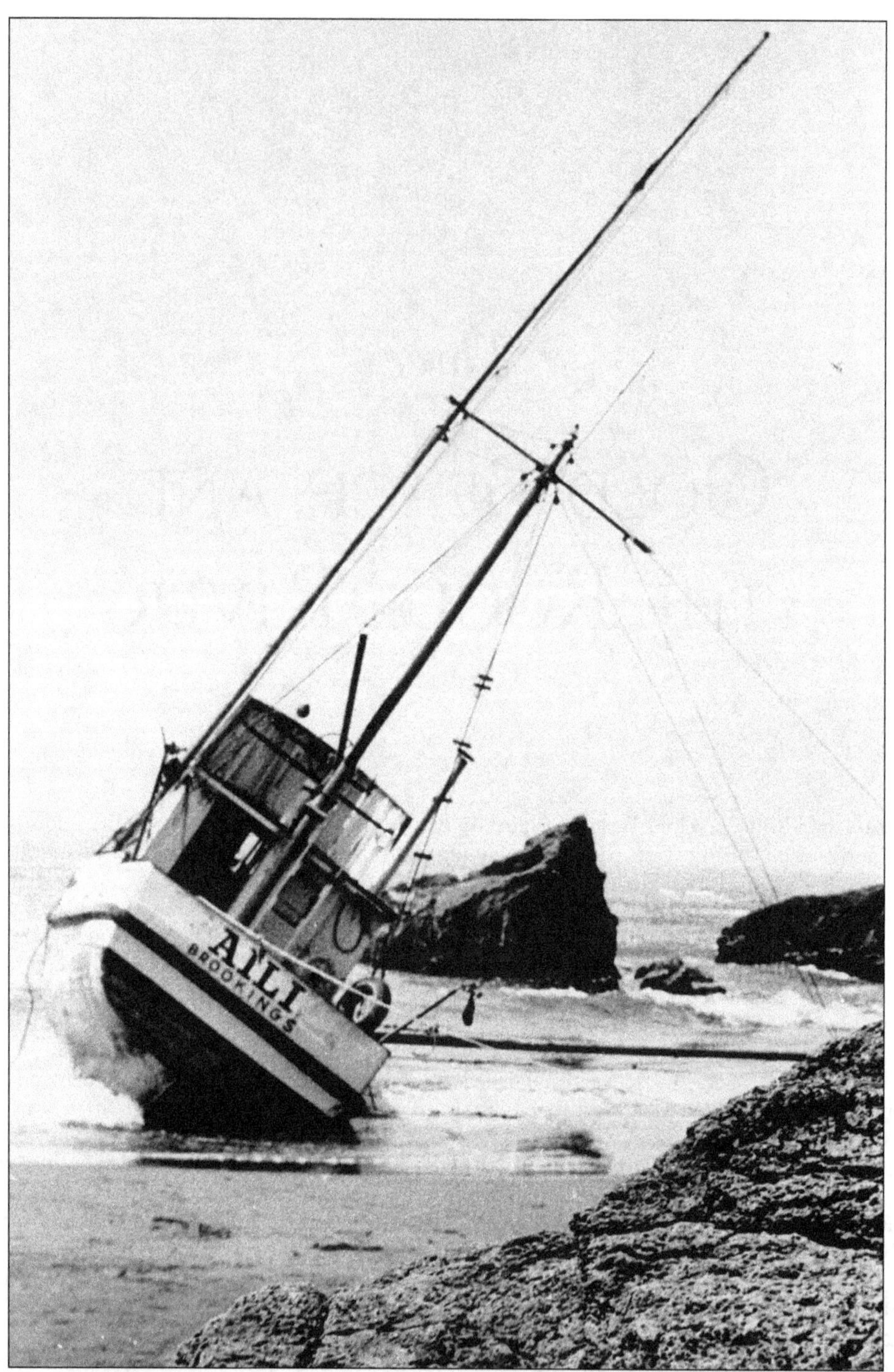

On August 6, 1969, the fishing vessel (F/V) *Aili* struck a rock off the southern Oregon coast. The pumps could not handle the amount of water rushing in through the large hole in the bow, so the captain intentionally ran the boat aground two miles south of Brookings to prevent it from sinking. The *Aili* was salvaged a few days later. It was soon repaired and returned to service. (CHM 009-16.1172.)

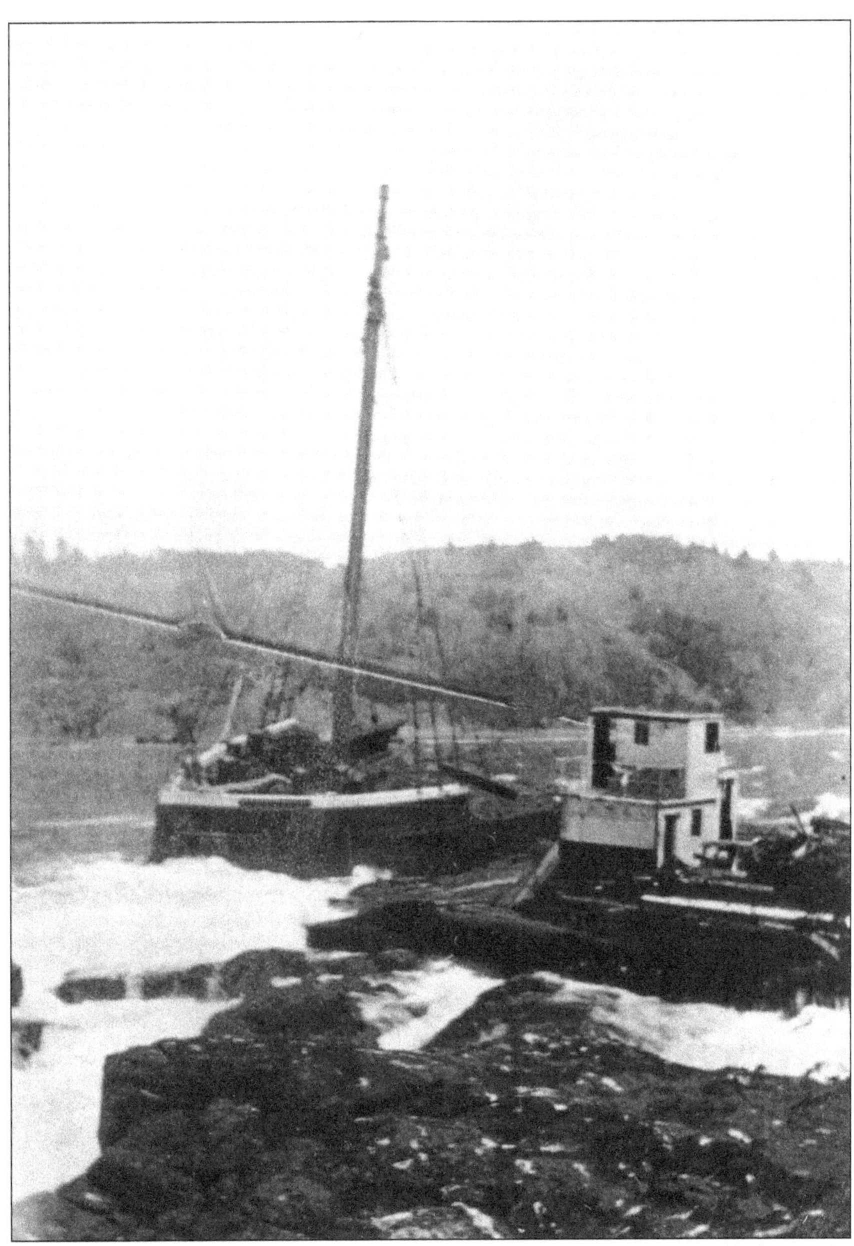

The gas schooner *Washcalore* was built by Kruse & Banks at their Stave Mill Shipyard in 1906. The wooden hulled vessel was 323 gross tons and 140 feet long with a 32-foot breadth and 10-foot depth. On May 21, 1911, the *Washcalore* was lost on Island Rock, a small reef just south of the mouth of the Rogue River. The ship encountered a gale while en route from San Francisco to the Siuslaw River with a cargo of general merchandise. Captain Peterson attempted to take shelter in a cove near Cape Sebastian. Unfortunately, the anchor chain broke and the ship drifted against Island Rock. The captain and 13 crew members sought shelter on the rock. They managed to salvage some supplies including several bottles of whiskey. The disabled ship soon broke into two pieces. Since Curry County did not have a lifesaving station, they had to wait 36 hours for the Coquille River Life-Saving Station crew to arrive from Bandon, 55 miles to the north, on the tug *Klihyam* to rescue them. (Bandon Historical Society 14622.)

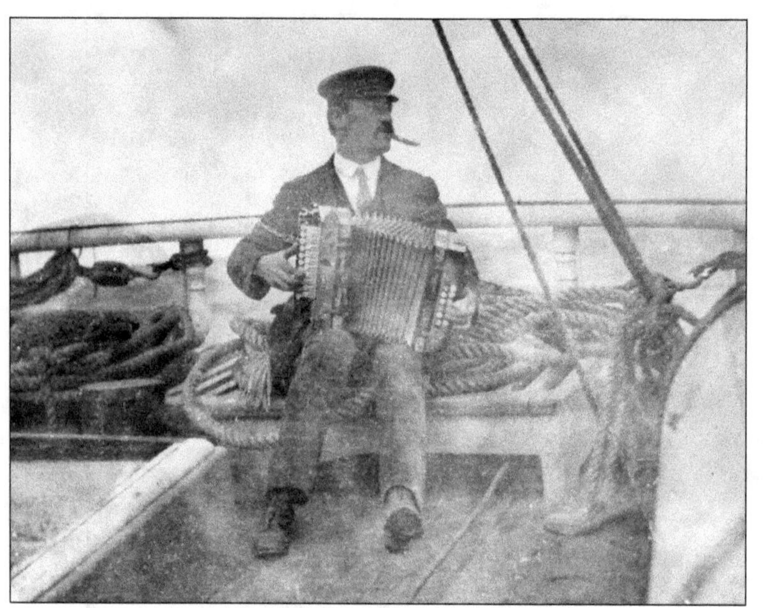

In this photograph, Capt. L. Christensen of the US Life-Saving Service takes a break from his duties to play the accordion and smoke a cigar. He is on board the tug *Klihyam*, which transported the Coquille Life-Saving Station crew to the site of the *Washcalore* wreck. (Bandon Historical Society 28064.)

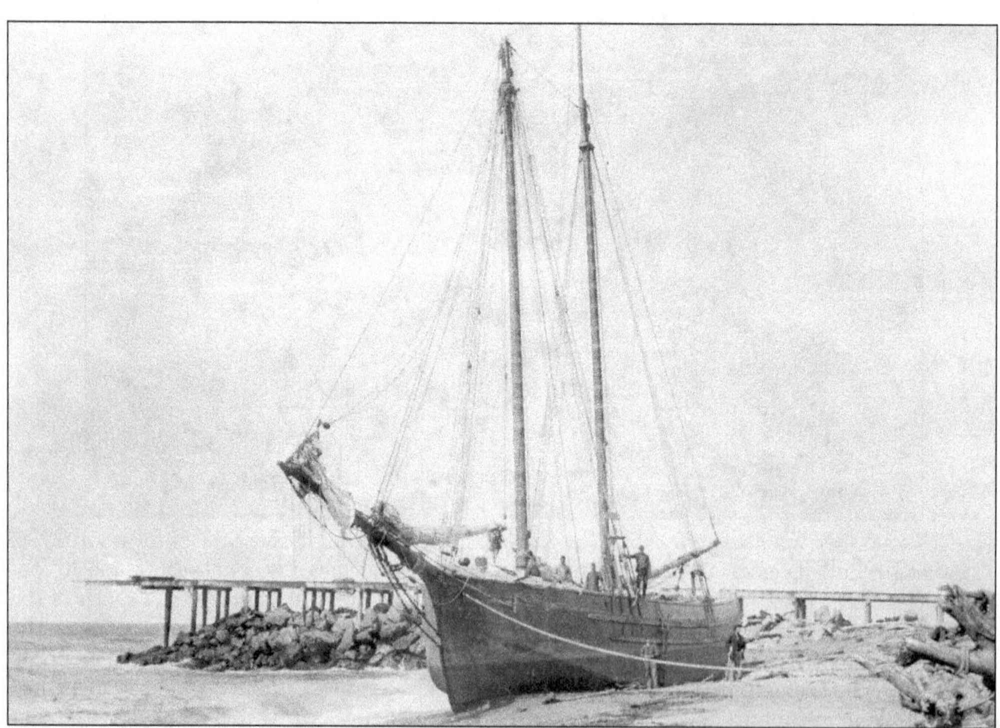

The two-masted schooner *Berwick* was built by Matthew Turner at Benicia, California in 1887. The vessel was 100 gross tons. The ship had a history of maritime mishaps, but it usually managed to avoid major damage. For instance, the *Berwick* ended up on the beach south of the Coquille River after a failed attempt to cross the bar on April 12, 1896. (Bandon Historical Society 28910.)

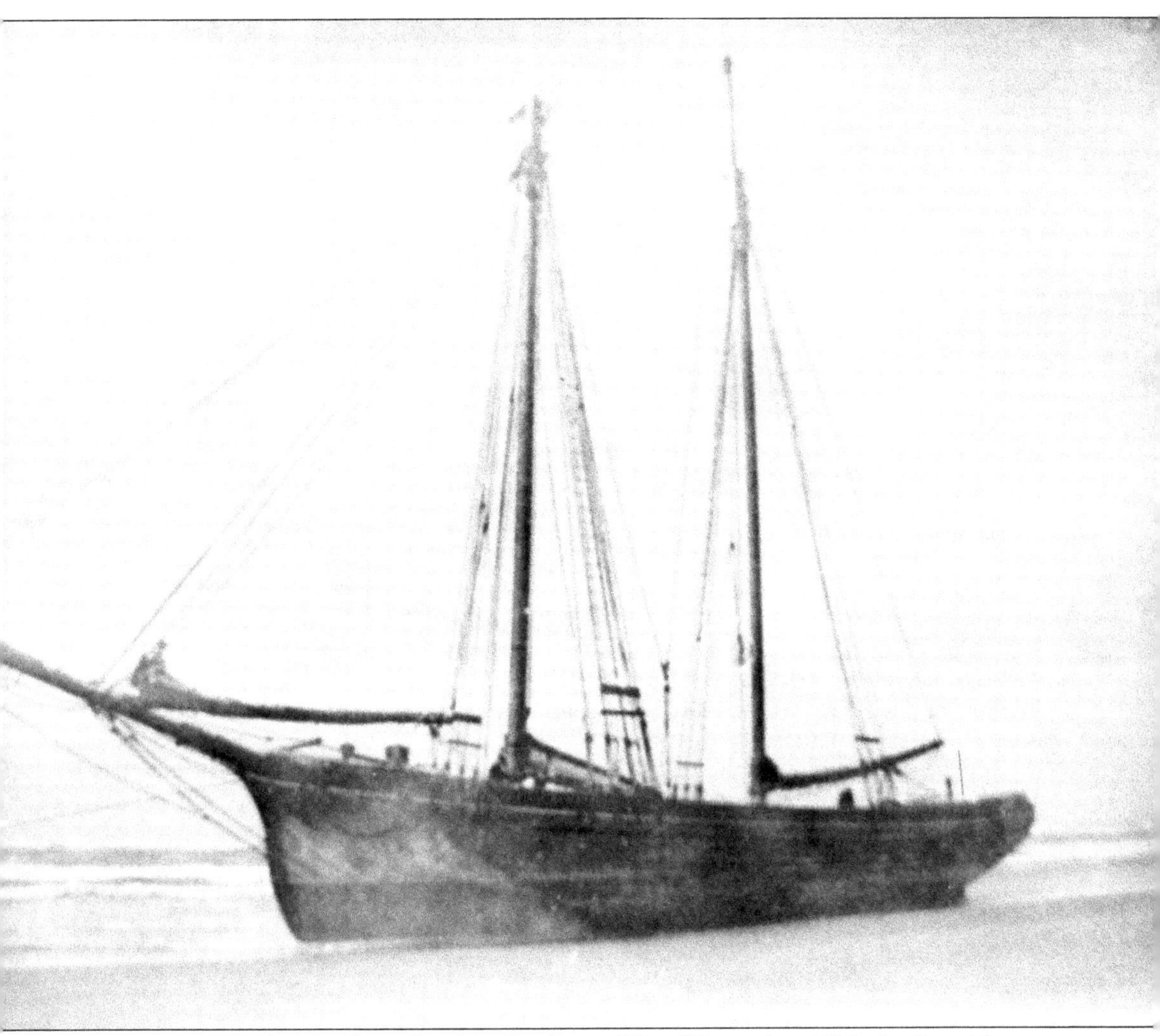

It took several months to refloat the ship. By the middle of December 1896, the *Berwick* was finally repaired and ready to return to service. The above photograph shows the schooner on the beach near Bandon. The *Berwick* ran into trouble on several separate occasions between 1900 and 1908. Many of these accidents involved stranding and being refloated. For instance, the *Berwick* stranded while attempting to enter the Siuslaw River while under tow by the steamer *Maggie* on February 5, 1900. (Bandon Historical Society 14624.)

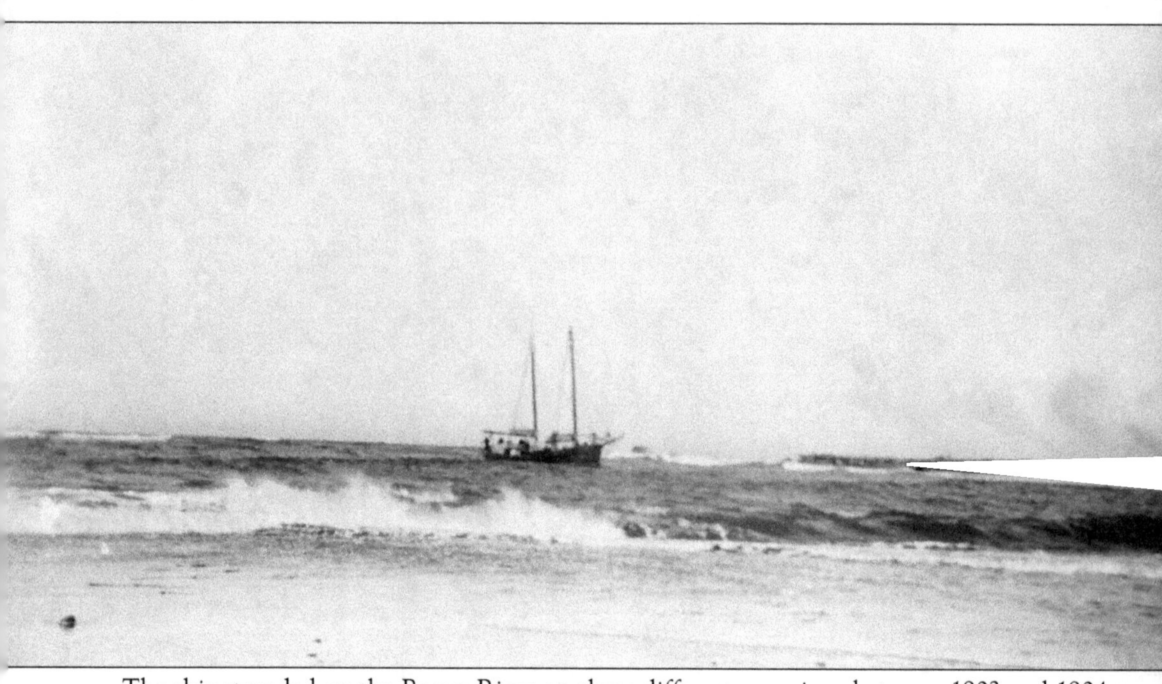

The ship stranded on the Rogue River on three different occasions between 1903 and 1904. The first occurred on May 28, 1903. The *Copper Queen* attempted to tow the schooner into the Rogue River, but a change in the channel caused the *Copper Queen's* propeller to become fouled up. Both vessels ended up on the beach. The *Berwick* remained on the beach for nearly a month. The ship was placed on rollers before it was refloated on the river. Although the *Berwick* was built as a sailing vessel, it later had two 50-horsepower standard gas engines installed. It wrecked for a final time in March 1908. It was having a rough year. The *Berwick* ran into trouble while at sea on February 24th. It visited the Kruse & Banks Shipyard to have its damaged rudder repaired. It departed Coos Bay on March 12th. (CHM 009-16.788.)

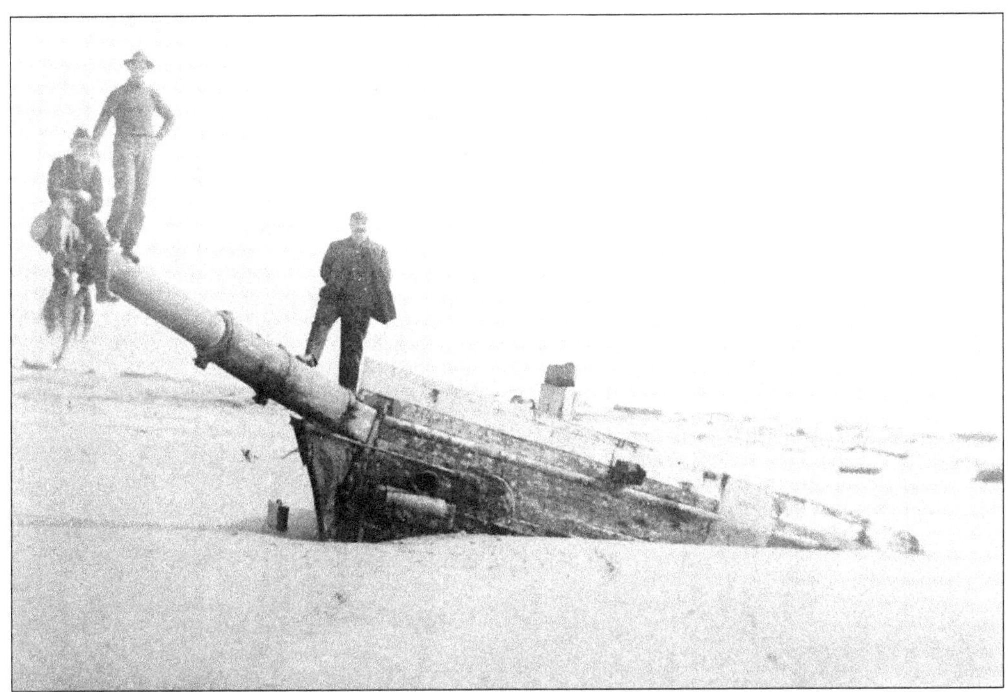

On March 13, 1908, the *Berwick* arrived off the coast of the Siuslaw River. The captain attempted to enter the river without the aid of a tug boat and ended up grounding the ship south of the river. The battered ship came to rest on the beach where it was high and dry at low tide. It became a total loss. (CHM 009-16.1474.)

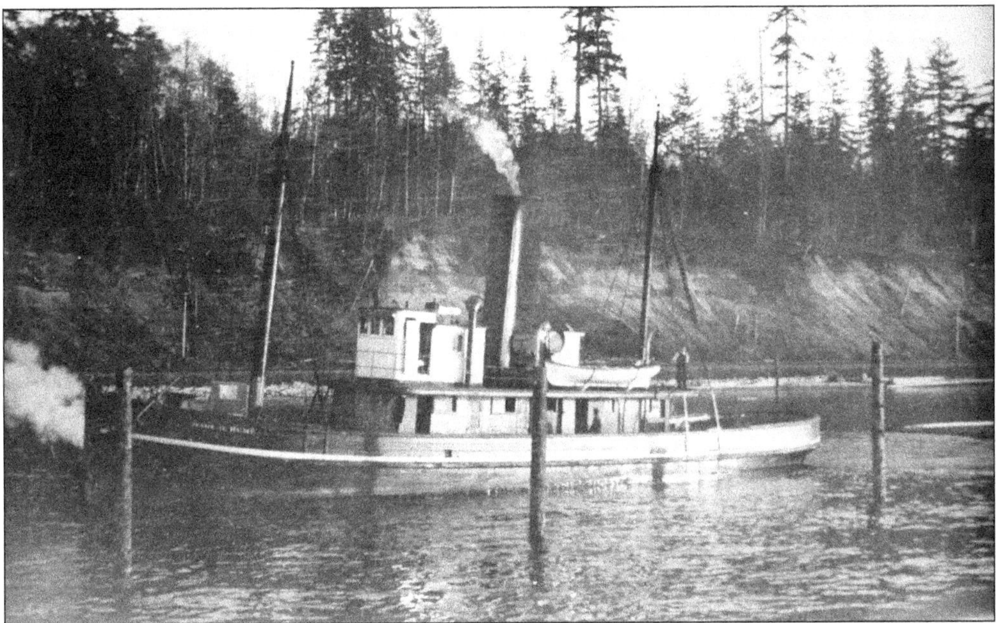

The *Mary D. Hume* holds the record for the longest time spent in active commercial sea service on the Pacific Coast. Its career spanned 97 years. The ship also stands out because it retained its original name throughout its career. Most ships changed names when they were sold to new owners. The *Mary D. Hume* is shown here at dock. (CHM 009-16.317.)

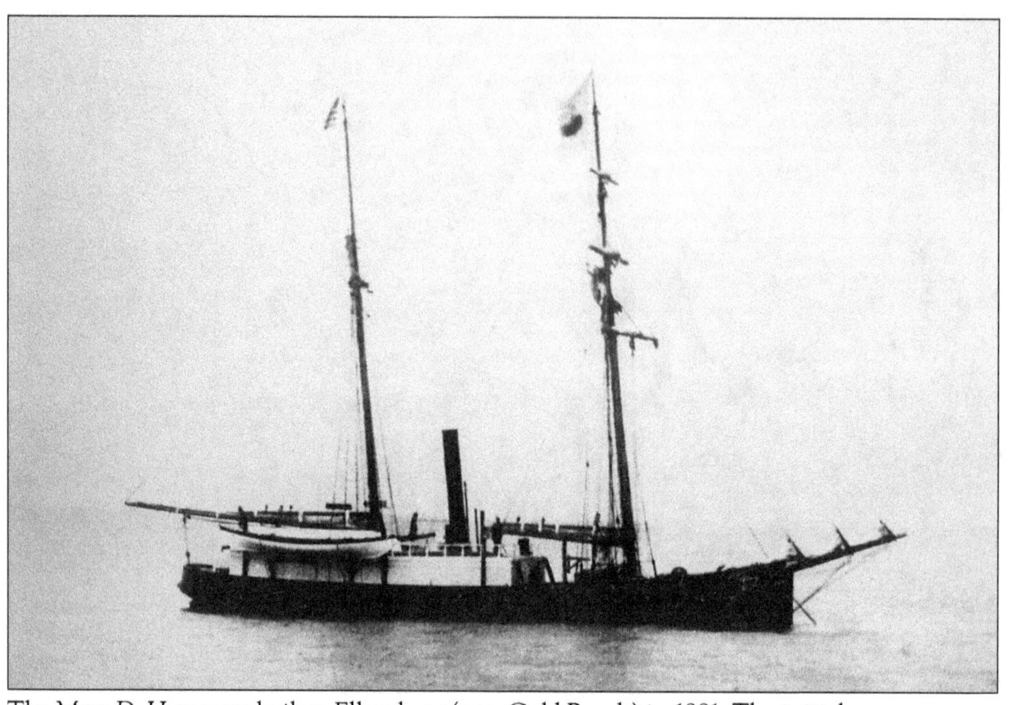

The *Mary D. Hume* was built at Ellensburg (now Gold Beach) in 1881. The initial measurements were 150 tons, 96 feet long, and 22 feet wide with a 9-foot depth. It was rigged as a two-masted auxiliary steam schooner. Its engine was salvaged from the wreck of the tug *Varuna*. It was built for R.D. Hume, who owned the first salmon cannery in Gold Beach. (CHM 009-16.316a.)

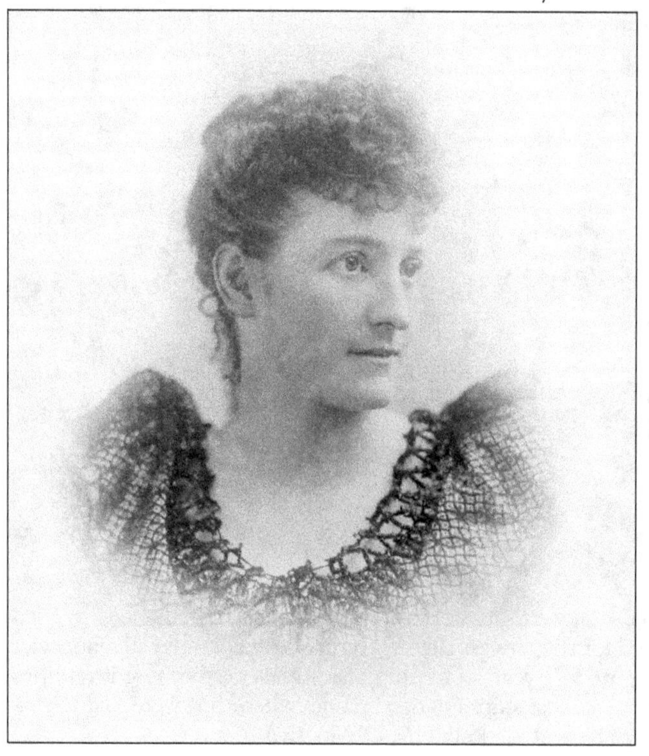

The boat was named after R.D. Hume's wife, Mary Duncan Hume. Throughout its career, the boat was modified several times to fulfill different tasks. The ship had a shallow enough draft that it could cross the mouth of the Rogue River. For the first 10 years of its career, the *Mary D. Hume* worked as a coastal freighter transporting goods to San Francisco. (CHM 988-P105.)

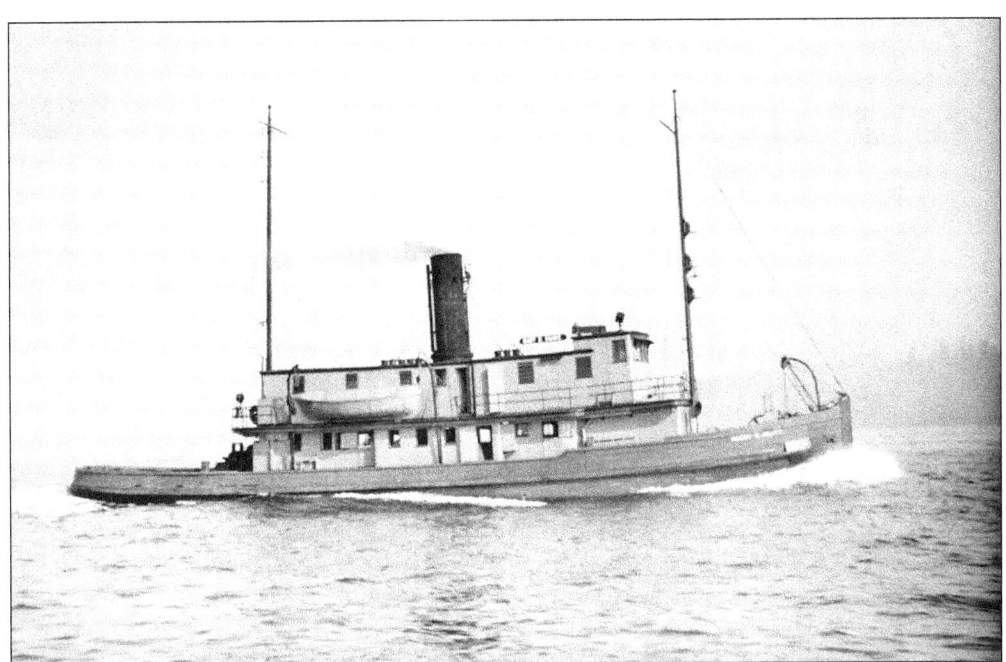

R.D. Hume was influential in the early development of the area. In addition to the cannery, he constructed and owned a can-making factory, pea-canning factory, hotels, several local newspapers, a fish hatchery, racetrack, and a sawmill. He also founded the town of Wedderburn, which was located north of the Rogue River. The *Mary D. Hume* is shown here as a steam tugboat. (CHM 009-16.318.)

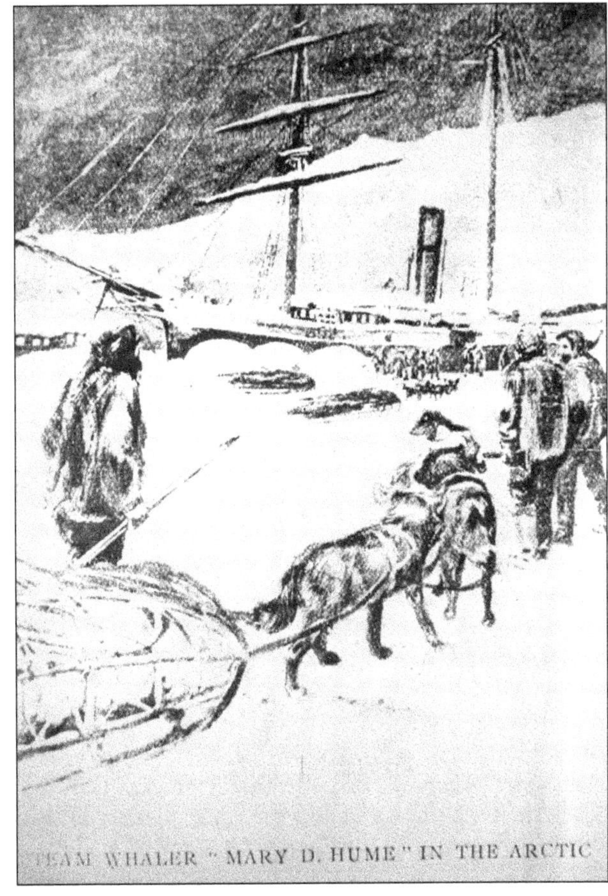

On December 5, 1889, the Pacific Whaling Company purchased the *Mary D. Hume* and put it to work as an Arctic whaling vessel. The ship set several records, including the largest catch of whale baleen (worth $400,000) and the longest whaling voyage (six and a half years). Several sailors died from scurvy and the cold during the voyage. (CHM 009-16.316.)

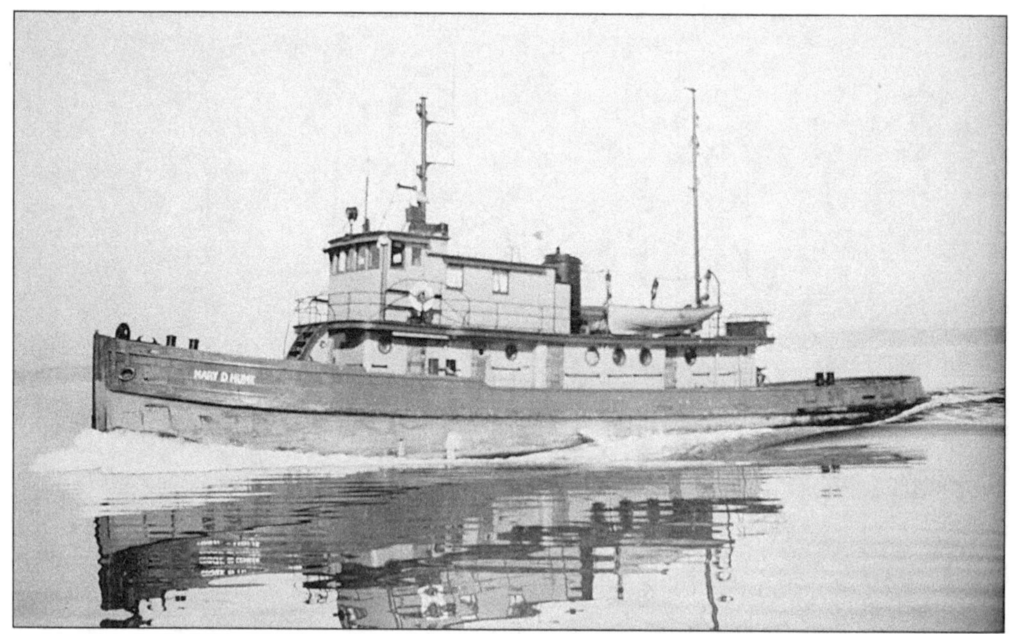

On May 20, 1909, the American Tug Boat Company purchased the *Mary D. Hume* and converted it into a tugboat. During 1914, it briefly worked in the Alaskan halibut industry. After losing money, the ship was returned to ocean towboat duty where it served under several owners over the next 60 years. In the 1970s, it was the oldest registered ship on the Pacific Coast. (CHM 009-16.319.)

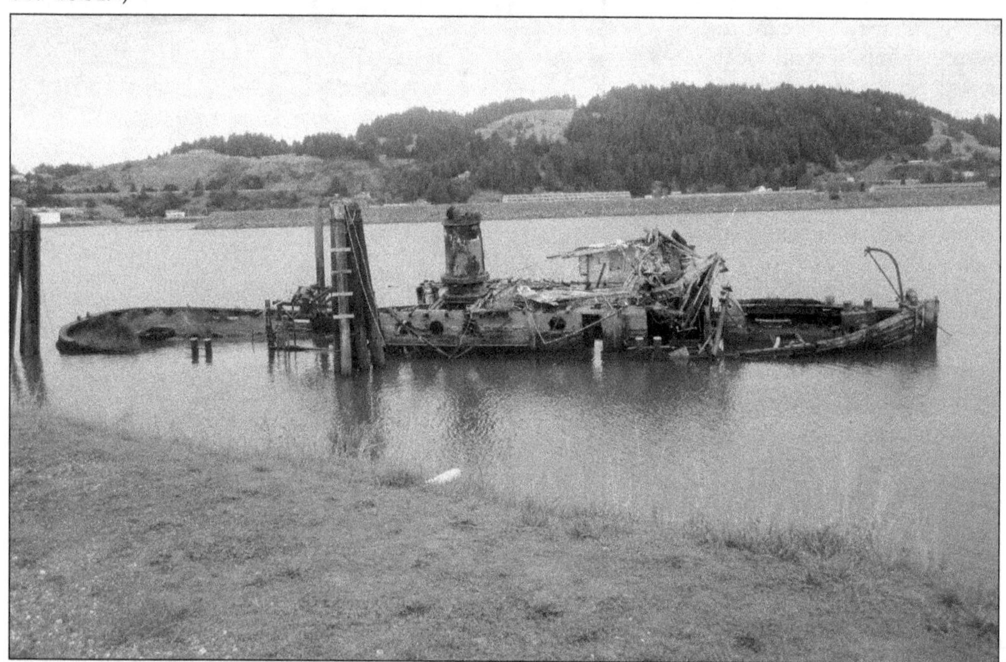

The *Mary D. Hume* was retired in the summer of 1978 and returned, under its own power, to Gold Beach. In 1979, it was given to the Curry County Historical Society. They intended to convert it into a museum ship. On August 1st, it was placed in the National Register of Historic Places. Unfortunately, things did not go according to plan. (Debbie Newman.)

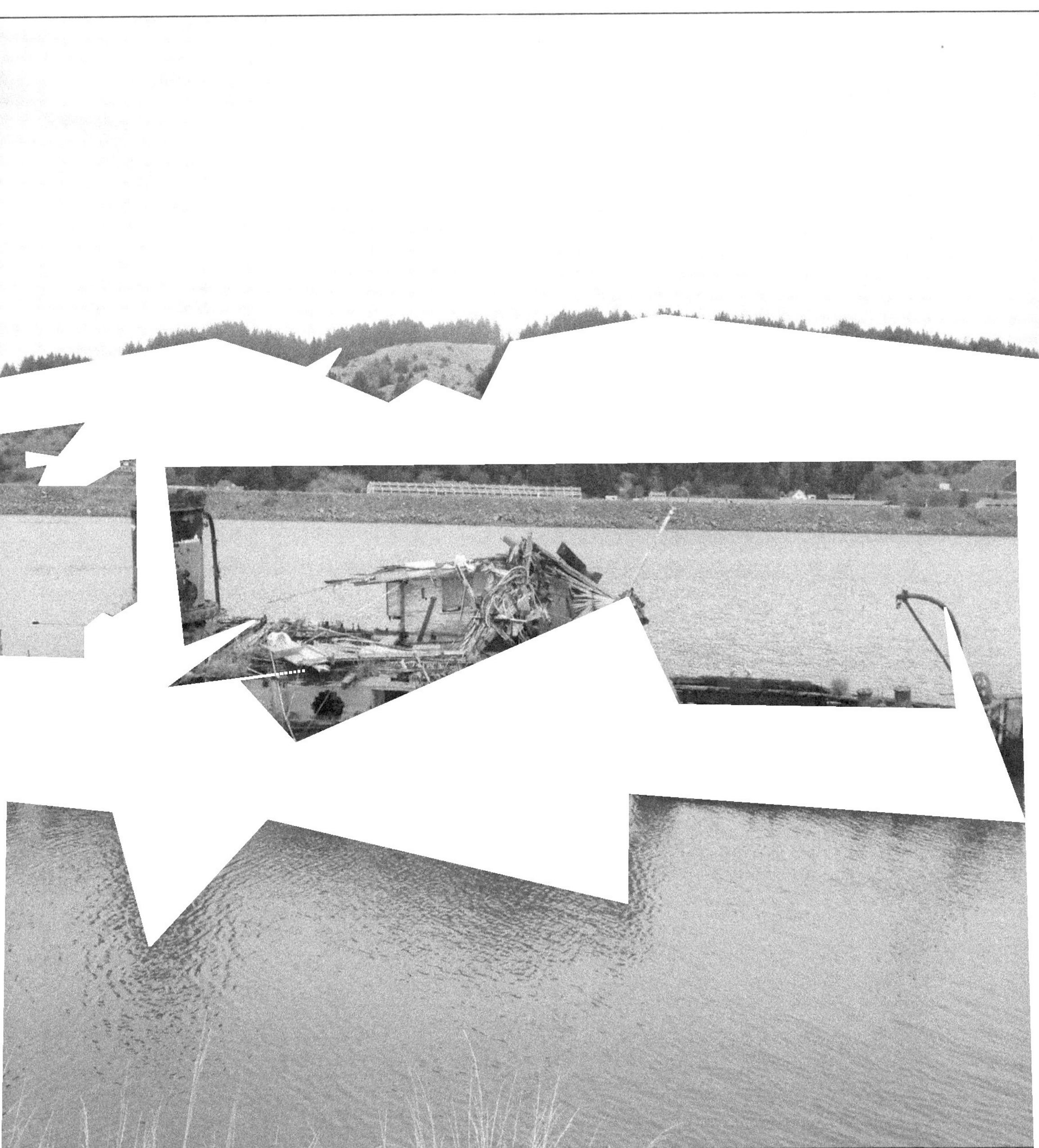

The Curry County Historical Society constructed a cradle beside the dock where they intended to display the *Mary D. Hume* as a museum ship. On November 13, 1985, they attempted to place the *Mary D. Hume* in the support cradle but it broke, causing the ship to sink in shallow water. There were several attempts to salvage it, but they all failed. (Author's collection.)

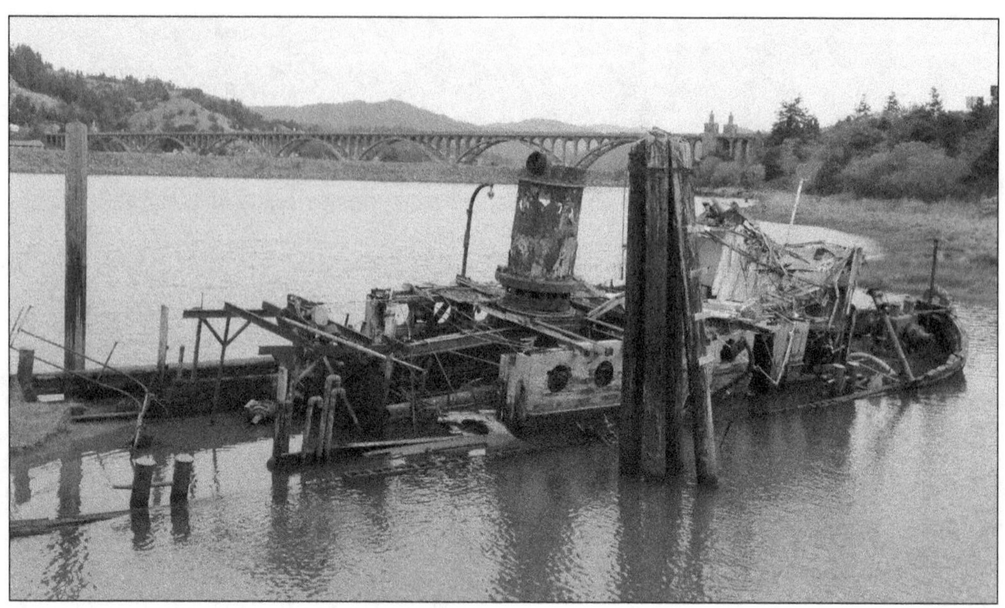

Prior to its retirement, the *Mary D. Hume* was the longest-serving commercial vessel on the West Coast. To this day, the wreck of the *Mary D. Hume* remains at a dock near the mouth of the Rogue River. The years have not been kind to the old ship, which is slowly falling apart. Regardless, it remains in the National Register of Historic Places. (Both, author's collection.)

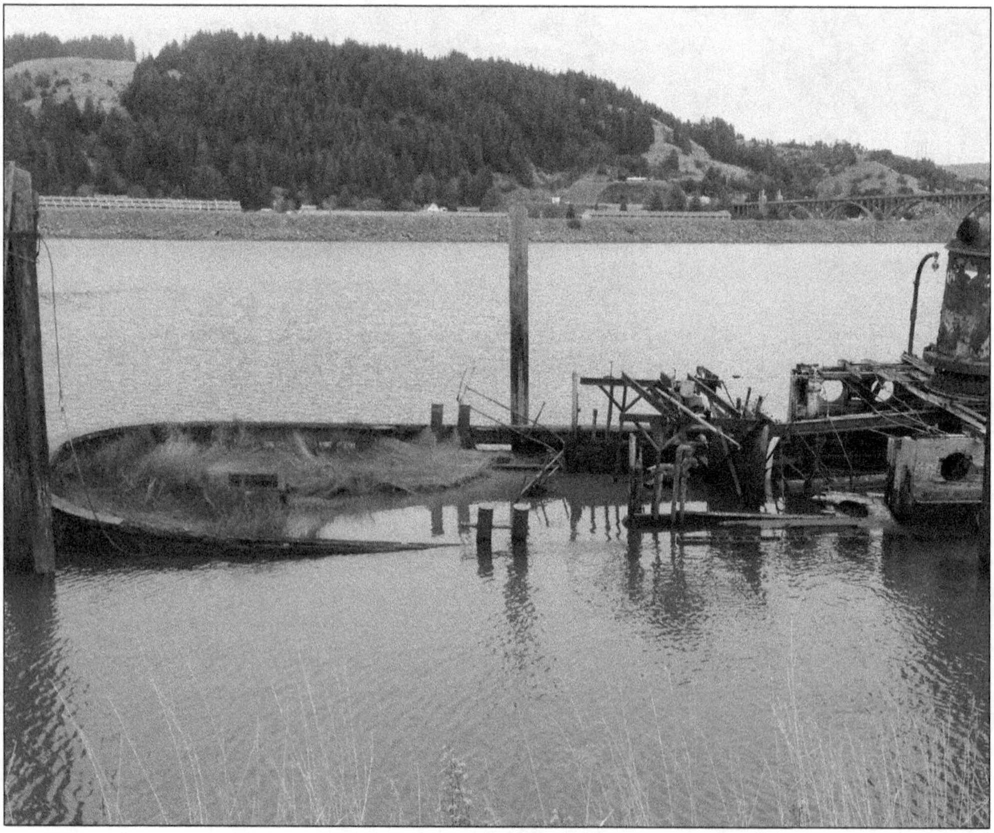

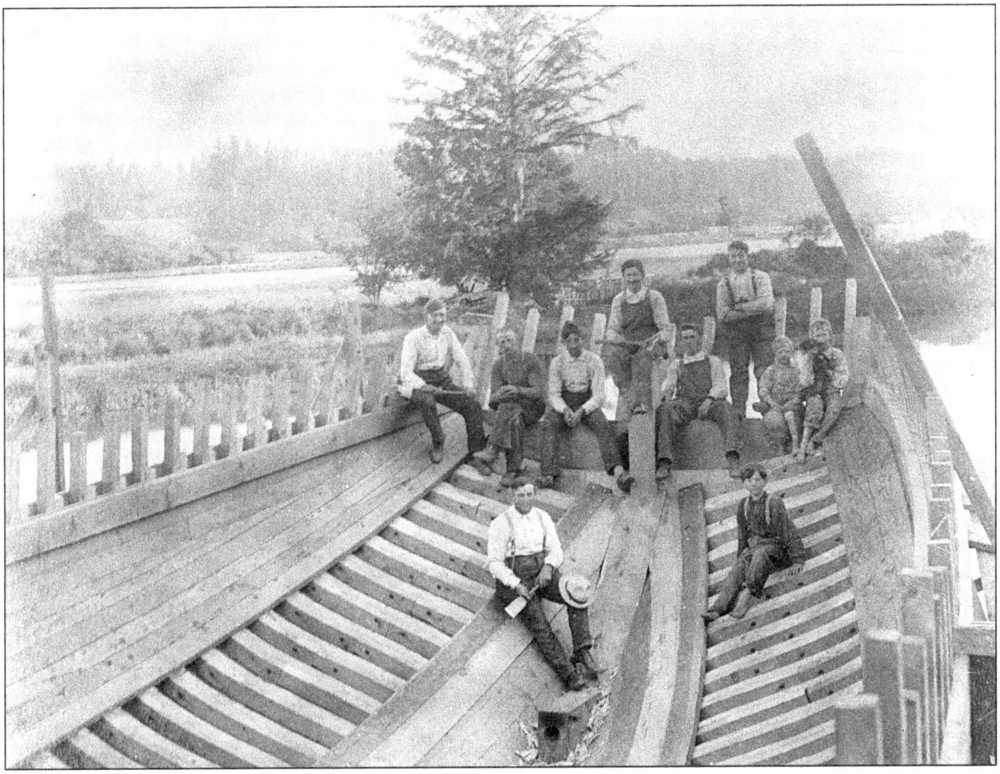

The gas schooner *Randolph* was constructed by the Herman Brothers Shipyard in Randolph (in Coos County) in 1910. The 42-ton vessel was 60 feet long with an 18-foot beam. Above, the crew has stopped construction of the ship long enough to pose for a photograph. Below, the *Randolph* is shown on an unidentified waterway. (Above, Bandon Historical Society 40015a; below, CHM 009-16.1711.)

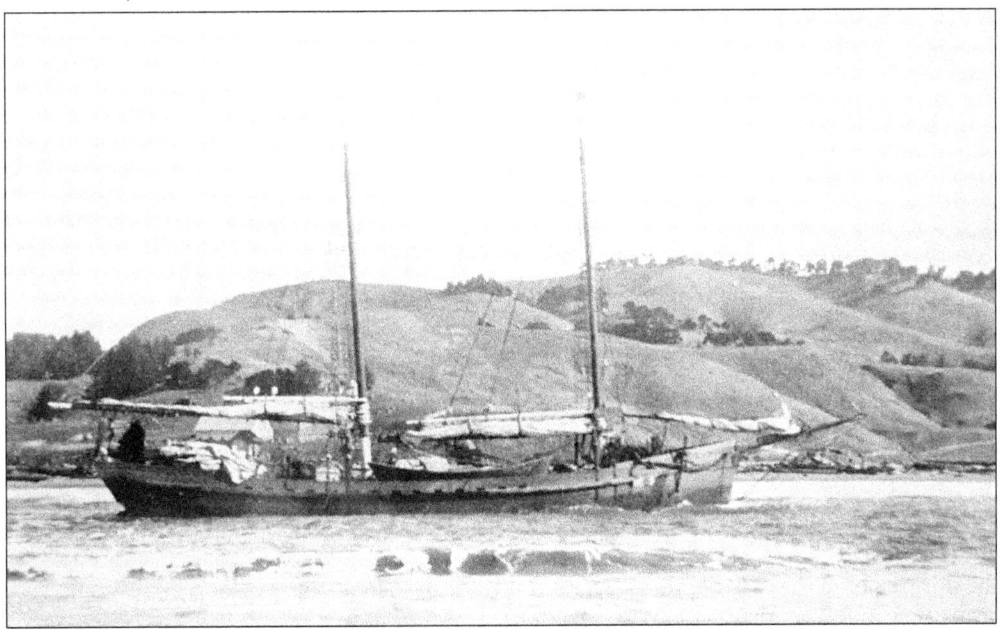

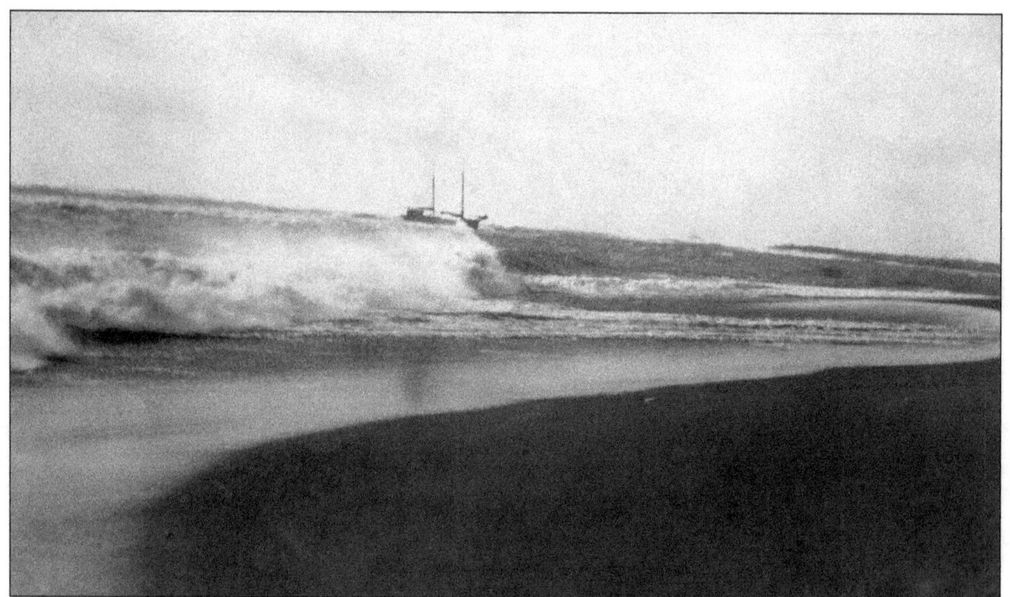

Throughout its short career, the *Randolph* was in numerous accidents. In June 1913, the *Randolph* grounded south of the Rogue River. The accident was blamed on the engineer, who carelessly left the plug out of the gasoline tank. As the ship tried to cross the bar, saltwater got into the tank and caused the engine to stall. The ship was refloated and repaired. (CHM 992-8-1673.)

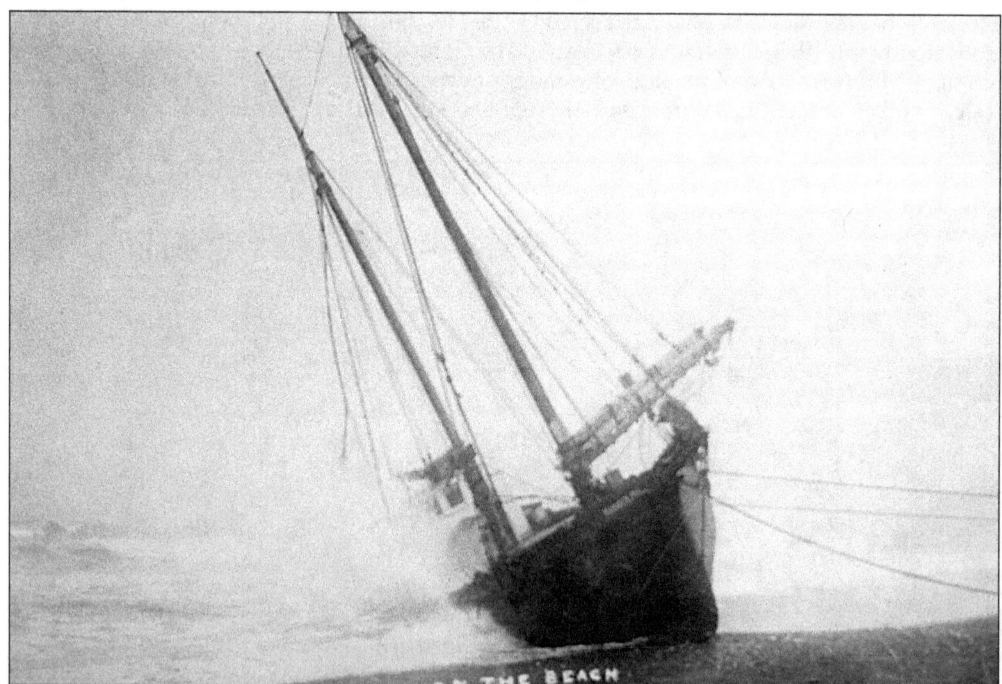

Tragedy struck the crew of the *Randolph* in 1914. Capt. John Anderson (who was a part-owner of the ship) fell from the gang plank, struck his head, and died. The ship was docked at Wedderburn at the time of the accident. (CHM 009-16.910.)

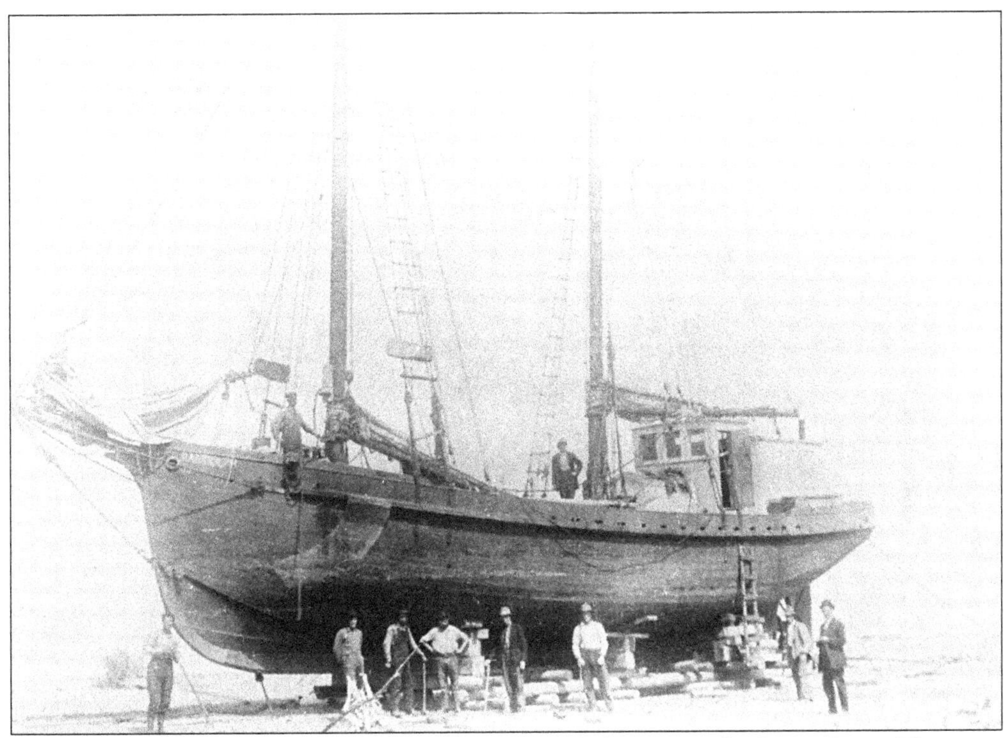

On May 1, 1914, the *Randolph* ran into trouble again while crossing the Rogue River. This time, the ship struck a sandbar and drifted onto the south spit. The *Randolph* is shown here ashore at Gold Beach. A cradle was built under the ship while it was being repaired. Several workers patched the damaged hull before the ship could be refloated. (CHM 009-16.1049.)

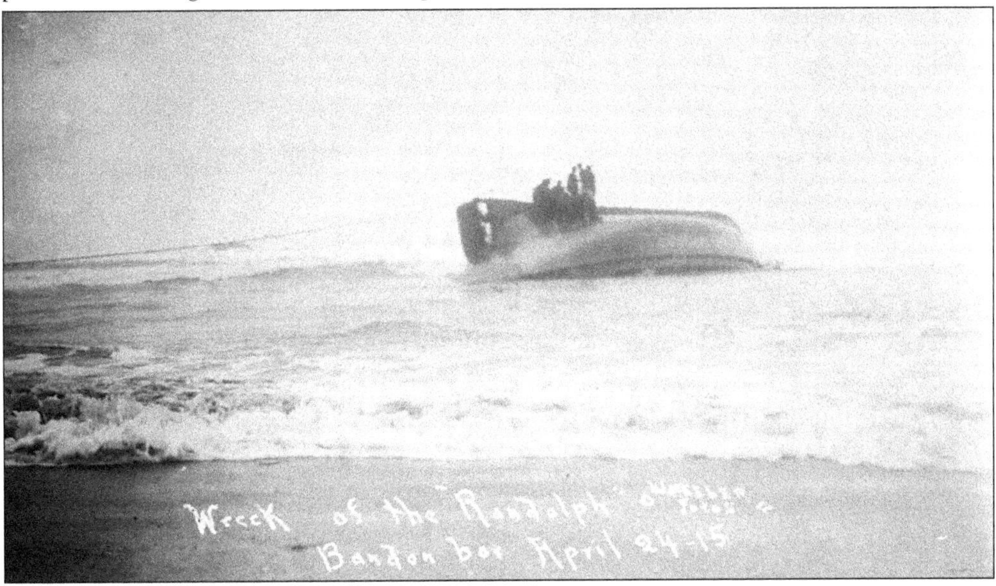

On April 24, 1915, the *Randolph* struck a rock while crossing the Coquille River bar and capsized. Three members of the crew died in the accident. One member of the crew managed to swim safely ashore, but two others became trapped in the ship's hull. Rescuers were forced to chop a hole in the hull of the submerged vessel in order to release the men. (CHM 992-8-1676.)

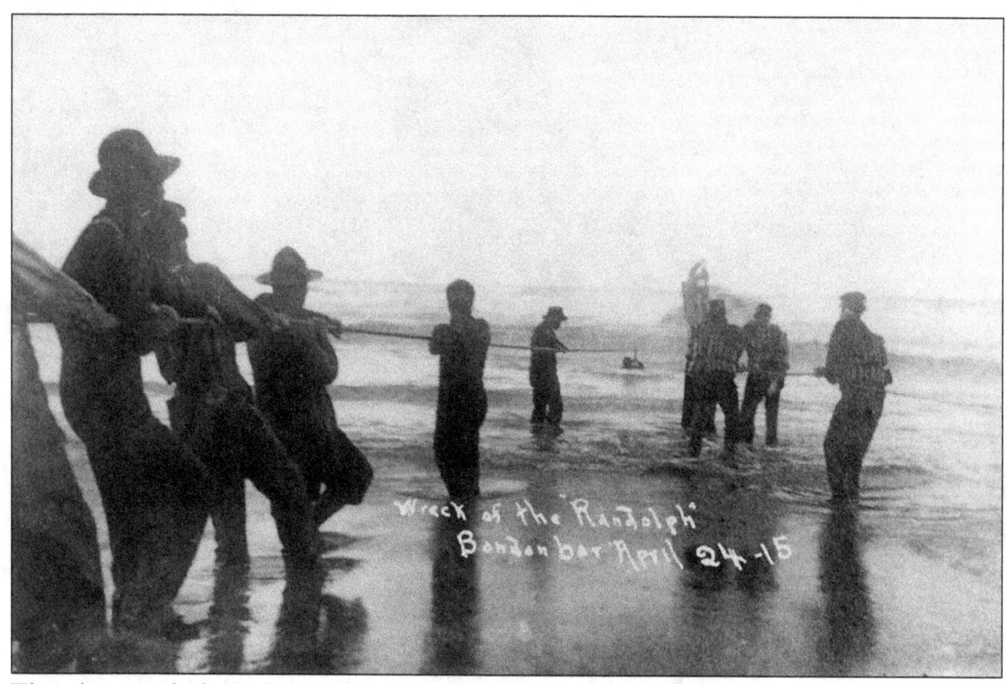

This photograph shows the *Randolph's* final wreck on April 24, 1915. Several men stand on the beach holding onto a rope that has been attached to the capsized hull, which is visible in the rough surf. Note the distinctive cork life vests worn by the members of the lifesaving crew. The *Randolph* was only five years old at the time of its loss. (Bandon Historical Society 28023.)

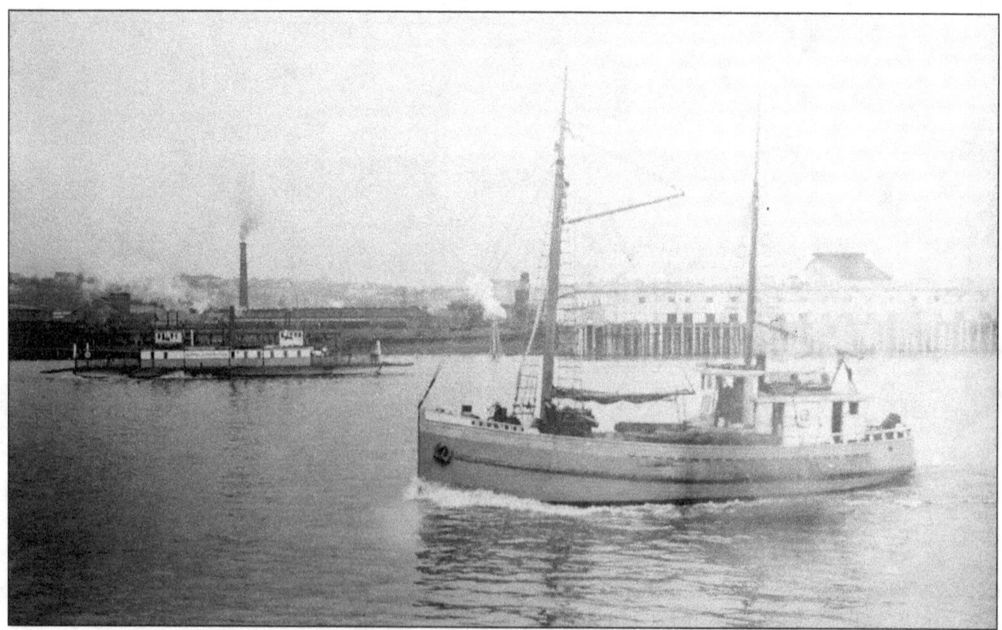

The gas schooner *Roamer* was built by Kruse & Banks at their North Bend shipyard in 1914. The 60-foot vessel was originally built for Peter Olson. It was mainly used to transport fish. The *Roamer* is shown here underway. (CHM 009-16.892.)

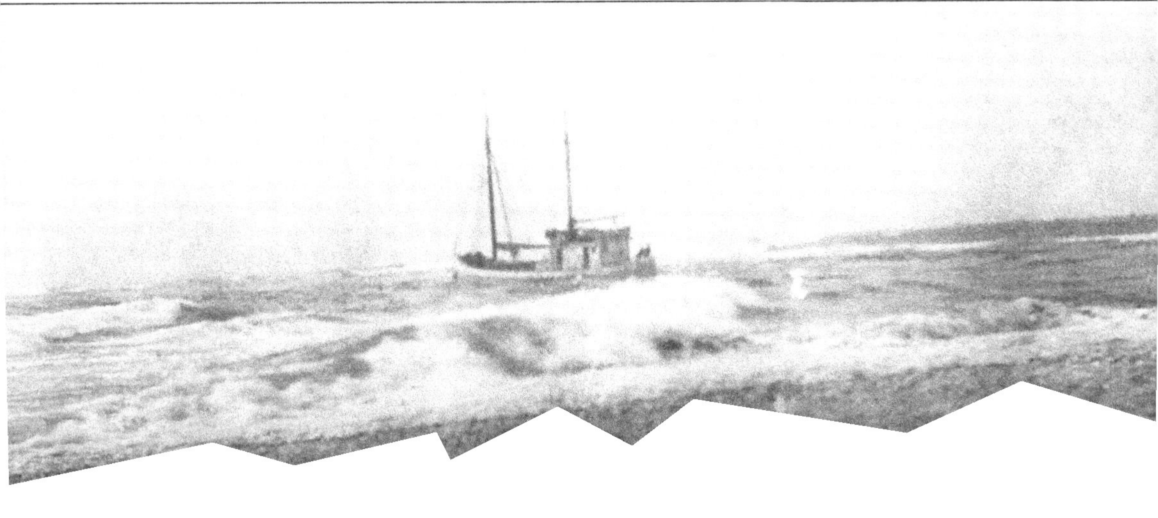

The *Roamer* regularly had trouble crossing the Rogue River bar. It ran into trouble on three separate occasions between 1916 and 1917. The first incident occurred on July 26th. The *Roamer*, under the command of Capt. Peter Olson, attempted to sail out of the Rogue River with a full cargo of fish. It is unclear what went wrong, but the ship ended up grounded on a sand spit. It was refloated with only minor damage. Then, on December 15th, the *Roamer* struck bottom while attempting to enter the Rogue River. Several waves crashed across the decks and washed away everything that was not secured. Once again, the ship survived with only minor damage. On January 4, 1917, the *Roamer* attempted to enter the river again. This time, it struck a sand spit that had formed in the main channel and grounded. Fortunately, the outgoing tide washed away enough sand to refloat the ship, which then fought the current as it continued up the river. Once again, the *Roamer* was barely damaged during the incident. (CHM 009-16.848a.)

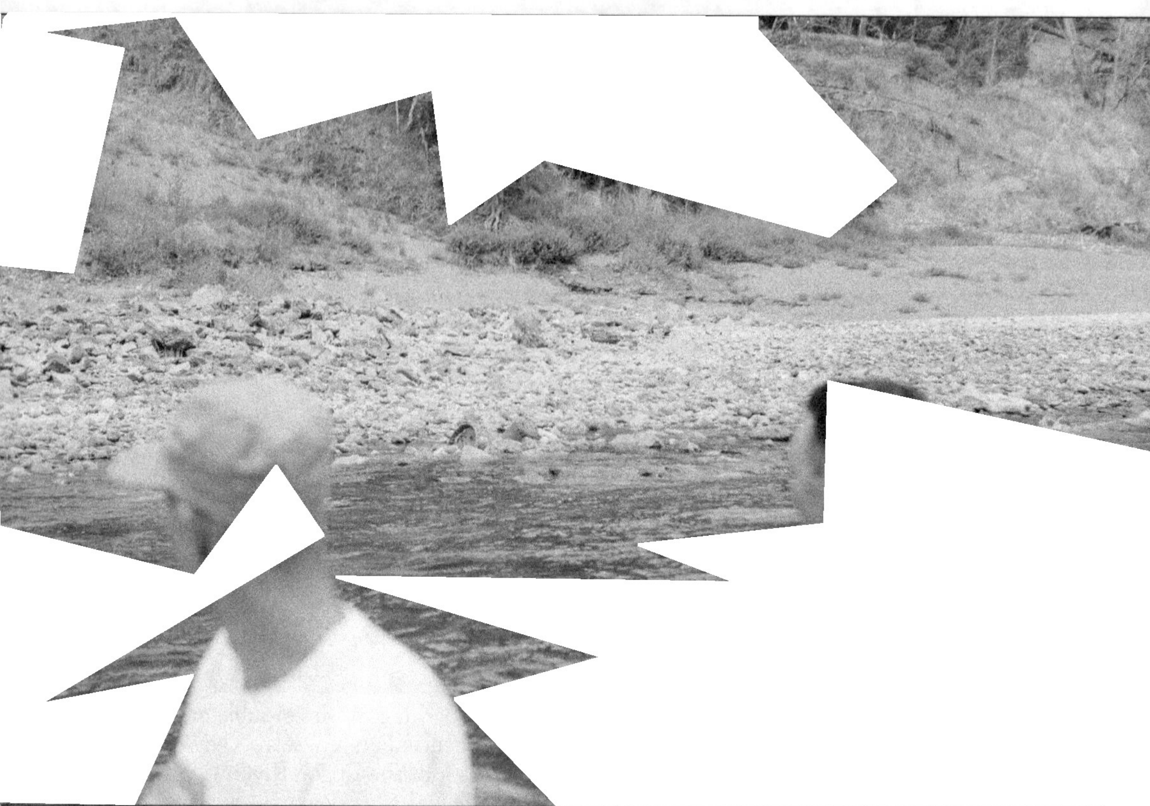

The sternwheeler *Rogue River* was built in Portland by Joseph Supple for the Rogue River Transportation Company in 1901. The 80-ton vessel was 66 feet in length with a 16-foot beam and a 4-foot depth. On November 16, 1902, the *Rogue River*, under the command of Capt. E. Burns, stranded 21 miles upriver. The boiler from the ship remained in the river for many years. The location was named "Boiler Rapids" as a result. According to Bill McNair of Jerry's Rogue Jets, the boiler was located on the rocks on the north side of the river until 1964, when it washed away during a flood and was never seen again. In this photograph, the boiler is just barely visible on the rocks at the edge of the river. It is in the center of the image between the two men in the boat. (CHM 009-16.420.)

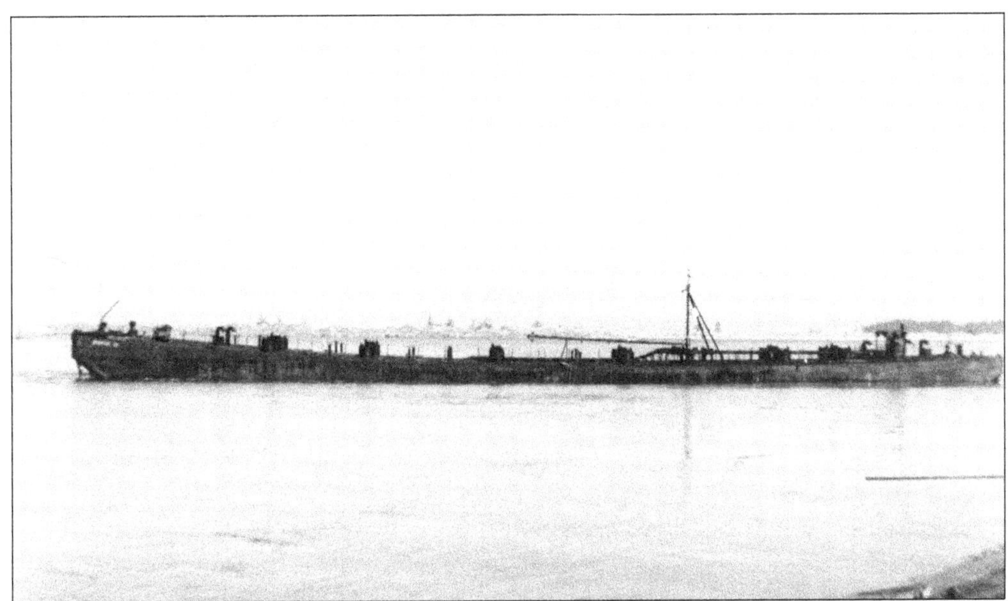

The 1,473-gross ton *Barge 14* was used to transport petroleum products. On January 15, 1956, the 245-foot-long vessel broke loose while being towed in stormy conditions. The tug *Sea Prince* was attempting to tow it from Puget Sound to California. Before it could be recovered, the barge drifted ashore south of Port Orford, where it broke into two pieces. The below photograph was taken after a previous incident. The tug *Sea Fox* attempted to tow *Barge 14* up the Coos Bay, but a towing wire became tangled in the propeller. The crew is seen helping diver Eddie Burroughs into his gear. He succeeded in untangling the wire from the propeller. (Above, CHM 009-16.1278c; below, CHM 009-16.1278a.)

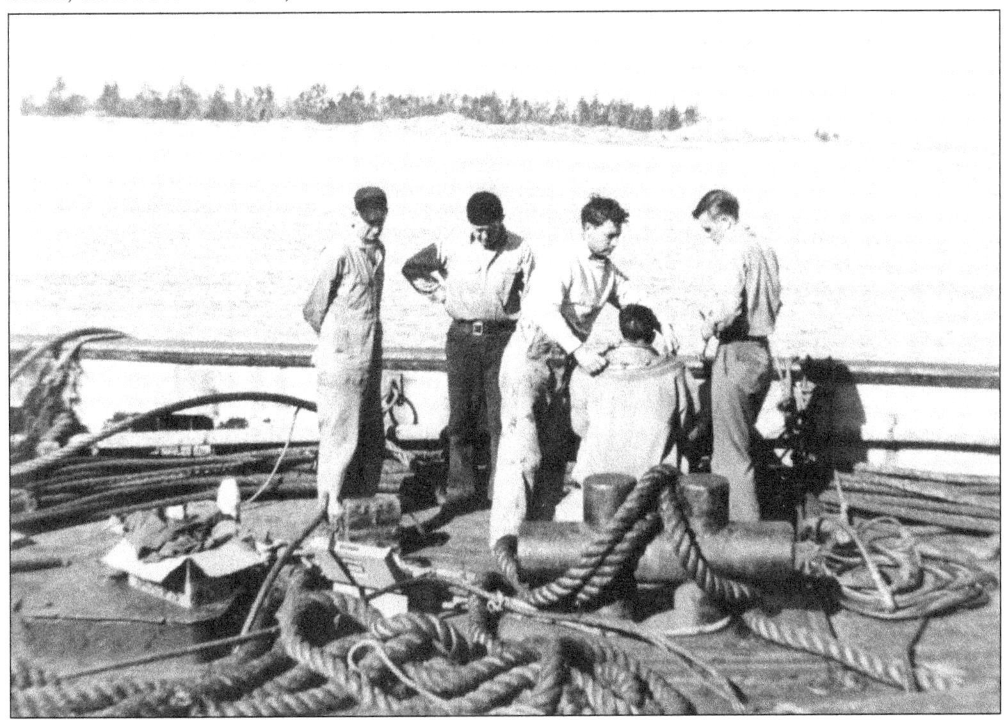

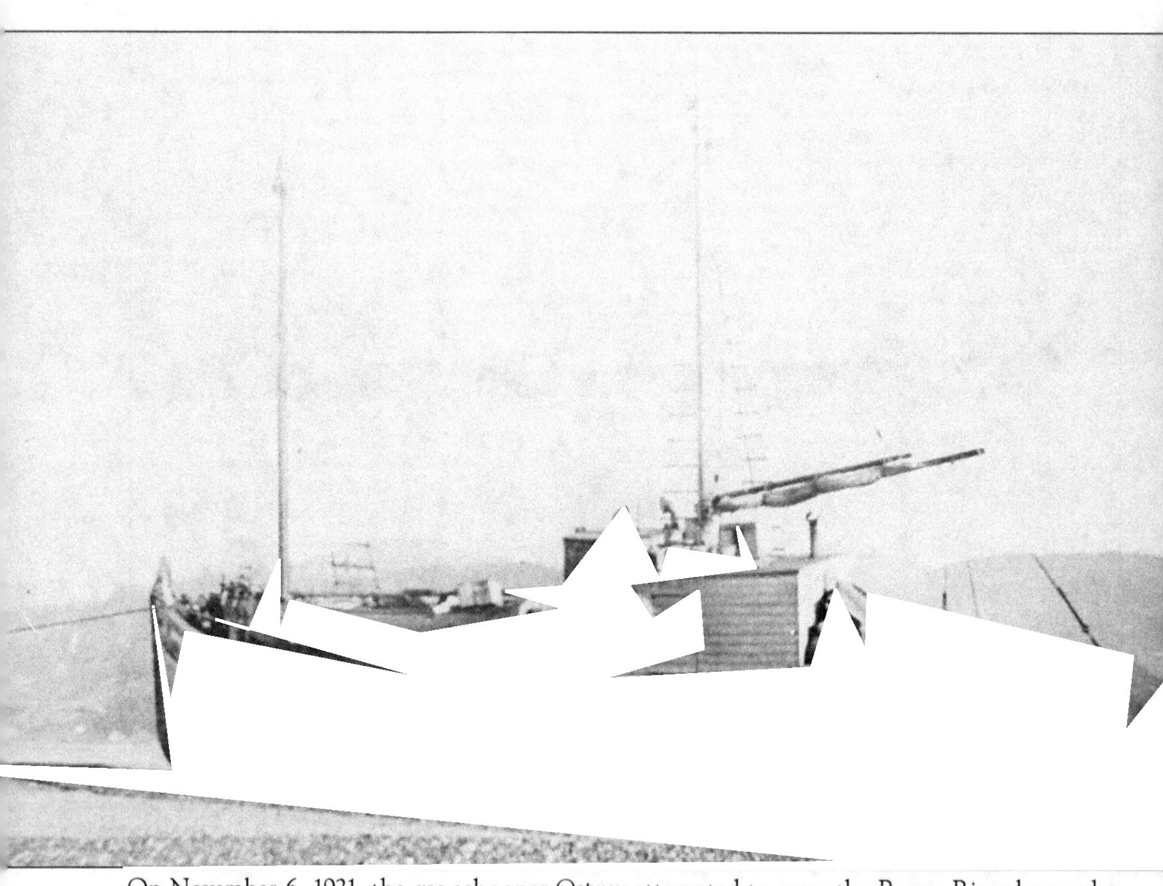

On November 6, 1921, the gas schooner *Osprey* attempted to cross the Rogue River bar under rough conditions. The ship ended up on the south spit. Fortunately, it did not sustain any major damage. The *Osprey* was refloated a short time later. It was reported that it only took a few hours of work to refloat the ship. (CHM 009-16.1712.)

Four

Coastal Wrecks

Ships often ran into trouble while traveling along the Curry County coastline, which is situated along the route between the larger ports in San Francisco, Portland, and Seattle. Although the shipping lanes were located fairly close to shore, there are sections of the coastline where it really is not safe for ships to travel closer than a mile and a half from the coastline. In these stretches, there are many potential striking hazards for mariners, including low rocky cliffs, reefs, and sea stacks. In addition, the weather can change without warning and can be hazardous for ships. Fog in particular has led to many shipwrecks. With their visibility limited, ship captains were in danger of striking submerged objects or even colliding with other ships. The area is known for its impressive wind gusts during the summer and powerful storms during the winter.

In addition to wrecks along the coastline, this chapter includes maritime accidents near Brookings, the Chetco River, and Harbor. Today, Brookings is the largest town in Curry County. As one of the warmest locations on the Oregon coast, it is sometimes referred to as the "banana belt." It is known for its flower bulb industry which was established in the 1940s. The Brookings Port District was created in 1956 with the development of the port as their main goal. The initial boat basin was constructed in 1958. A year later, the port extended the boat basin upstream. For years, there was discussion of turning Chetco Cove into a deepwater harbor. As early as the 1920s, a bill requesting the construction of a harbor and two jetties was presented to Congress. Despite their efforts, the work was not completed until the late 1950s. In modern times, the Chetco River is dredged regularly and protected by two stone jetties.

All of these improvements have helped decrease the number of maritime accidents in the area.

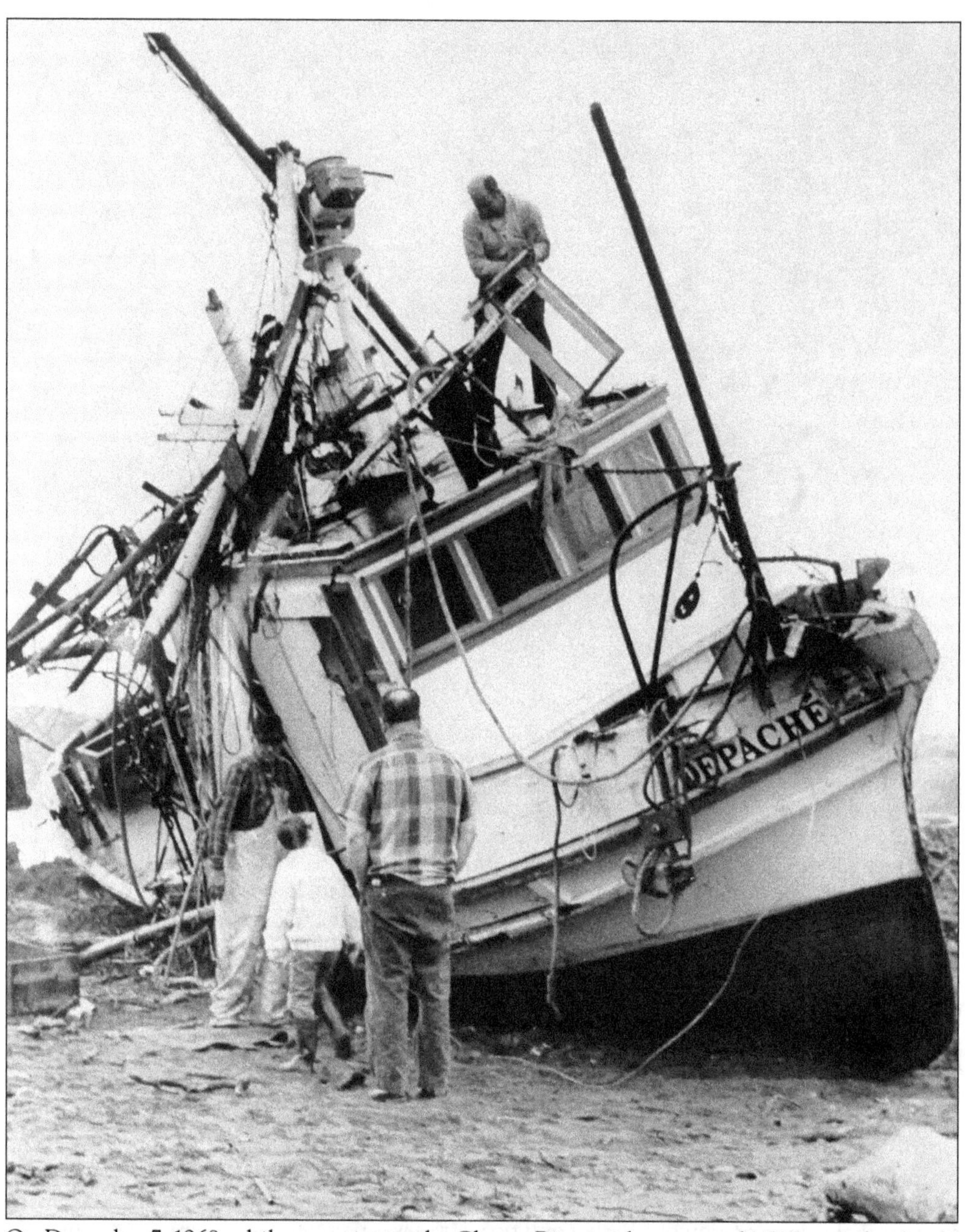

On December 7, 1968, while returning to the Chetco River with a cargo of 1,500 pounds of crab, the fishing vessel *De Pache* was struck by a freak wave which turned it broadside to the seas before flipping it over on its side. A second wave struck the vessel before it could right itself and flipped it upside down, trapping two of the three crewmen in the cabin. With the water pressure holding the door shut, they had to kick it open in order to escape. The third crewman was thrown into the water. All three were later rescued—two by the Coast Guard and one by a tug boat. The *De Pache* drifted ashore near the Chetco south jetty. A few months earlier, the crew of the *De Pache* responded to a distress call from the fishing vessel *Mary E*, which had struck a submerged object and was taking on water. They rescued the two crewmen minutes before their boat sank off the coast of Brookings. (CHM 009-16.1140.)

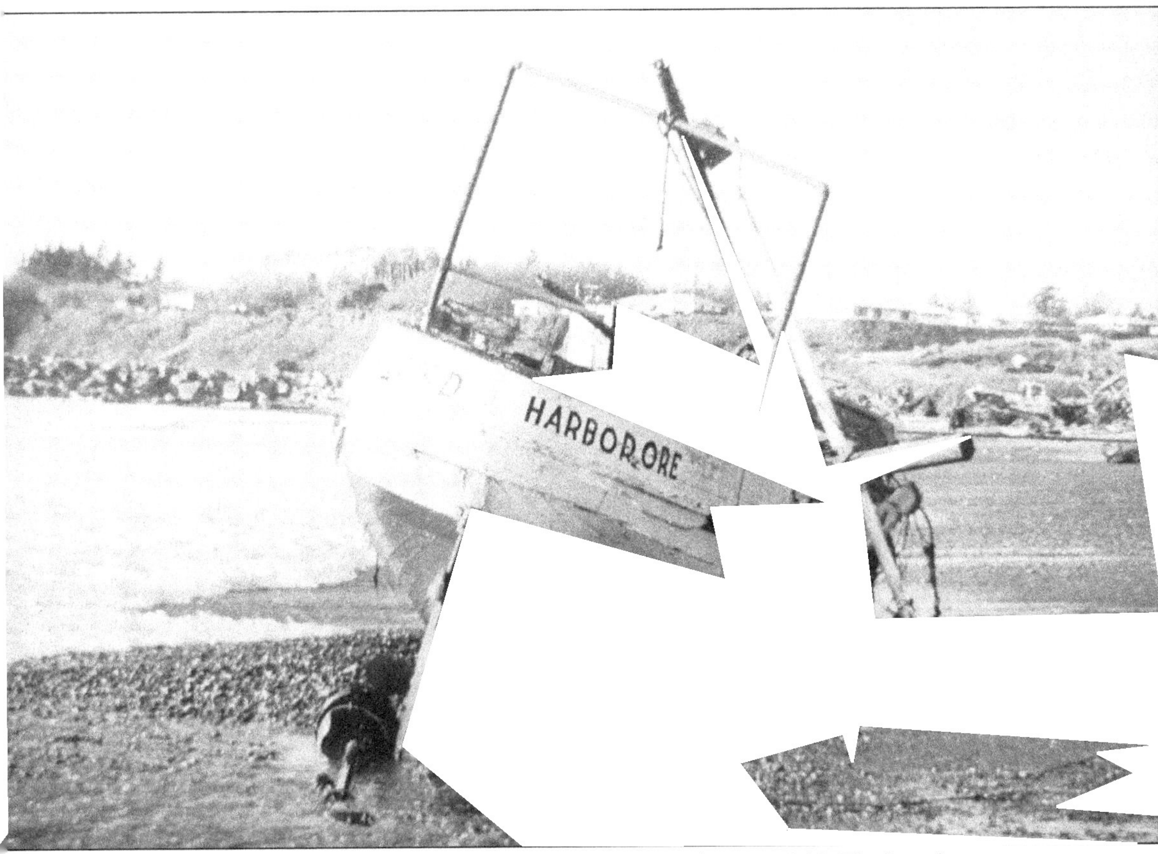

The 38-foot fishing vessel *Francis D.* ran into trouble on December 28, 1966. The boat lost power three miles south of the Chetco River. The Coast Guard attempted to tow the boat into the river. Unfortunately, during the attempt, both vessels were struck by several powerful waves in the rough surf, which disabled the lifeboat. The *Frances D.* was struck by a wave with so much force that it damaged the boat and tossed one of the crewmen into the water. He succeeded in swimming to shore safely. The Coast Guard boat managed to return to port, but the *Frances D.* washed up on the beach a total wreck. (CHM 009-16.1727.)

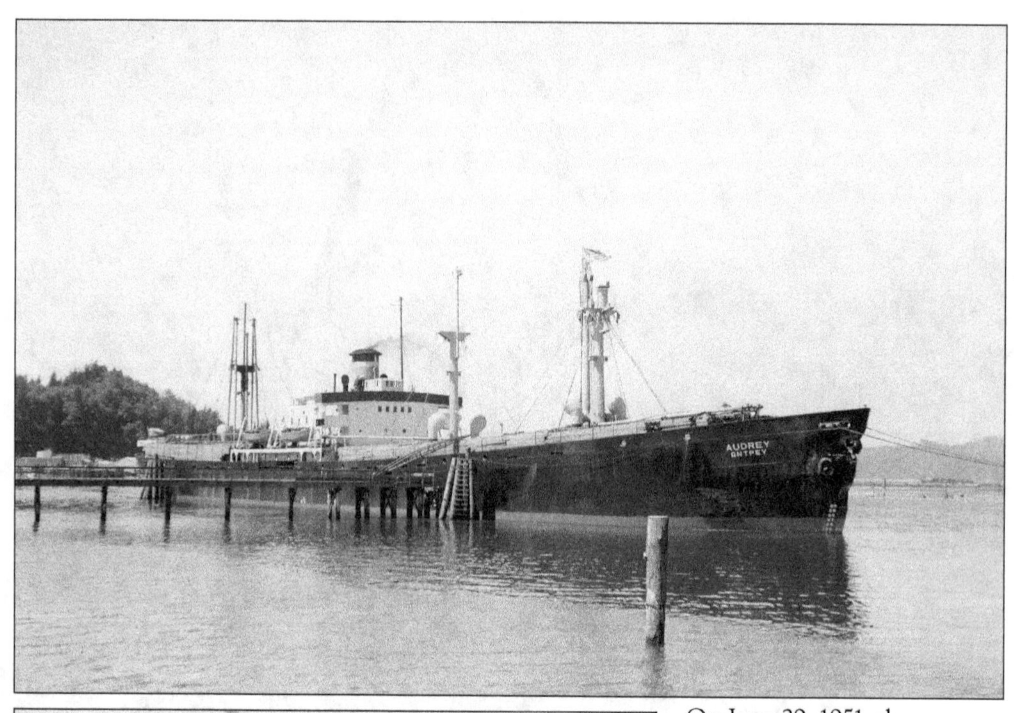

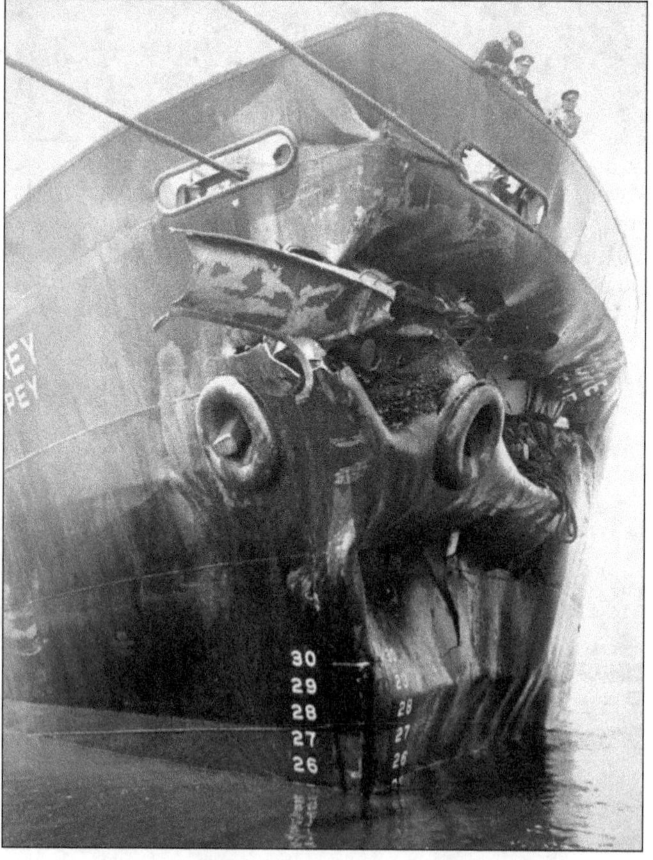

On June 29, 1951, the Greek steamer *Audrey* and the American tanker *Alen Seegar* collided in thick fog off Cape Blanco. The above photograph shows the *Audrey* prior to the accident. At left, three men stand on the deck of the *Audrey* and examine the extensive damage to the bow. Much of the metal has been bent inward from the force of the collision. There is a large gaping hole on the port side revealing the interior hull of the ship. In the center, a piece of metal (presumably from the other ship) is still attached to the hull. Despite the damage, the ship was not rendered inoperable. It continued north to the port of Coos Bay, where it received temporary repairs. It made another stop in Vancouver, British Columbia, before continuing on to Egypt. (Above, CHM 009-16.411; below, CHM 009-16.756.)

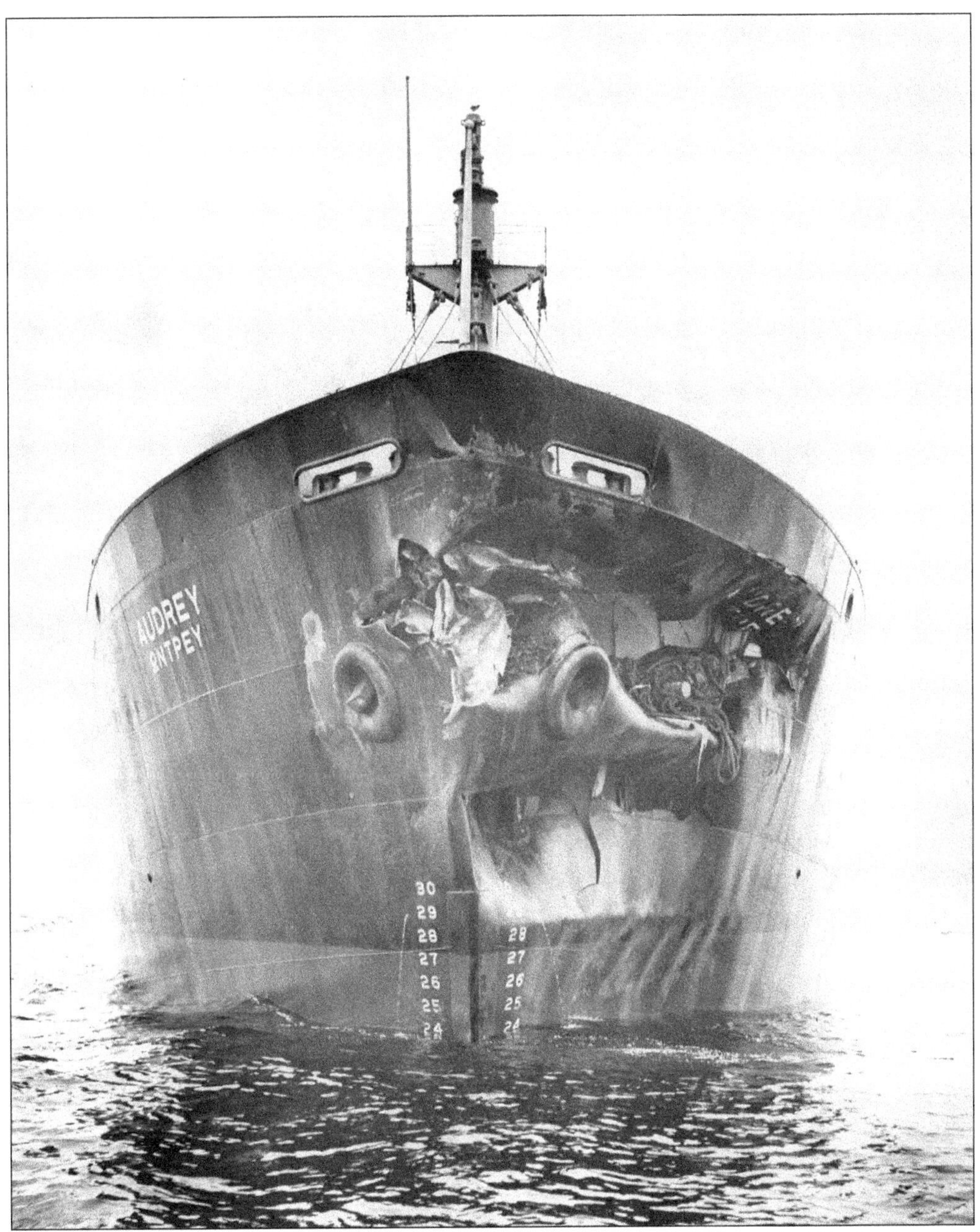

Although both vessels sustained damage, neither was rendered inoperable. While the *Alen Seegar* continued on to the Columbia River, the *Audrey* made a stop at Coos Bay for temporary repairs. This stunning photograph depicts the extensive damage to the bow of the *Audrey* after the collision. Several large, gaping holes in the side of the hull are clearly visible. Portions of the inner hull are also visible. It is fortunate that the ship sustained the blow at a point above the waterline. Had the ships collided in a different location, the *Audrey* may not have been able to remain afloat. (CHM 013-8.12d.)

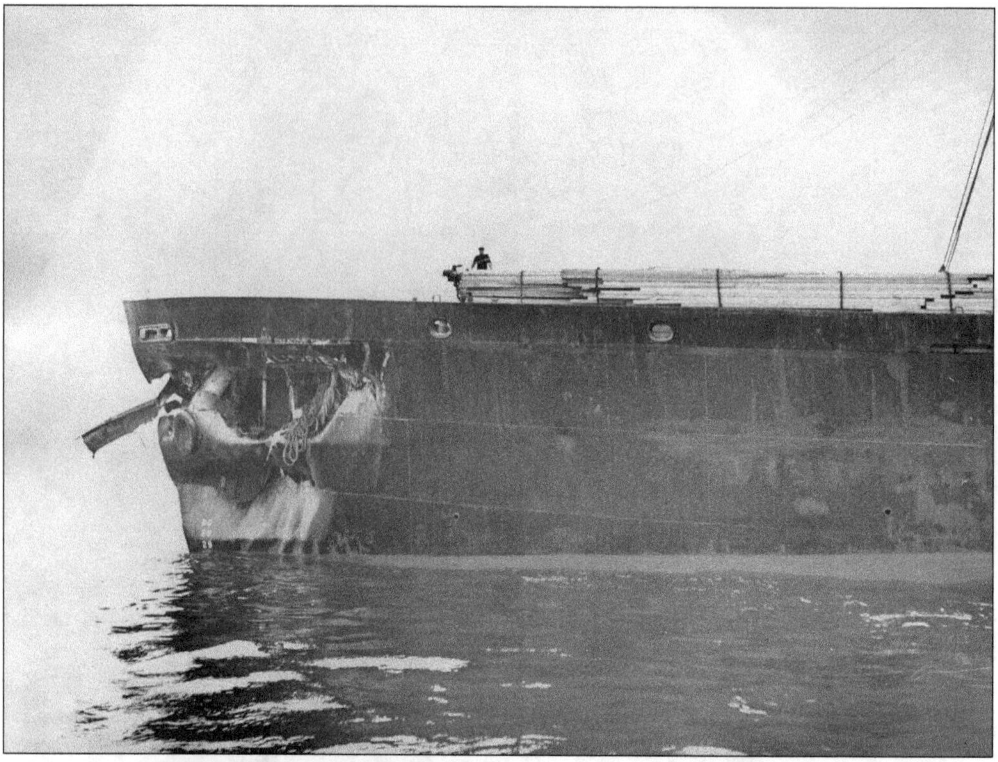

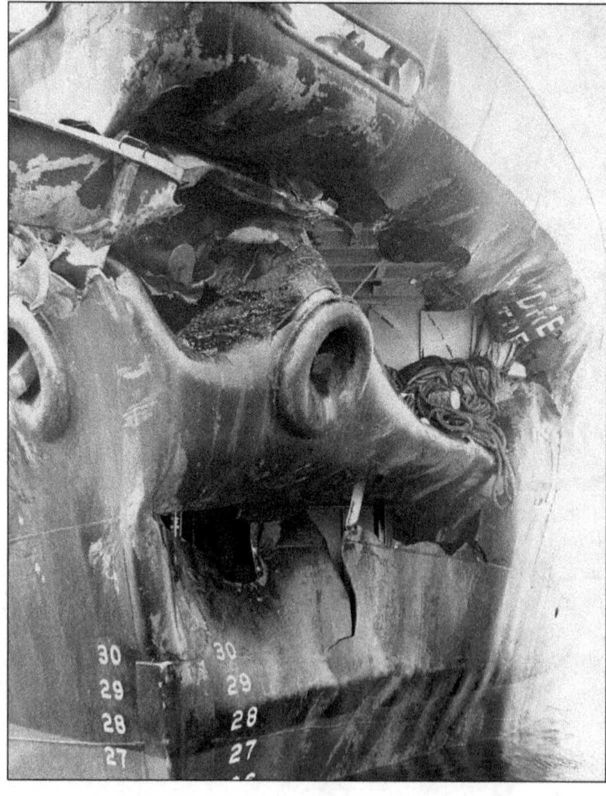

The side of the ship is visible in the above photograph, which was taken from a nearby ship. The man standing on the deck helps to demonstrate the scale of the damage. He is standing beside the deck load of lumber that the ship was transporting. The photograph at left provides a close-up of the damage to the bow of the Greek steamer *Audrey*. (Above, CHM 013-8.12g; below, CHM 013-8.12h.)

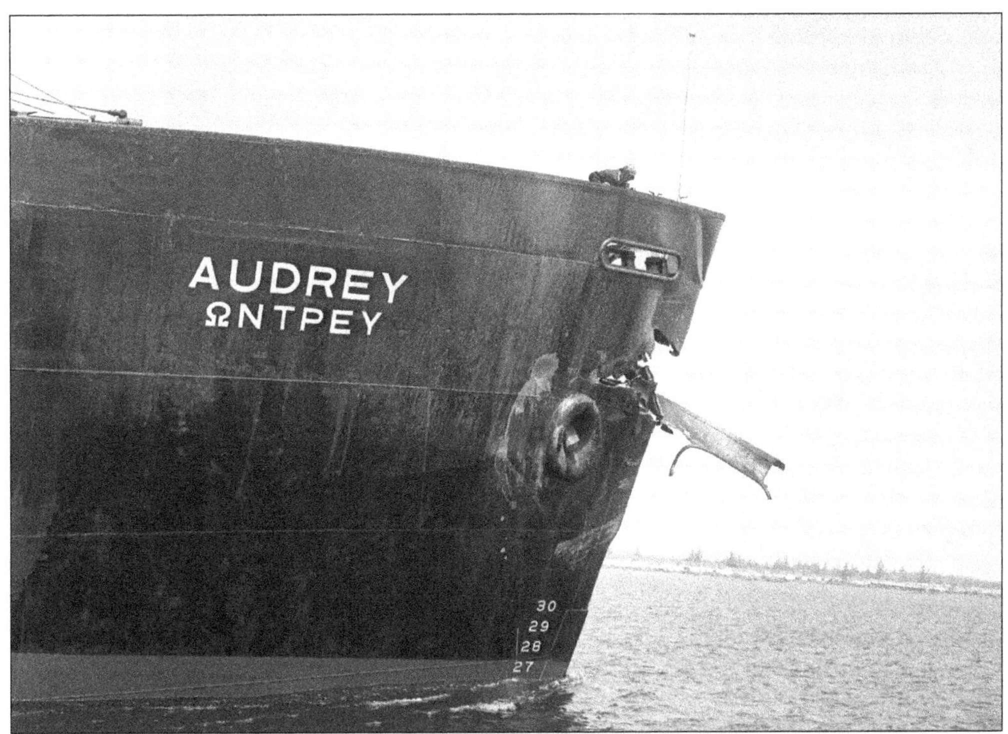

The photographs on this page are of each side of the steamer *Audrey*. The majority of the damage occurred on the port side of the ship. Above, a large piece of metal from the other ship, the *Alen Seegar*, is visible jutting out of the side of the *Audrey*'s hull. Below, there is a long gash along the side of the vessel. (Above, CHM 995-1.14501.1; below, CHM 995-1.14419.2.)

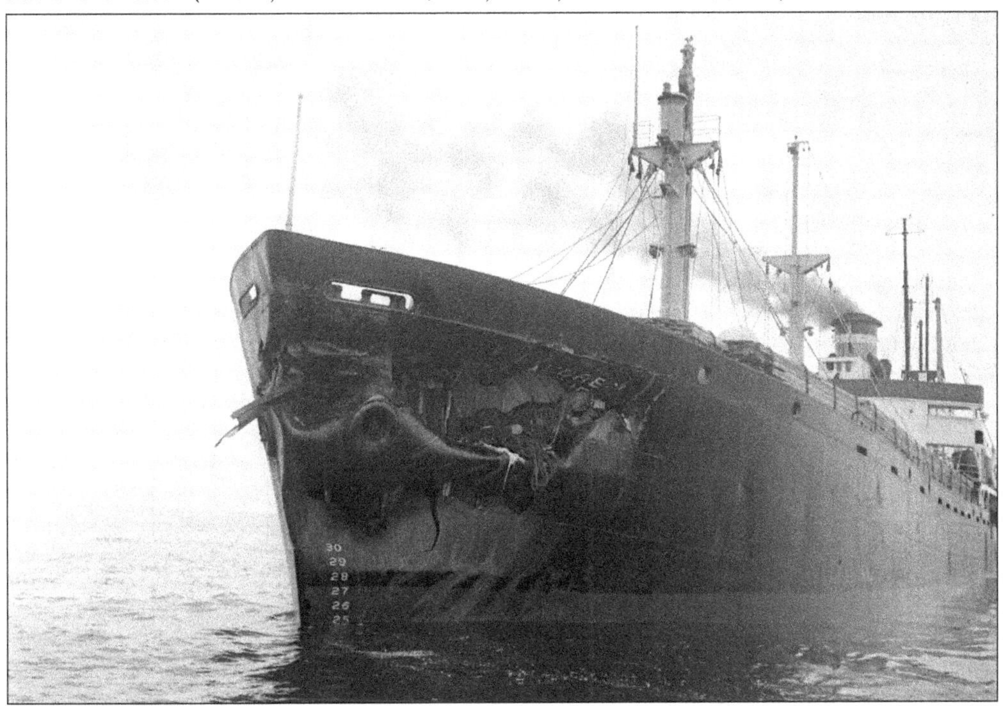

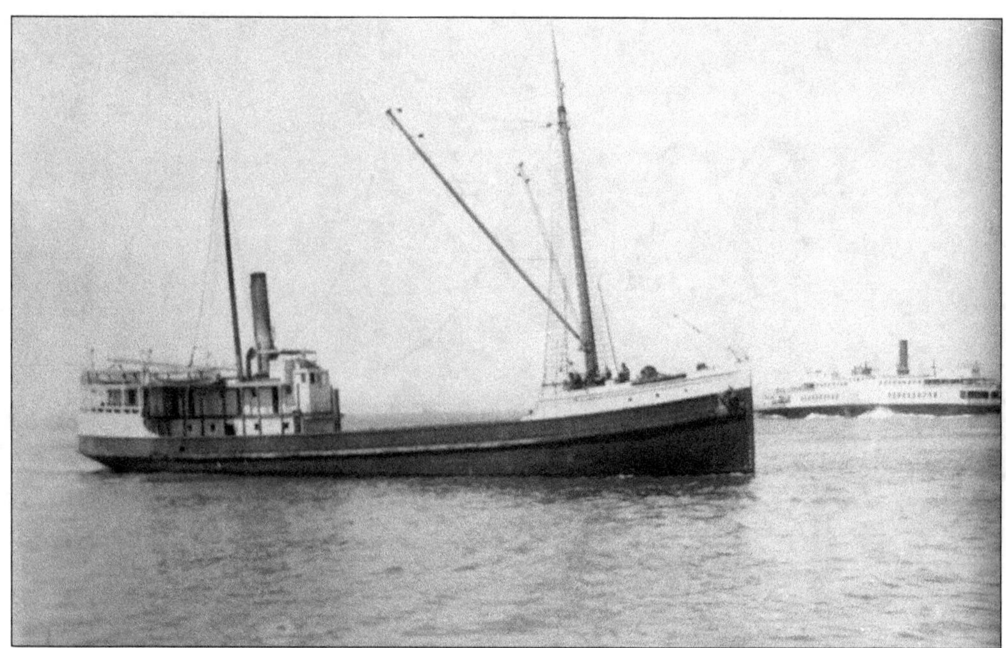

John Lindstrom built the wooden steam schooner G.C. *Lindauer* at Aberdeen, Washington, in 1901. The ship was 453 gross tons and 158 feet long with a 36-foot beam and 11-foot depth. It was equipped with a 400-horsepower compound engine. The lumber carrier had a capacity of 490,000 board feet of lumber. (CHM 009-16.4574.)

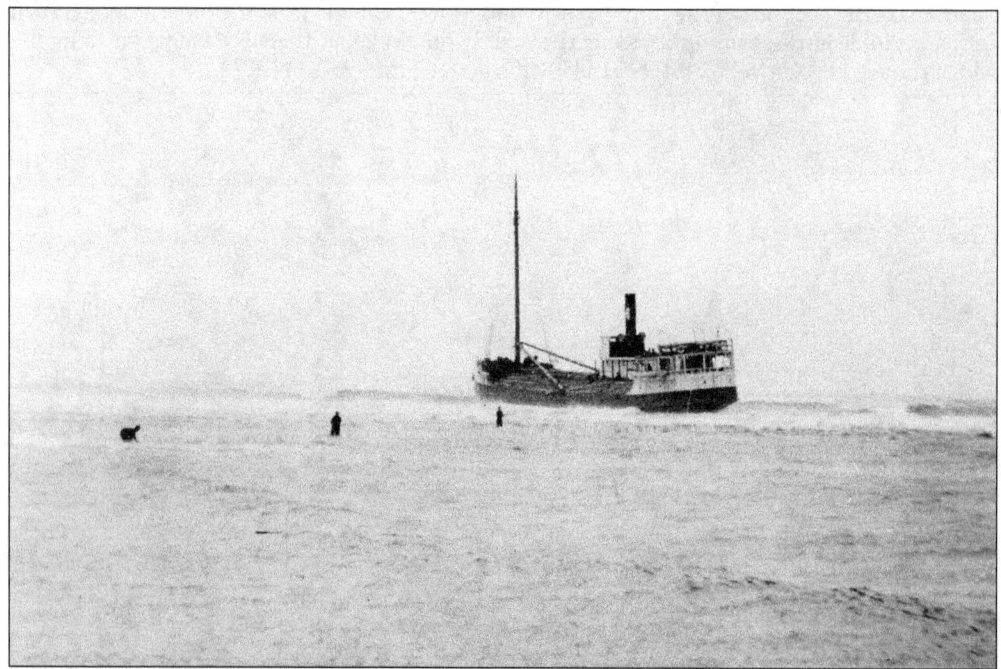

The G.C. *Lindauer* ran into trouble on several different occasions. On May 22, 1916, the engine became disabled in rough seas off Cape Blanco. After being towed partway, the engine was repaired and it was able to continue to San Francisco under its own power. It is shown here just off the beach after one of its accidents. (CHM 009-16.993.)

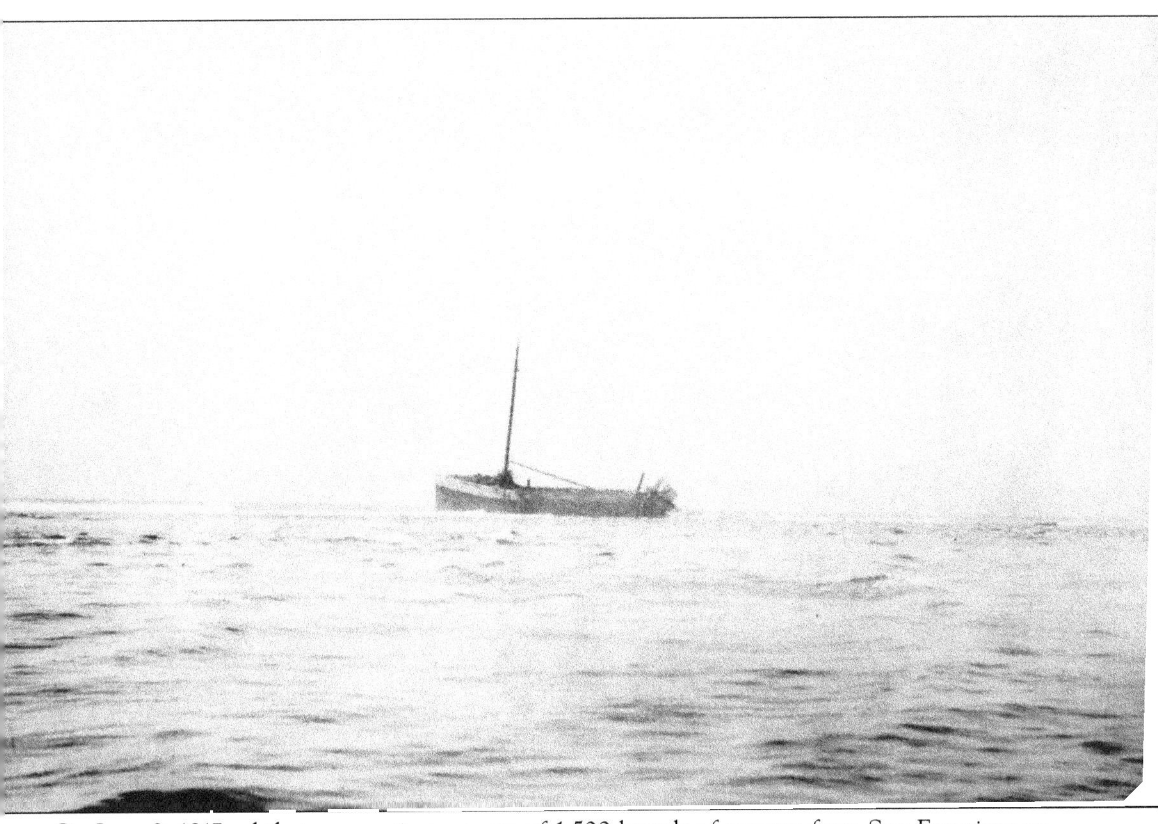

On June 9, 1917, while transporting a cargo of 1,500 barrels of cement from San Francisco to Coos Bay, the G.C. *Lindauer* struck an uncharted rock off Cape Blanco. The waterlogged ship managed to continue on to Coos Bay. The cement was later used to pave Central Avenue. Three-fourths of the cargo was salvaged. The G.C. *Lindauer*'s luck ran out on May 16, 1924. The ship, under the command of Capt. Axel Hendrickson, loaded 500,000 board feet of lumber at Reedsport, Oregon. The G.C. *Lindauer* stranded on the south spit after attempting to cross the Umpqua River bar. It broke into two the next day. The pilot, A.W. Reed, was blamed for the loss after an inspection by government officials. He was charged with ignorance of the bar, tides, and currents. (CHM 009-16.354.)

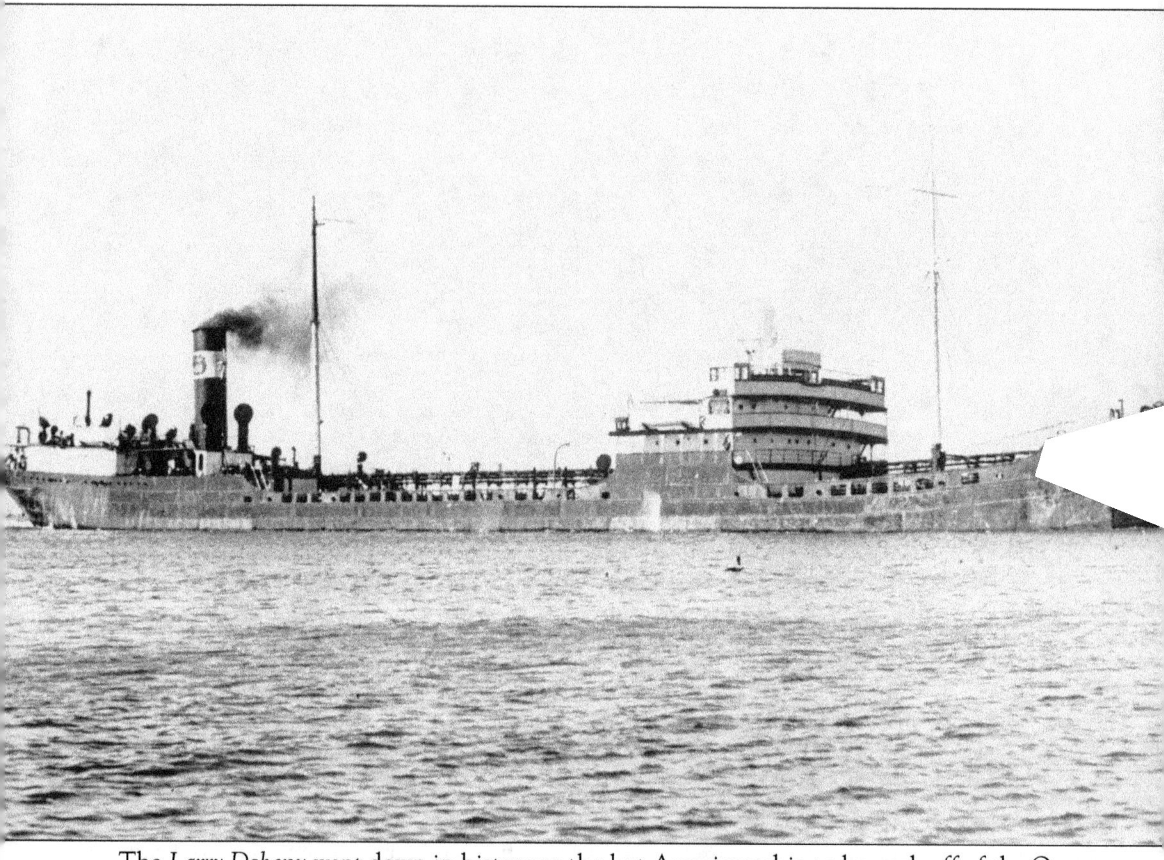

The *Larry Doheny* went down in history as the last American ship to be sunk off of the Oregon coast during World War II. The American tanker was built at Chester, Pennsylvania, in 1921. It was 6,805 gross tons and 430 feet long with a 59-foot beam and a 33-foot depth. It was owned by the Richfield Oil Company. In October 1942, the *Larry Doheny* travelled between San Pedro, California, and Portland, Oregon, with a cargo of 66,000 barrels of fuel oil. On October 5, 1942, the tanker *Larry Doheny* was torpedoed by the Japanese submarine *I-25* off of Cape Blanco. Six of the forty-six crewmen lost their lives. (CHM 009-16.1106.)

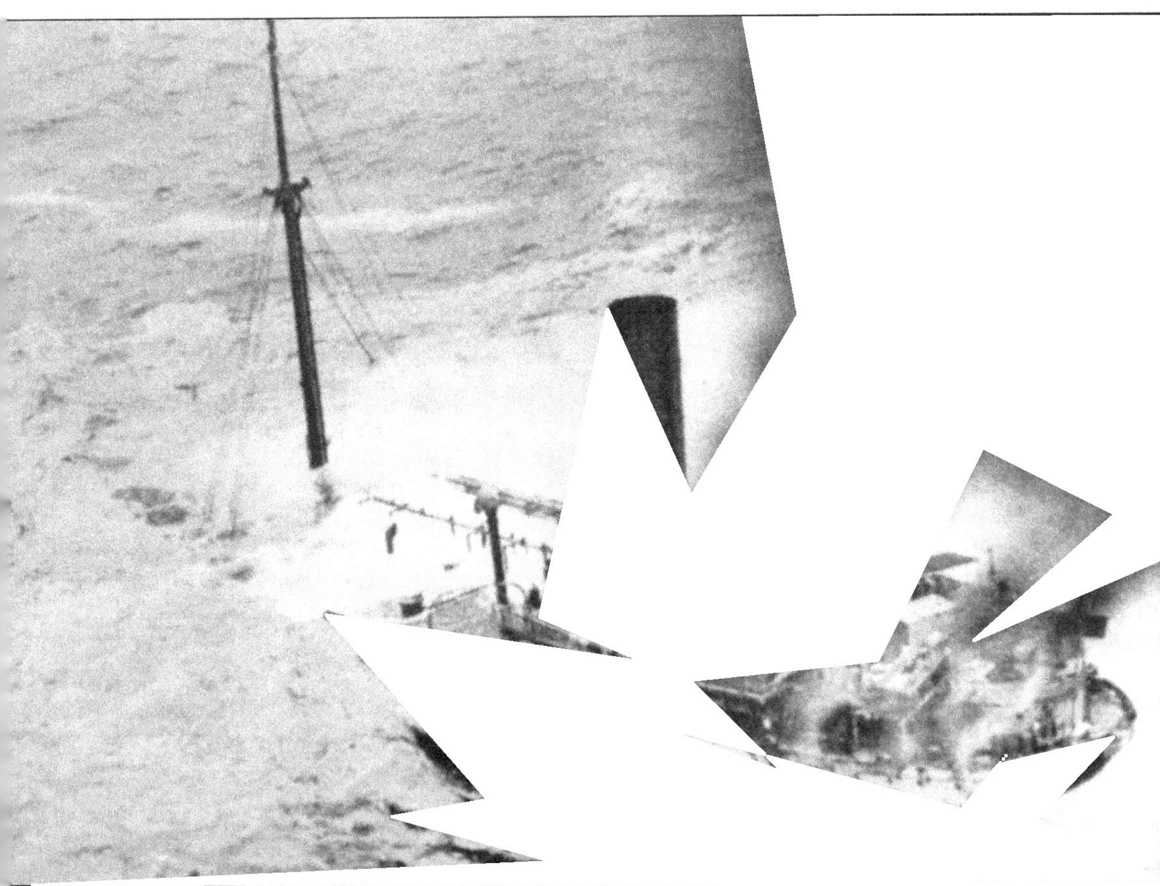

The torpedo struck the *Larry Doheny* on the port side, just forward of the bridge, and the entire length of the ship became engulfed in flames. The fire burned so hot that the ship's machine gun ammo began exploding. Capt. Olaf Breiland and his crew were forced to abandon ship. The crew was unable to transmit a distress call before leaving their ship. The survivors spent a cold night in lifeboats within sight of their burning vessel. In the morning, the ship slipped beneath the surface of the water. The steamer *Coos Bay* rescued the crew and transported them to Port Orford. The US Navy Q-ship *Anacapa AG-49* arrived at the scene and tried to lure the sub to the surface. The Q boats (also known as decoy ships) were merchant ships with concealed weaponry. They were designed to lure submarines into making surface attacks. Once they surfaced, the Q boats could try to sink them. The *Anacapa AG-49* continued to circle the tanker all night, but their attempts failed. (CHM 007-25.370).

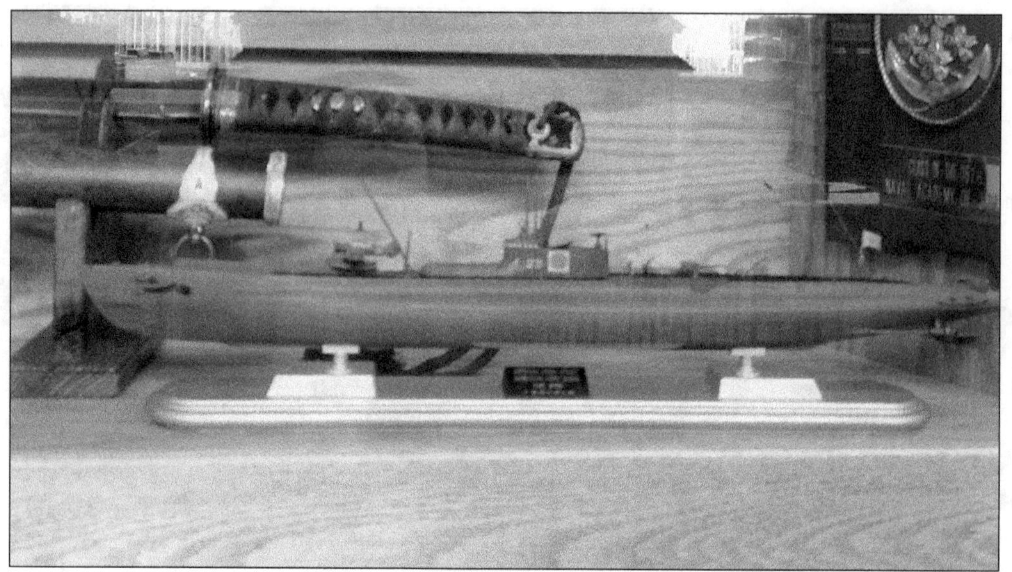

The *I-25* was having a busy week. The day before it torpedoed another ship, the American tanker *Camden*, off the Washington coast. The submarine model in this photograph is part of a display at the Chetco Community Library in Brookings. (Author's collection.)

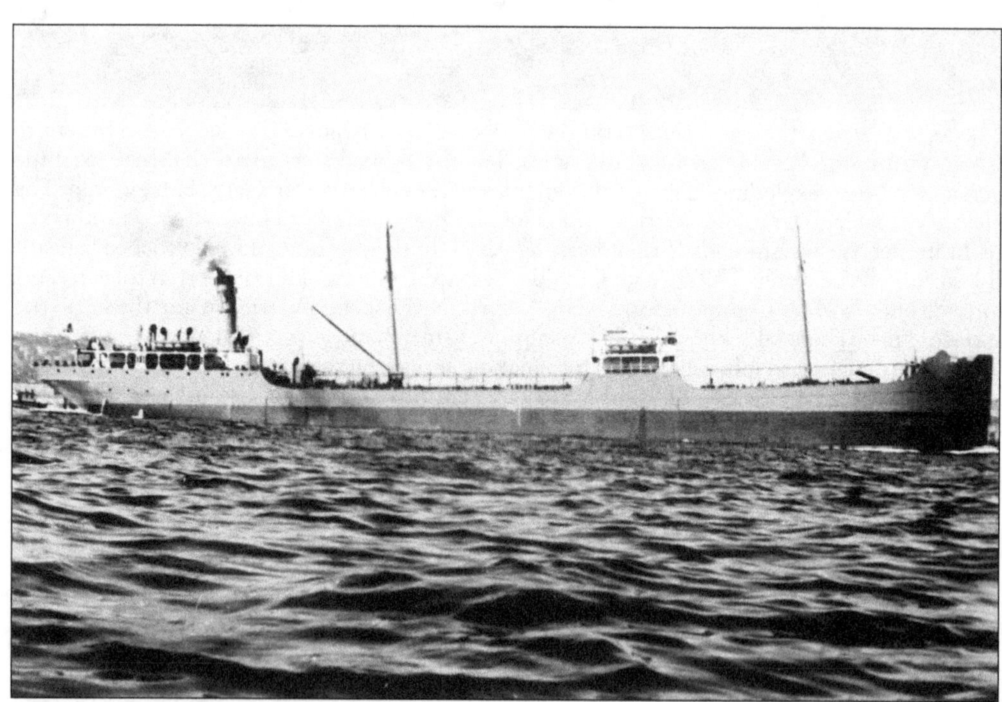

The steel hulled tanker *Camden* was built in 1921 at Camden, New Jersey. The 6,653-gross-ton vessel was 419 feet long with a 56-foot beam and a 33-foot depth. It was owned by Charles Kurz and Company but leased to the Shell Oil Company. (CHM 009-16.1213.)

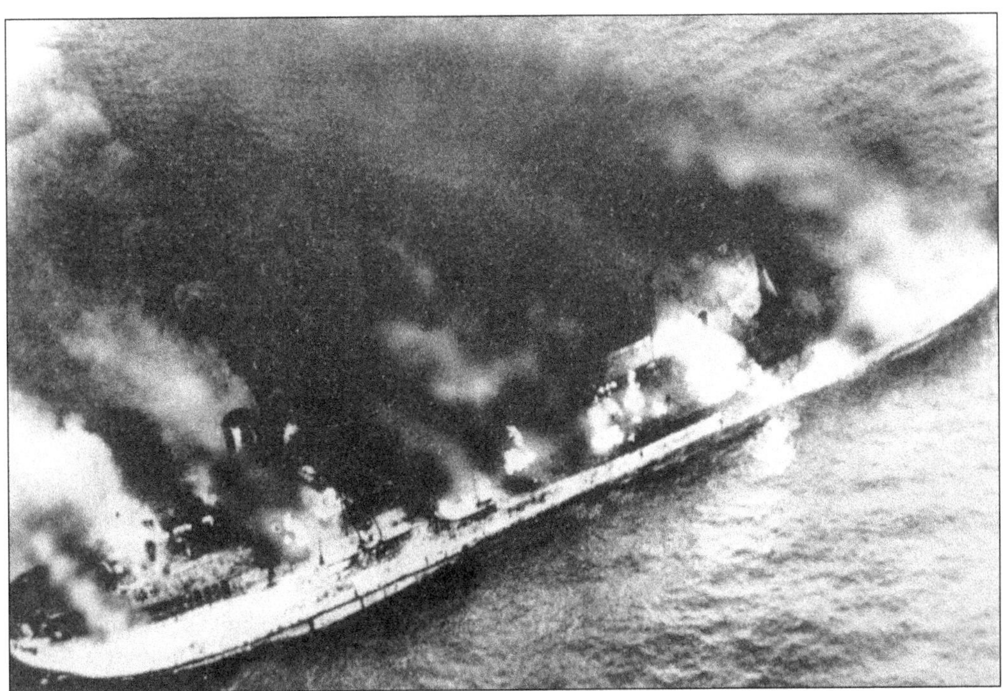

On October 4, 1942, the *Camden* was torpedoed by the Japanese submarine *I-25* off Willapa Bay with the loss of one life. The ship, under the command of Capt. D.M. Davidson, had stopped 50 miles north of Cape Blanco to complete minor repairs to the main engine. It was en route from San Pedro to Puget Sound with 76,000 barrels of petroleum products. (CHM 007-25.522.)

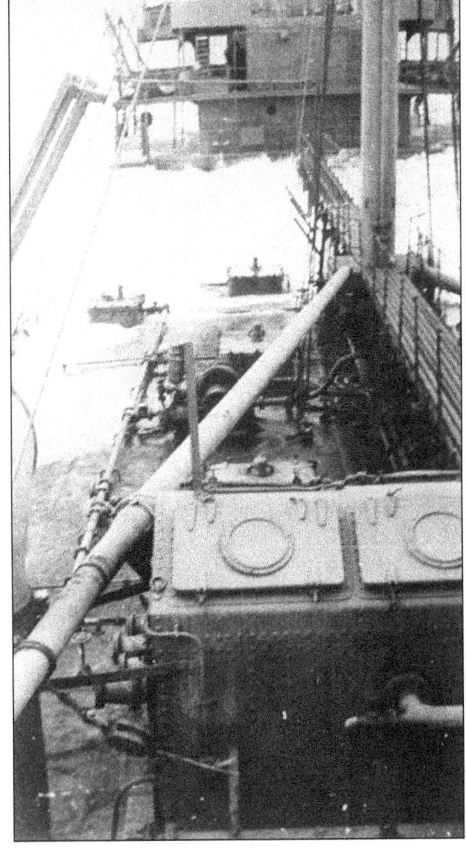

Within minutes, the deck was awash as far as the aft bridge. The captain gave the order to abandon ship. The crew was picked up by the Swedish *Kootaburra* and transported to Port Angeles, Washington. The tug *Kenai* found the *Camden* and attempted to salvage it. On October 10th—after nearly a week of towing—the *Camden* burst into flames and sank 60 miles off Grays Harbor. (CHM 009-16.1051a.)

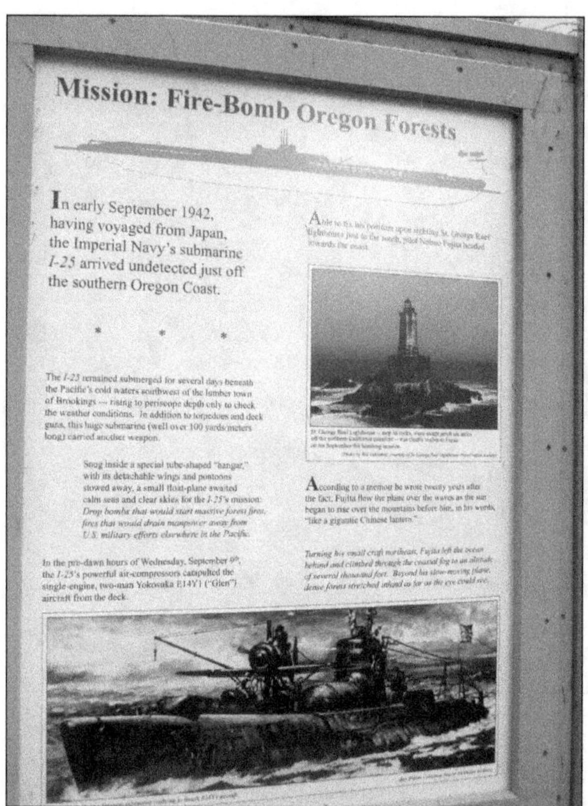

The 356 foot B1 Scouting Class submarine was responsible for several other attacks. On June 21, 1942, the *I-25* shelled Fort Stevens on the northern Oregon coast. The sub was also an aircraft carrier. It transported a small reconnaissance plane in a watertight compartment on its deck. In September 1942, the plane dropped four bombs over the forests in Curry County, making it the only location in the contiguous United States to be attacked by the Japanese Air Force during World War II. The bombs were intended to start forest fires since we relied on our forests to build ships and planes for the war effort. Fortunately, they failed. Although they did start a few small fires, they were quickly extinguished. These photographs were taken at the bomb site memorial. (Both, Debbie Newman.)

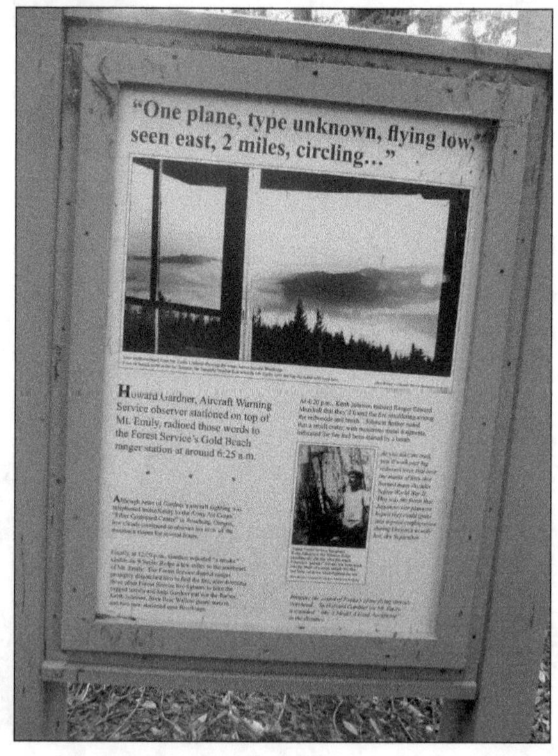

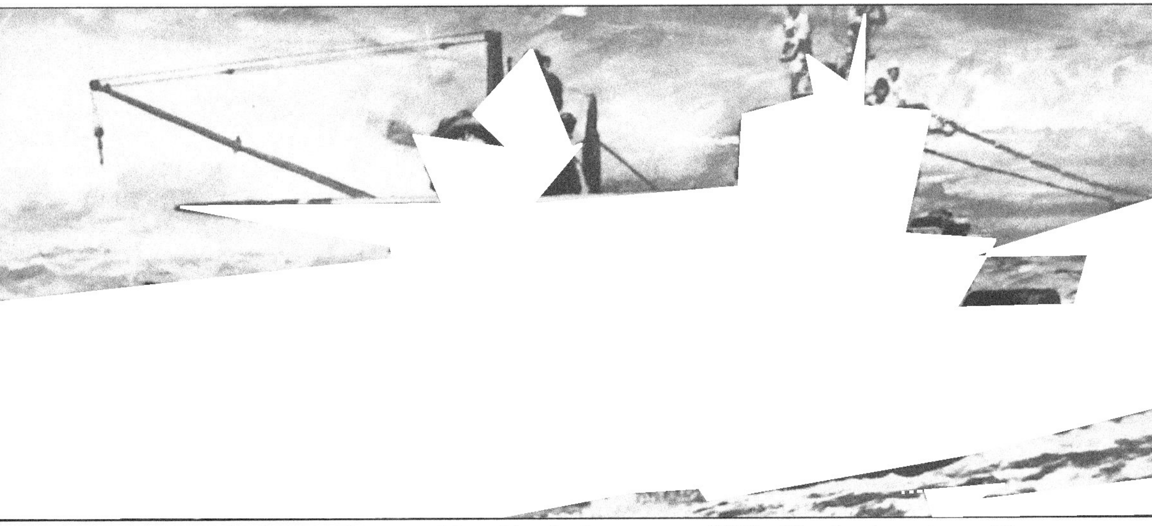

The 28-foot plane had two nicknames: "Geta" by the Japanese and "Glen" by the Americans. The plane was mostly metal but the wing and tail surfaces were covered in fabric. It was designed to be stored in a watertight compartment on the deck of the submarine, but it had to be partially disassembled in order to fit. It was launched using an air-driven catapult and equipped with pontoons so it could land on water. A small crane would then lift it into the submarine. With a wingspan of 36 feet and a cruising speed of only 90 miles per hour, the plane was too slow for combat missions. Initially, it was used for reconnaissance flights. Modifying the plane to carry bombs was the idea of the pilot, WO Nobuo Fujita. He made two flights over southern Oregon forests, dropping two incendiary bombs on each flight. On September 3, 1943, the USS *Ellet* and USS *Patterson* sank the *I-25* near Espiritu Island, 1,100 miles east of Australia. (Debbie Newman.)

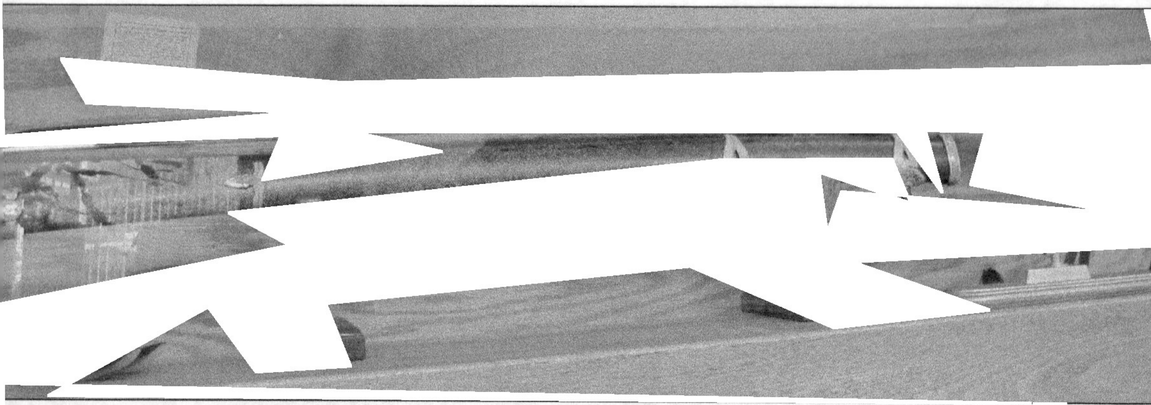

Many years later, Nobuo Fujita expressed regret for his role in the bombings. In 1962, the Brookings-Harbor Jaycees invited Fujita to the Azalea Festival with the intention of improving relations between the countries and to generate publicity for the area. It was the beginning of an international friendship. Although the initial public reaction was mixed, the invitation helped to foster good will between the former wartime enemies. On his first visit, Fujita donated his samurai sword to the City of Brookings as a "sign of goodwill." There is a Japanese tradition of giving a samurai sword to a former enemy in order to foster peace and friendship. He visited several more times and hosted several American high school students on a visit to Japan. On January 8, 1992, fifty years after the bombing, Fujita planted a redwood tree at the bomb site. On May 28, 1994, an historical marker was dedicated in Brookings to commemorate the bombings. After Fujita's death in 1997, a portion of his ashes were buried at the bomb site. (Debbie Newman.)

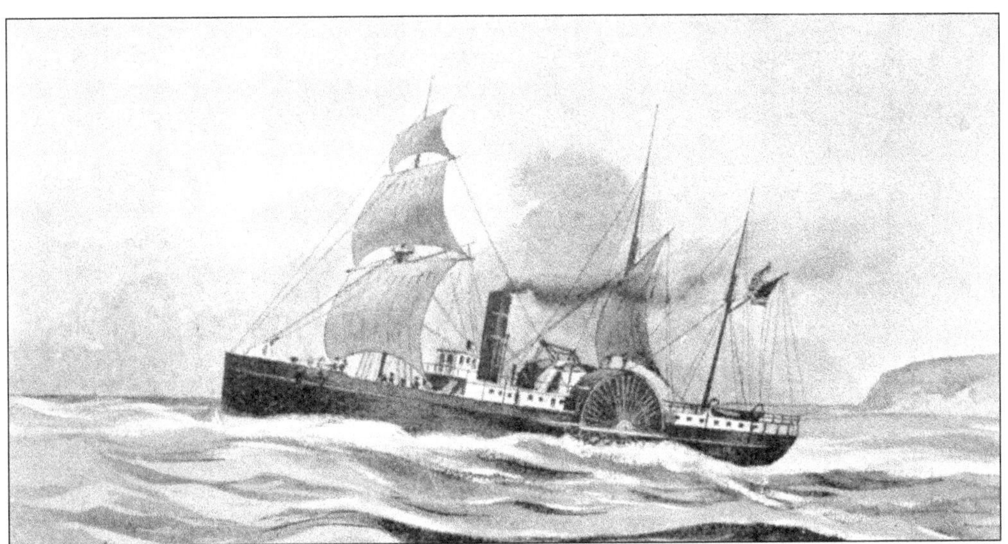

The American sidewheel steamer *Brother Jonathan* was built by Perrine, Patterson, and Stack at Williamsburg, New York, in 1851. The 1,181-gross-ton vessel was 214 feet long with a 34-foot beam and a 19-foot depth. Its wheels were 33 feet in diameter and driven by a vertical beam engine with a 72-foot diameter cylinder and 11-foot stroke. It was originally named the *Commodore*. (CHM 009-16.2933.)

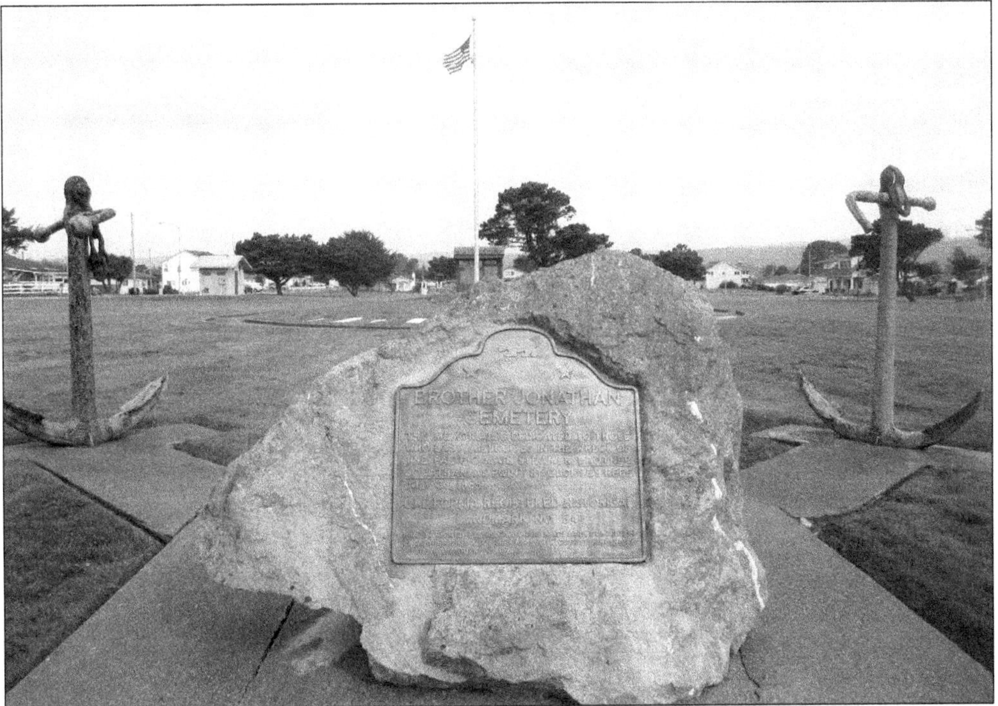

On July 30, 1865, the *Brother Jonathan* encountered a storm while traveling from San Francisco to Portland. There are discrepancies, but it is estimated that 244 people were on board. With the ship struggling, the majority of the passengers seasick, and rumors of the Confederate pirate ship *Shenandoah* nearby, Capt. Samuel DeWolf decided to turn around near the Oregon-California border and return to Crescent City. (Debbie Newman.)

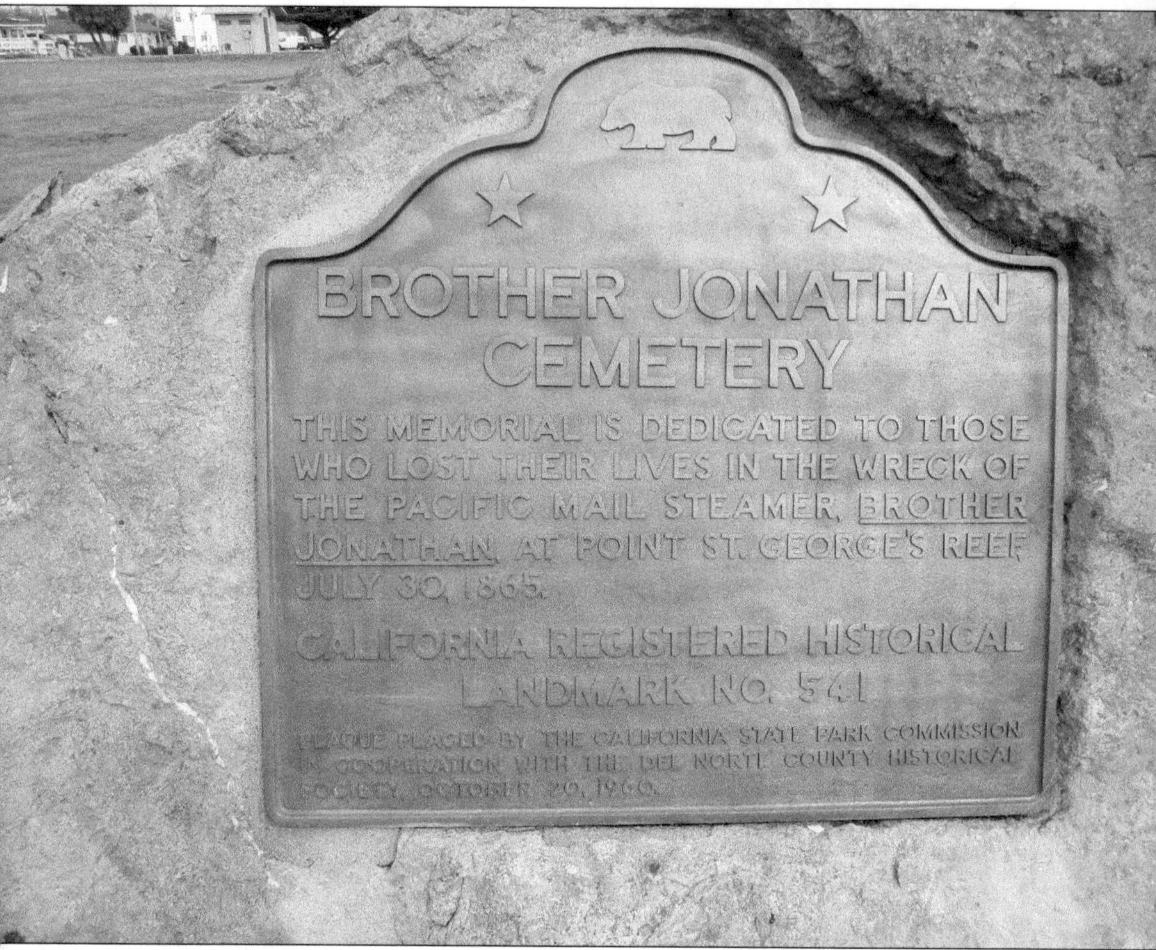

The *Brother Jonathan* struck a submerged rock less than an hour later. Only three lifeboats were launched. The first capsized, and the second was smashed against the side of the ship. The third lifeboat, containing 19 people, was the only one to make it safely to shore. A total of 225 passengers and crew were lost. After the wreck, there were rumors and speculation concerning the cause of the tragedy. Some claimed that the ship, which was carrying 750 tons of cargo (including 346 barrels of whisky), was overloaded. Others blamed the wreck on damage the ship sustained in a collision with the *Jane A. Falkenberg* on the Columbia River on June 14, 1865. Although the *Brother Jonathan* was repaired, some people thought the work may have been substandard and left the ship in a weakened condition. This photograph was taken at the shipwreck memorial in Crescent City. (Debbie Newman.)

PASSENGER LIST OF THE BROTHER JONATHAN

On her final voyage just before sinking off the coast of Del Norte County, California

(Source: California Shipwrecks: Footsteps in the Sea, by Don B. Marshall, Superior Publishing Company, Seattle)

PASSENGERS

B. Matherson
Mrs. Luckey, 2 children
Major E.W. Eddy, USA
G. Canel
Moses Beitier
Joseph Orseli
H. Definnie
George W. Annis
J. Strong-body recovered
S.P. Craig
Mary A. Tweedale*
Patrick Dwyer
John Adams
2 Unknown Indians
R.S. Manly
Henry Abrams
Thomas Gullan
C. Bisner
Issac Weil-body recovered
Ed De Rutte
Mrs. Mina Bernhart & child*
Mrs. Martha Stott & son*
Mrs. Martha E. Wilder*
Mr. Leach-body recovered
E.J. Lount-body recovered
D. Parrish-body recovered
Joseph Lord
J. Anchoine-body recovered
William Perkins-body recovered
Robert M. Frazer
John R. Craig
William Bilinsky
J.S. Bonn
Gilman Cilndruaid
Mrs. Woodlock
James Lynch
Conrad Adams
A. Ingraham, M.D., USA
James P. Richards-body recovered
Fred A. Pound
Victor Smith
Miss E.P. Snow
James Connell
J.G. Gar & Wife
Miss Shiser, nurse-body recovered
M.L. Hefron

SHIP'S CREW

Samuel J. DeWolf, Captain
W.H. Allen, 1st Officer
J.D. Campbell, 2nd Officer
James Patterson, 3rd Officer*
John S. Benton, purser
Albert Dyer, freight clerk-body recovered
Elijah Mott, chief engineer
J. Francis, 2nd engineer
G. White, 1st engineer
William Anderson, oiler
G.W. Hill, 3rd engineer
Patrick Lynn, fireman*
A. Collenburg, fireman
Frederick Malers, fireman
Arthur Harvey, fireman
J. Thompson, fireman
William Lowery, fireman
John Hensley, fireman
John Gorman, coal passer
John Clinton, coal passer
John Hilton, coal passer
James Perkins, seaman
Jacob Yates, seaman*
Henry Walker, seaman
A. Gonzels, seaman
William Penn, seaman
L. Domingo, seaman
J. Silva, seaman
William Foster, seaman
Frederick Douglas, seaman
James Fowler, seaman
D. Deas, pantryman
Thomas Tierney, porter
Henry Miller, baker*
Ed Shields, waiter*
Charles Rice, waiter
Manuel Herrila, waiter
C.F. Laurend, watchman
Richard Daulton, steward
H.G. Brown, steward
David Farrell, steerage steward*
John Miller, pantryman
Charles Law, cook-body recovered
James Law, cook
Henry Lee, cook
C. Stevenson, stewardess

Due to the circumstances of the accident, the location of the wreck of the *Brother Jonathan* remained a mystery for over 125 years. There were few survivors, the stormy conditions made visibility difficult, and there were no other ships nearby to witness the accident. The lifeboat containing the only survivors came ashore eight miles from Chetco Harbor. Debris from the wreck (including the bodies of victims) was spread out over a large area including Southern Oregon, Northern California, and several miles out to sea. (Debbie Newman.)

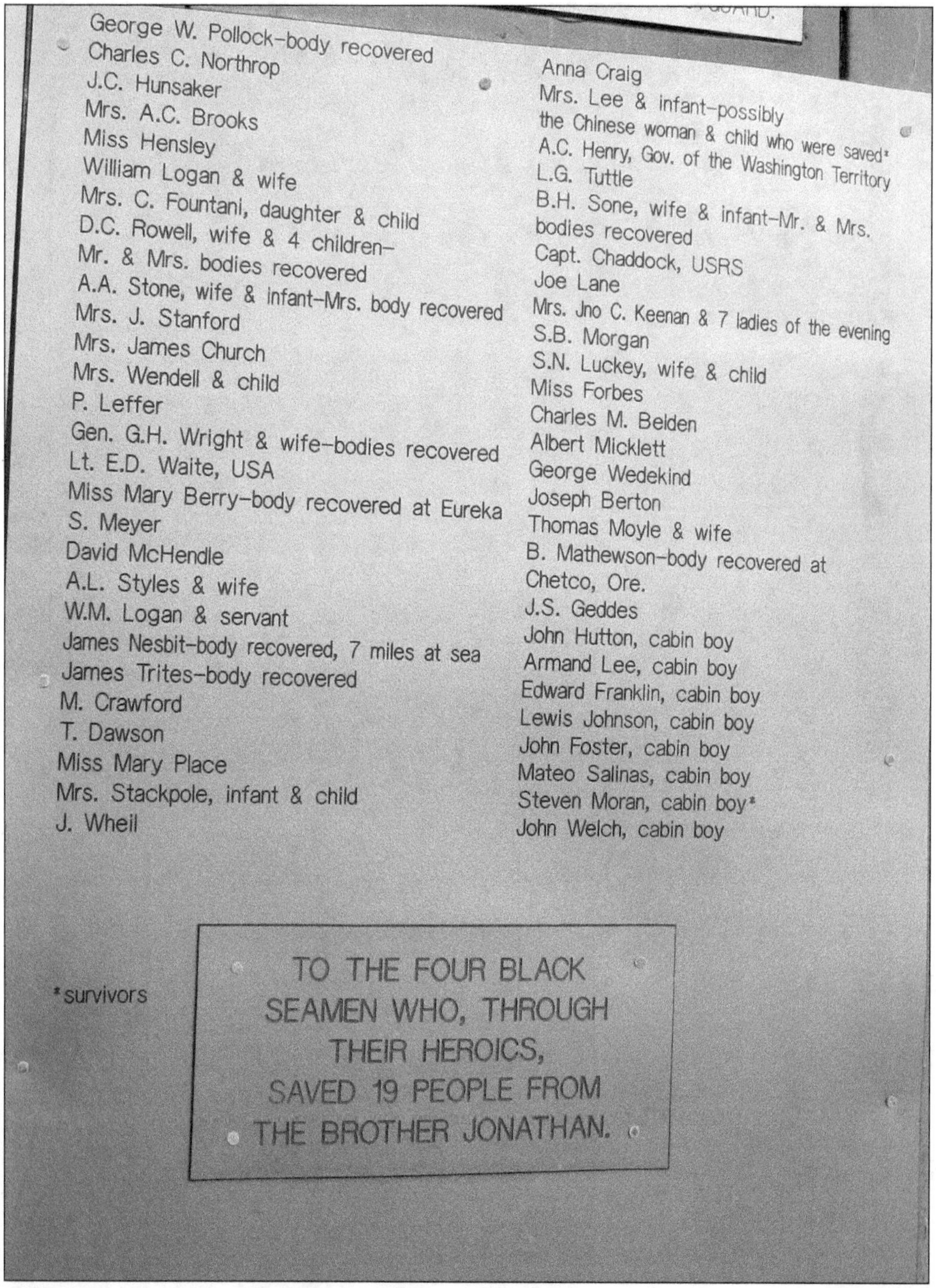

George W. Pollock–body recovered
Charles C. Northrop
J.C. Hunsaker
Mrs. A.C. Brooks
Miss Hensley
William Logan & wife
Mrs. C. Fountani, daughter & child
D.C. Rowell, wife & 4 children–
Mr. & Mrs. bodies recovered
A.A. Stone, wife & infant–Mrs. body recovered
Mrs. J. Stanford
Mrs. James Church
Mrs. Wendell & child
P. Leffer
Gen. G.H. Wright & wife–bodies recovered
Lt. E.D. Waite, USA
Miss Mary Berry–body recovered at Eureka
S. Meyer
David McHendle
A.L. Styles & wife
W.M. Logan & servant
James Nesbit–body recovered, 7 miles at sea
James Trites–body recovered
M. Crawford
T. Dawson
Miss Mary Place
Mrs. Stackpole, infant & child
J. Wheil

Anna Craig
Mrs. Lee & infant–possibly the Chinese woman & child who were saved*
A.C. Henry, Gov. of the Washington Territory
L.G. Tuttle
B.H. Sone, wife & infant–Mr. & Mrs. bodies recovered
Capt. Chaddock, USRS
Joe Lane
Mrs. Jno C. Keenan & 7 ladies of the evening
S.B. Morgan
S.N. Luckey, wife & child
Miss Forbes
Charles M. Belden
Albert Micklett
George Wedekind
Joseph Berton
Thomas Moyle & wife
B. Mathewson–body recovered at Chetco, Ore.
J.S. Geddes
John Hutton, cabin boy
Armand Lee, cabin boy
Edward Franklin, cabin boy
Lewis Johnson, cabin boy
John Foster, cabin boy
Mateo Salinas, cabin boy
Steven Moran, cabin boy*
John Welch, cabin boy

*survivors

TO THE FOUR BLACK SEAMEN WHO, THROUGH THEIR HEROICS, SAVED 19 PEOPLE FROM THE BROTHER JONATHAN.

Capt. Francis Connor of the *Sierra Nevada* reported seeing shipwreck debris 25 miles north of Crescent City. Once the story hit the papers, several people came forward claiming they heard distress cannons or saw the ship in trouble. These stories always placed the wreck in a different location. Since the *Brother Jonathan*'s cargo included both gold coins and gold bars, many people searched for it over the years. It was not discovered until October 1, 1993. It is now known that the ship sank eight miles from Crescent City. (Debbie Newman.)

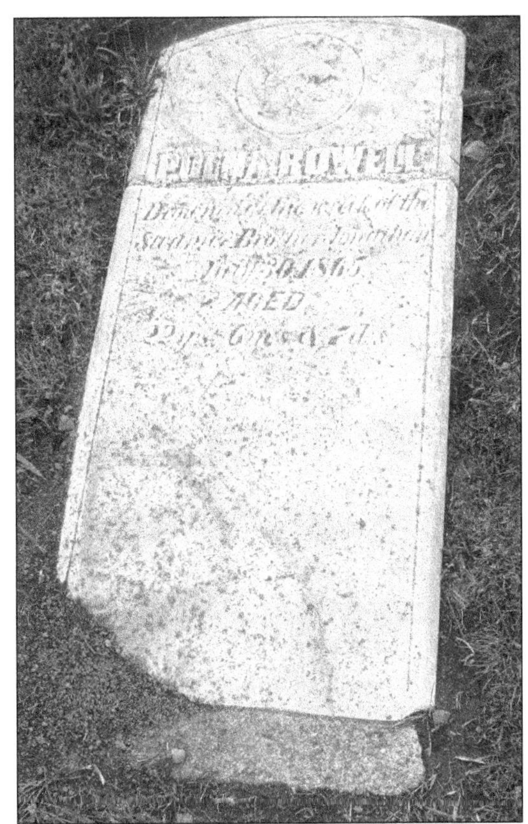

These headstones mark the graves of Polna Rowell (age 22) and her husband, Daniel C. Rowell (age 38), who both died during the shipwreck of the *Brother Jonathan* on July 30, 1865. They were buried at the ship memorial in Crescent City. Tragically, their entire family (including their four children) died in the accident. Only the parents' bodies were recovered. (Both, Debbie Newman.)

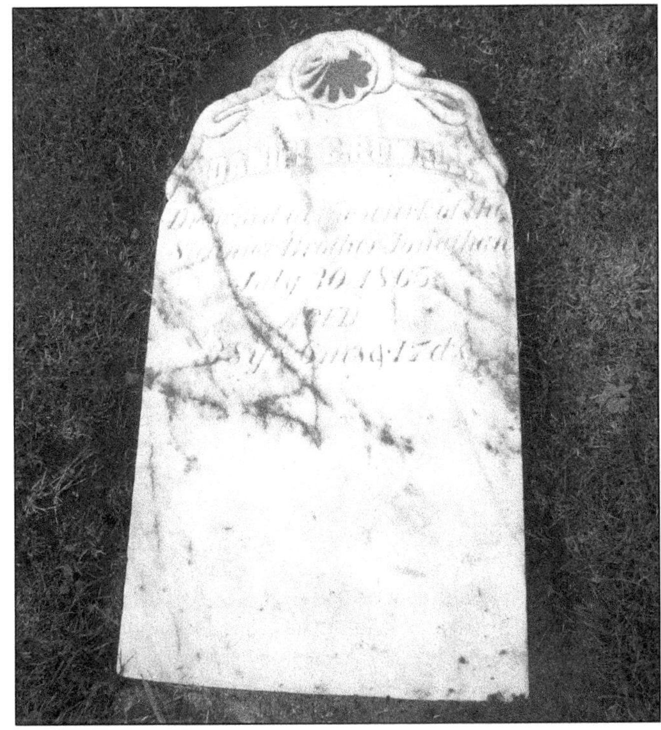

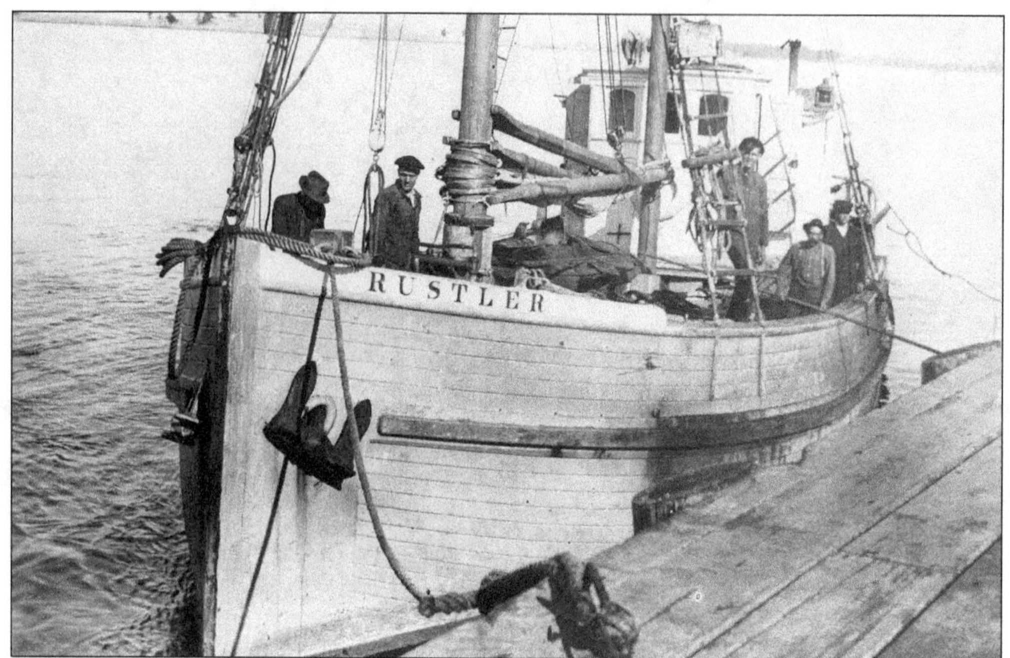

The American gas screw *Rustler* was built by Kruse & Banks at North Bend, Oregon, in 1911. The 39-gross-ton vessel was 61 feet long with a 20-foot breadth and 6-foot depth. The Macleay Estate Company owned it. (CHM 009-16.89.)

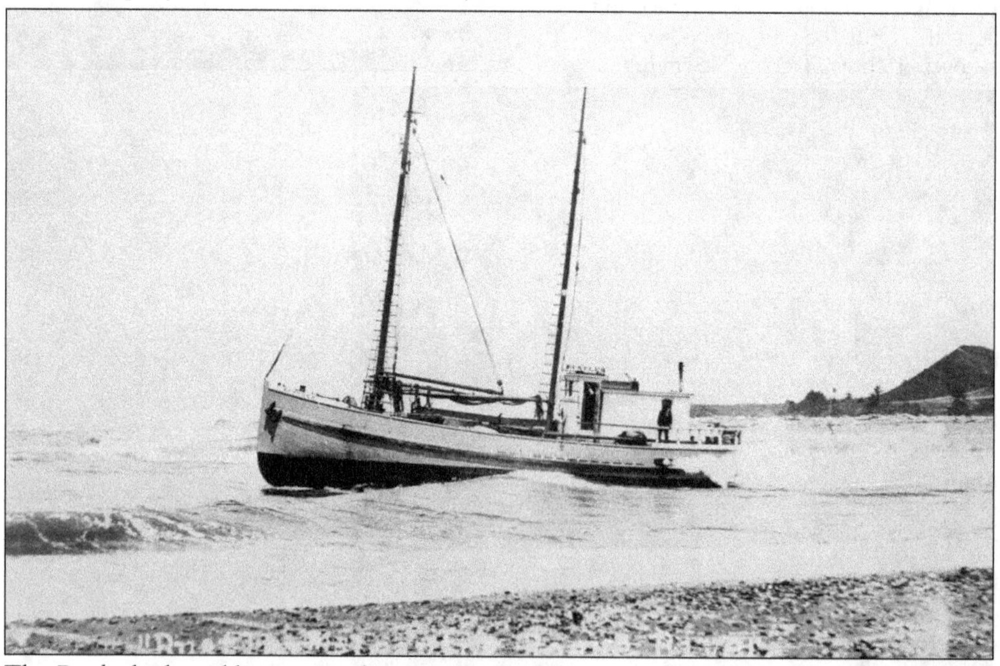

The *Rustler* had trouble on several occasions. On February 24, 1917, it attempted to cross the Rogue River bar under rough conditions. A swell flooded one of the engines. Captain Colvin tried to continue onward, but the ship struck bottom and then veered toward the south spit. He then tried to return to sea, but the second engine died. The ship grounded north of the river. It was refloated on March 1st. (CHM 009-16.2038.)

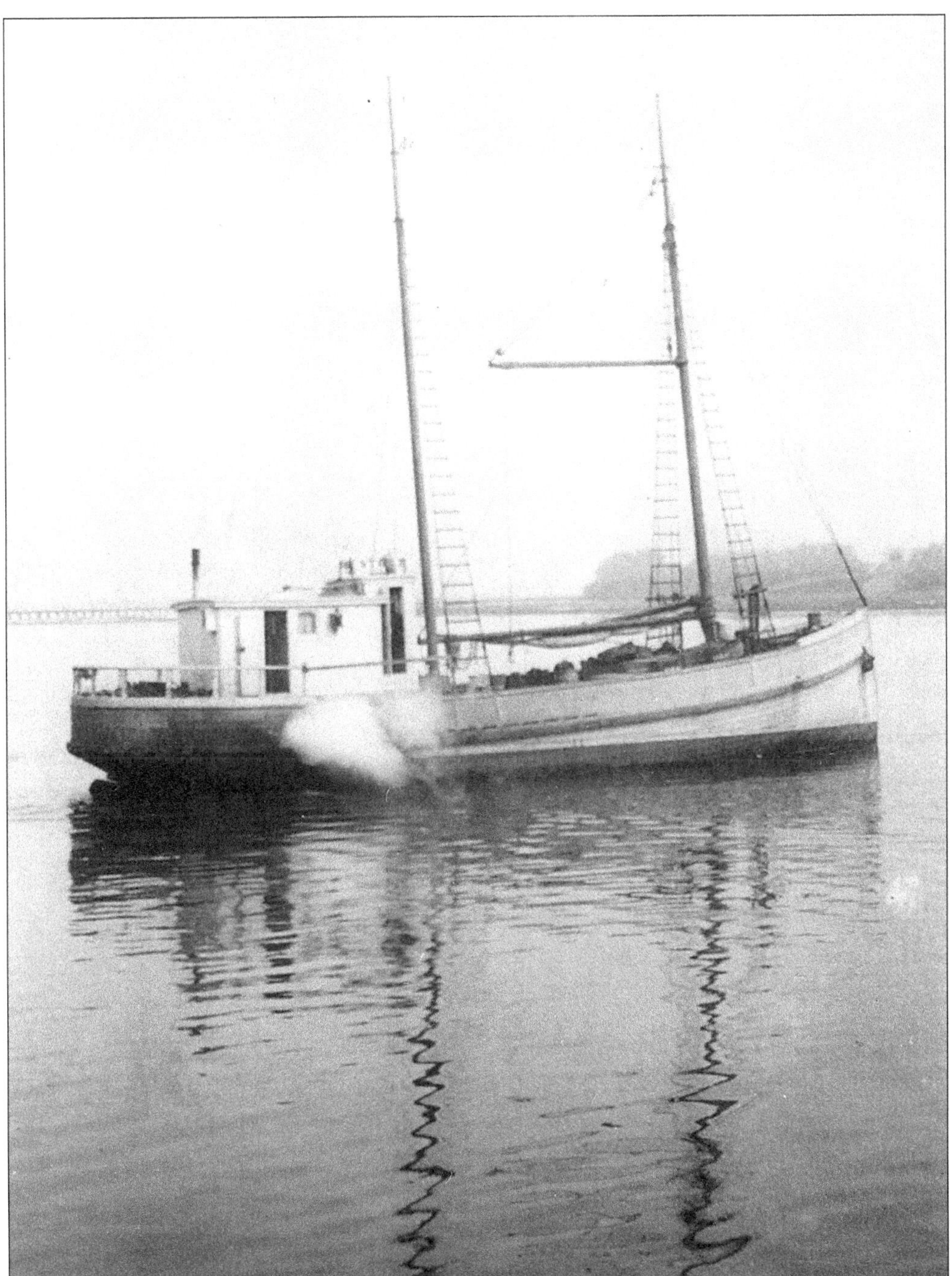

The *Rustler* grounded on Cape Blanco reef in 1918 but was refloated. Finally, on August 23, 1919, the *Rustler*'s luck ran out. While traveling from the Rogue River to Coos Bay, the ship's engine backfired before catching on fire. It was located approximately four miles south of Fox Creek. The crew of four was forced to abandon ship after their attempts to extinguish the fire failed. They reached the shore safely after spending 12 hours in their lifeboat. The *Rustler* was carrying a cargo of 788 cases of salmon and seven tons of fresh salmon. It became a total loss. (CHM 007-25.368.)

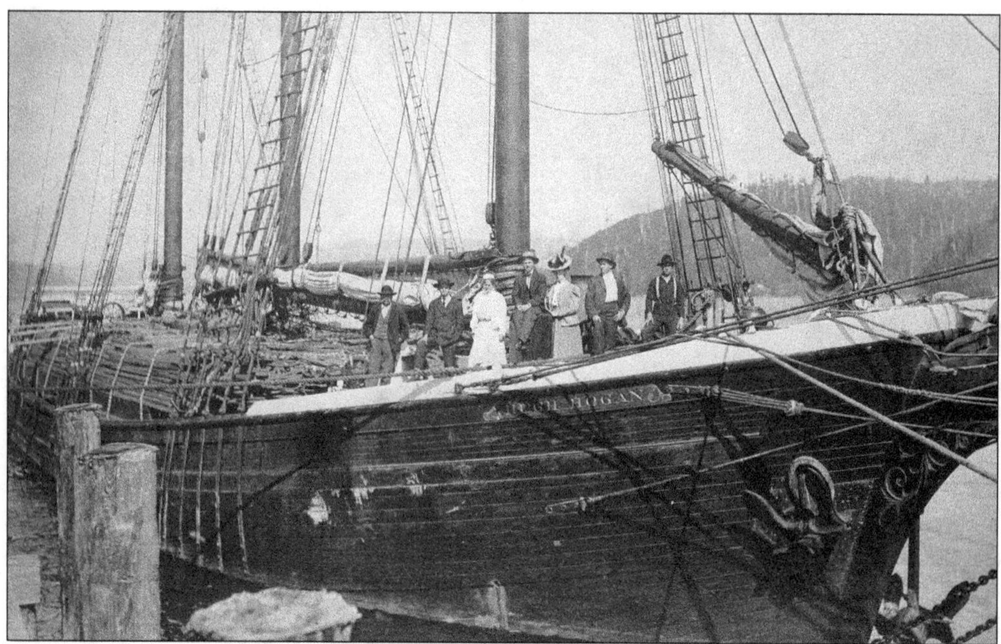

The three-masted schooner *Hugh Hogan* was built by K.V. Kruse at his Marshfield shipyard in 1904. The 765-gross-ton wooden-hulled vessel was 160 feet long with a 38-foot breadth and 9-foot depth. In 1918, the ship was renamed *Ozmo*. Just before World War II, a gas engine was installed. (CHM 992-8-1586.)

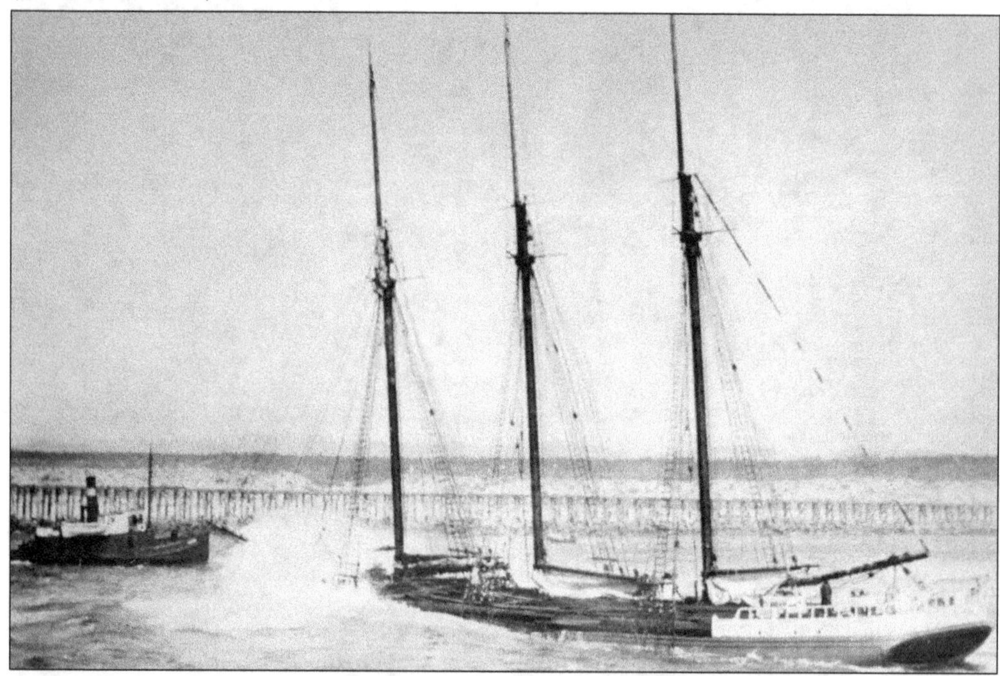

On April 28, 1914, a rope broke while the *Hugh Hogan* was being towed across the Siuslaw River bar by the tug *L. Roscoe*, causing the ship to ground. Captain Hill and his second mate had their wives with them. Both women chose to remain on board. After the deck load of lumber was thrown overboard, the ship was light enough to be refloated and repaired. (CHM 009-16.419.)

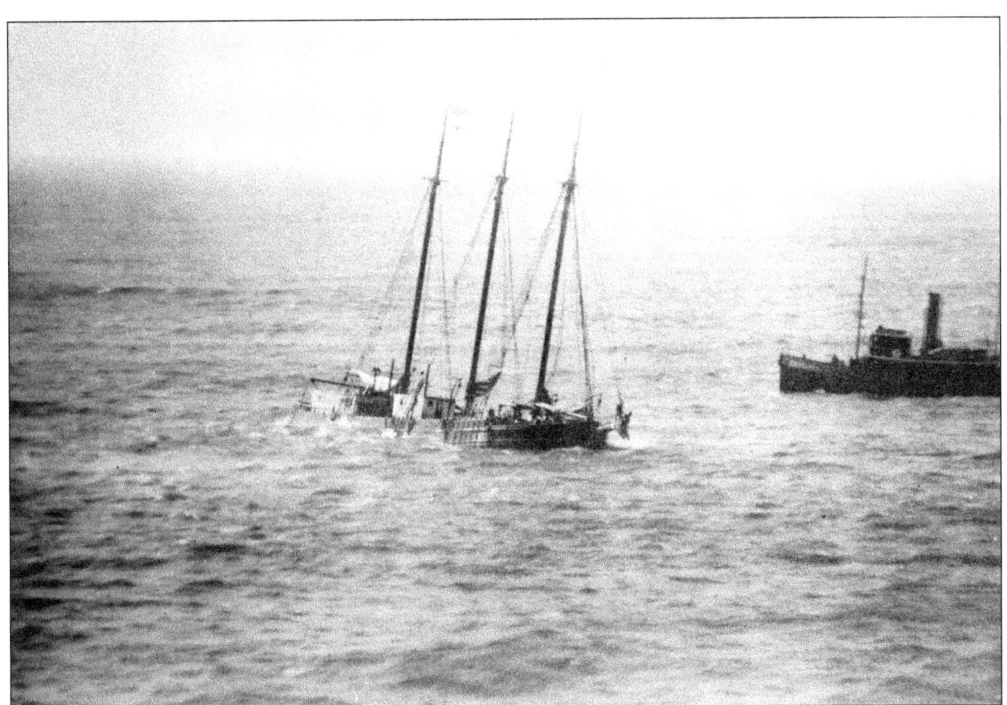

On May 17, 1922, the *Ozmo* (formerly *Hugh Hogan*) struck Orford Reef near Cape Blanco and began to take on water. It was traveling from San Francisco, California, to Bethel, Alaska, with a cargo of general merchandise. The accident was blamed on fog and strong currents. The steam schooner *Daisy* arrived the following day and took the *Ozmo*'s crew and one passenger, the chief engineer's wife, on board. Above, the *Ozmo* is shown partially submerged with another ship nearby. The photograph below shows the flooded deck and debris after the accident. (Above, CHM 009-16.921; below, CHM 009-16.1165.)

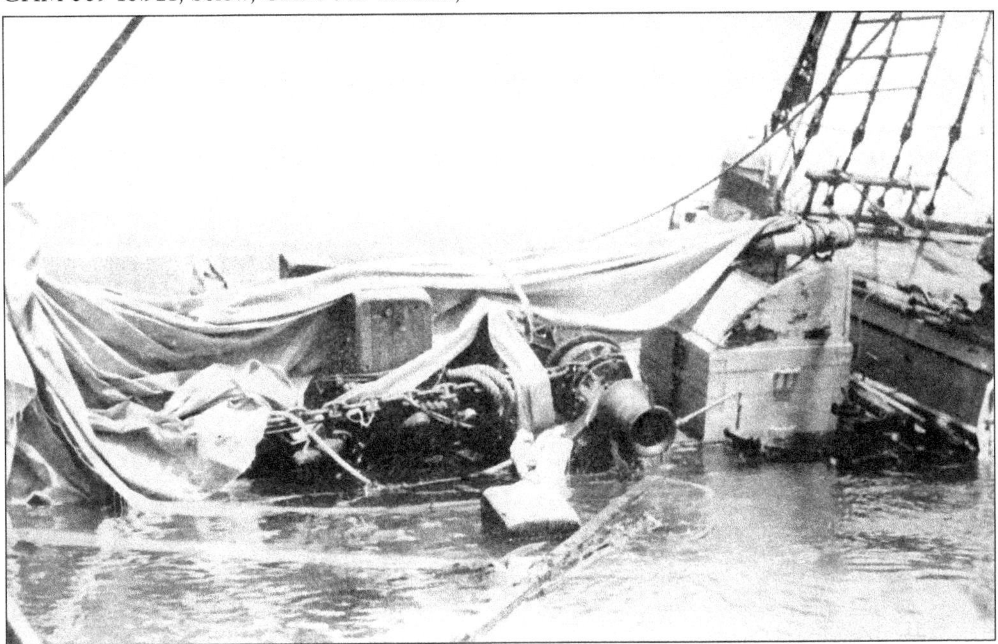

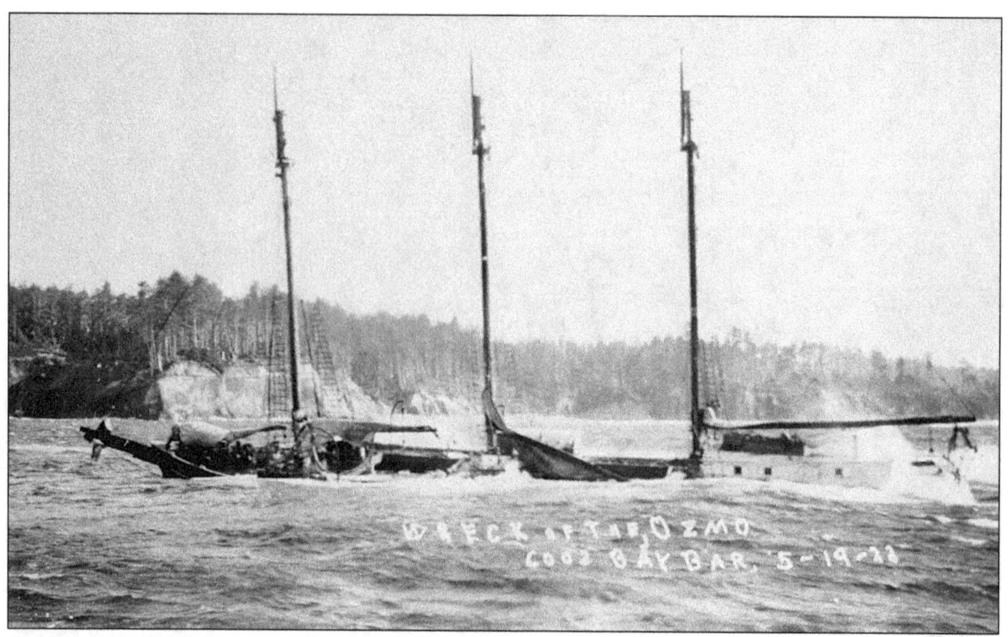

On May 19, 1922, Captain Worth and his chief engineer remained on board the *Ozmo* while the *Daisy* attempted to tow the disabled ship across the Coos Bay bar. Unfortunately, the steam schooner was unable to control the waterlogged vessel, which got caught in a strong current and drifted onto the south spit. The Coast Guard rescued the two men on board the *Ozmo*. (CHM 009-16.349.)

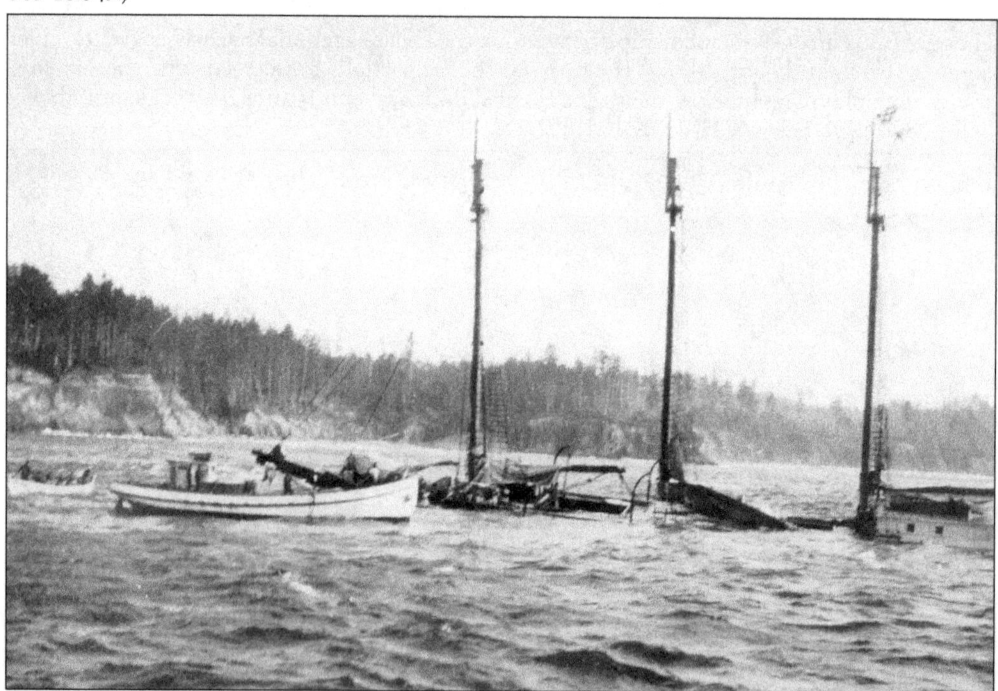

On May 22nd, the tide refloated the beached *Ozmo*, and it drifted toward the Coos Bay. The gas boat *Zebra* helped the tug *Fearless* to get a line aboard the disabled vessel and tow it across the bar and up the bay. The *Ozmo* was later found to be damaged beyond repair. (CHM 007-25.542.)

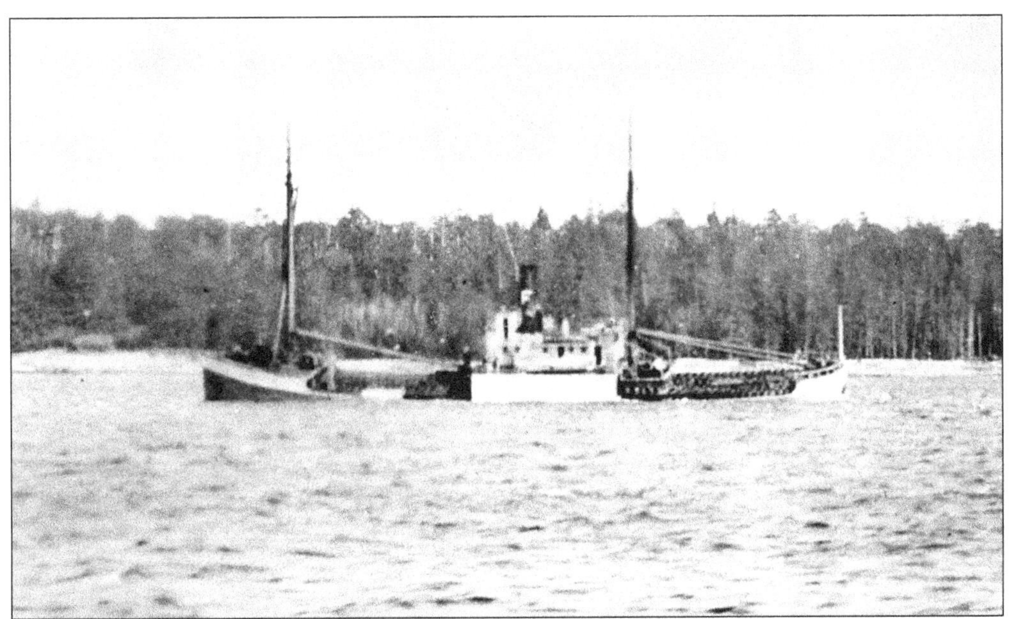

The steam schooner *Daisy* became disabled on the Coos Bay bar while towing the waterlogged auxiliary schooner *Ozmo* into the bay on May 18, 1922. The disabled vessel is visible in the above photograph. The boat beached inside the bar. It was later repaired and returned to service. (CHM 007-25.30.)

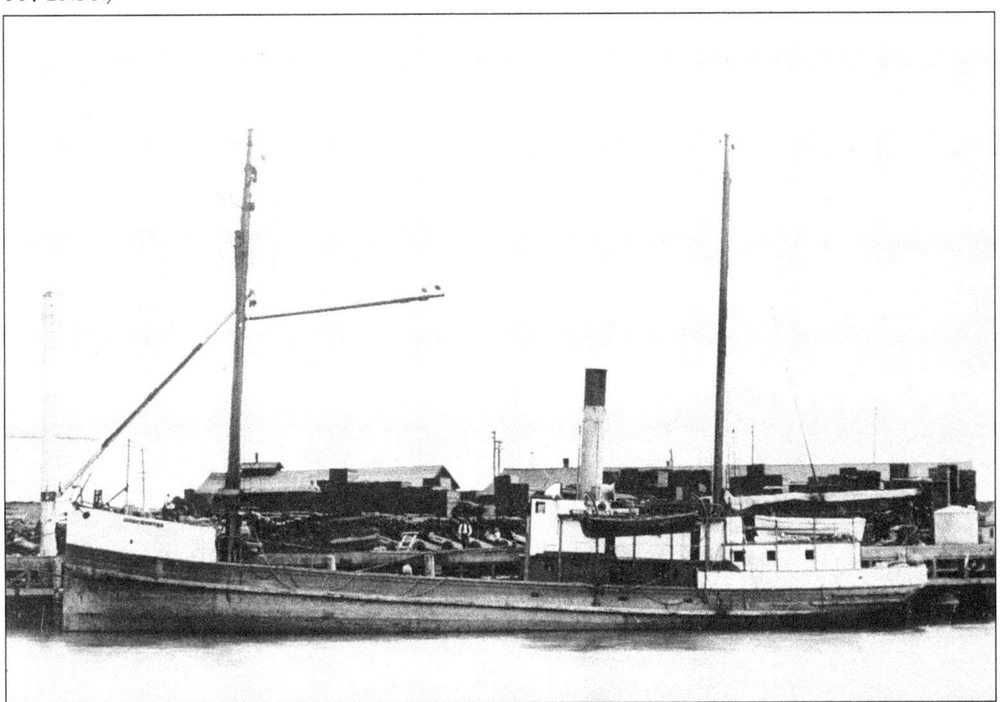

The loss of the *South Coast* remains a mystery. The steam schooner was built by C.G. White at San Francisco in 1887. The wood-hulled vessel was 302 gross tons, 131 feet long with a 32-foot breadth and a 10-foot depth. It was powered by a 190-IHP engine. With a capacity of 295,000 board feet, it ran in the coastal lumber trade. (CHM 009-16.395a.)

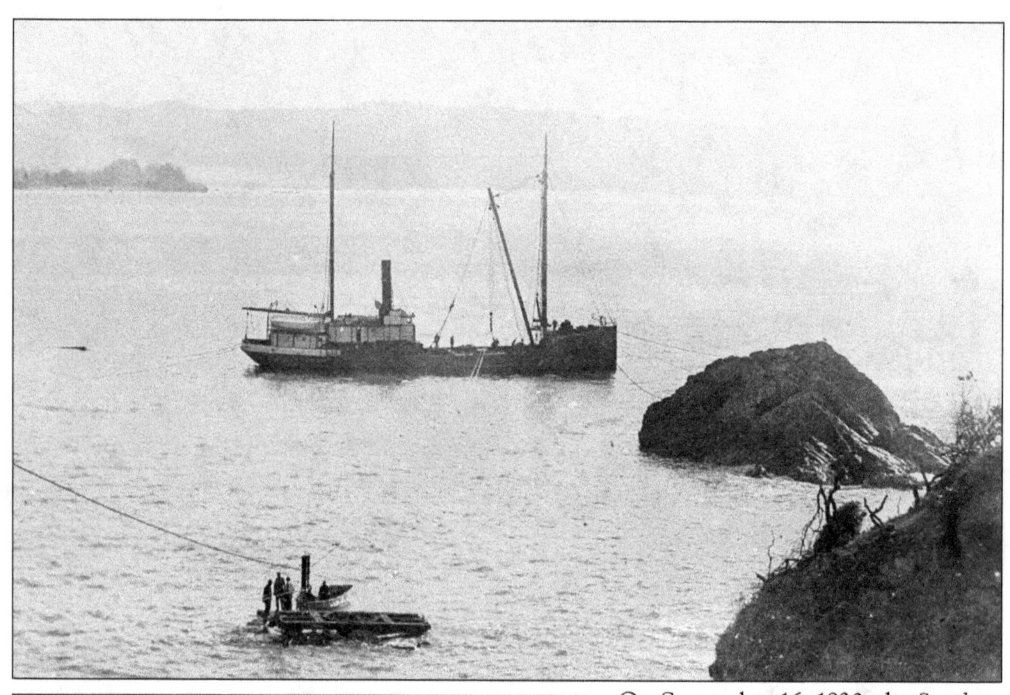

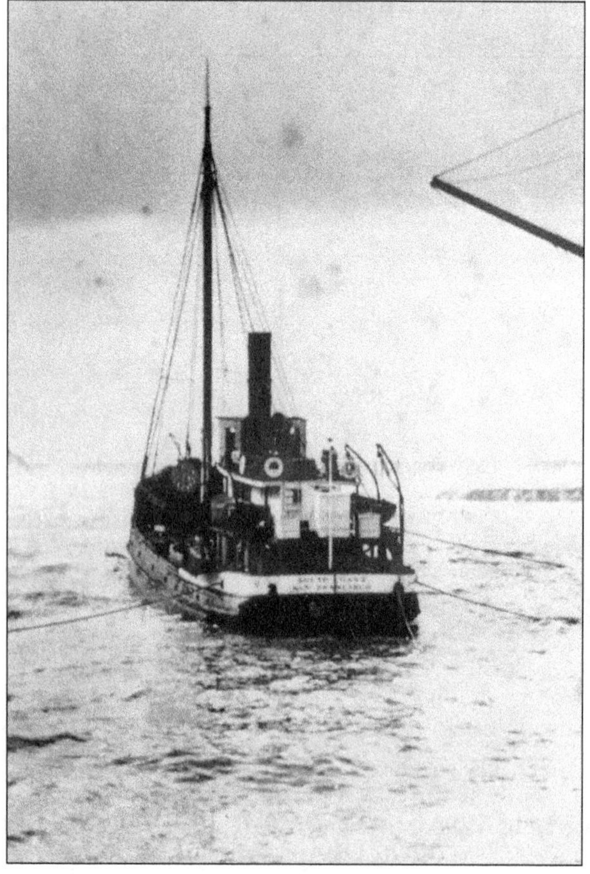

On September 16, 1930, the *South Coast*, commanded by Capt. Stanley Sorenson, left Crescent City on its way to Coos Bay with a crew of 19 and a cargo of cedar. It was never seen again. There are no photographs of the actual shipwreck since no one witnessed it, and there were no survivors. All of these photographs of the *South Coast* were taken beforehand. (CHM 009-16.2123.)

A small amount of wreckage was discovered off shore between Brookings and Gold Beach on September 18th, including a lifeboat and part of the wheelhouse. Numerous cedar logs were discovered off the Rogue River. There are many theories concerning the loss of the *South Coast*. Some speculated it foundered during a storm. Others believed that the ship's boilers might have exploded. (CHM 009-16.395b.)

The steam schooner *Solano* was built by Andrew Peterson at Raymond, Washington in 1913. The wooden hulled vessel was constructed for W.H. Wood of San Francisco. The 943-gross-ton ship was 198 feet long with a 43-foot breadth and 14-foot depth. It was powered by a 650-IHP triple-expansion engine and had a cargo capacity of one million board feet of lumber. The Hart-Wood Lumber Company ran the ship in the coastal lumber trade. The *Solano* experienced at least two maritime mishaps during its career, but only one accident occurred in Curry County. The first accident occurred in 1926 when the *Solano* wrecked at Point Purisima, California. The ship was repaired and returned to service. (Right, CHM 009-16.4545; below, CHM 009-16.1984.)

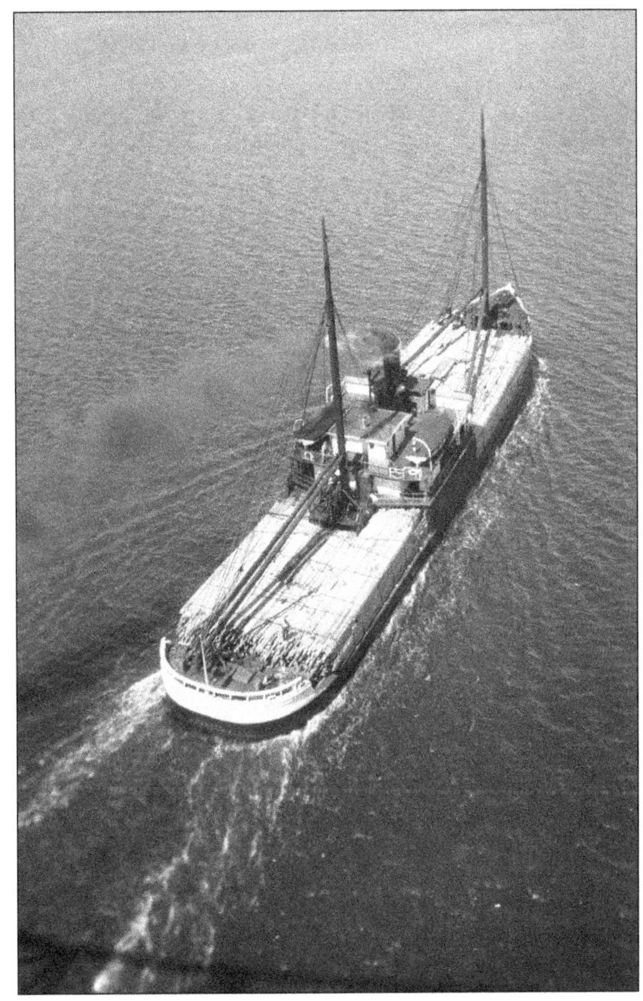

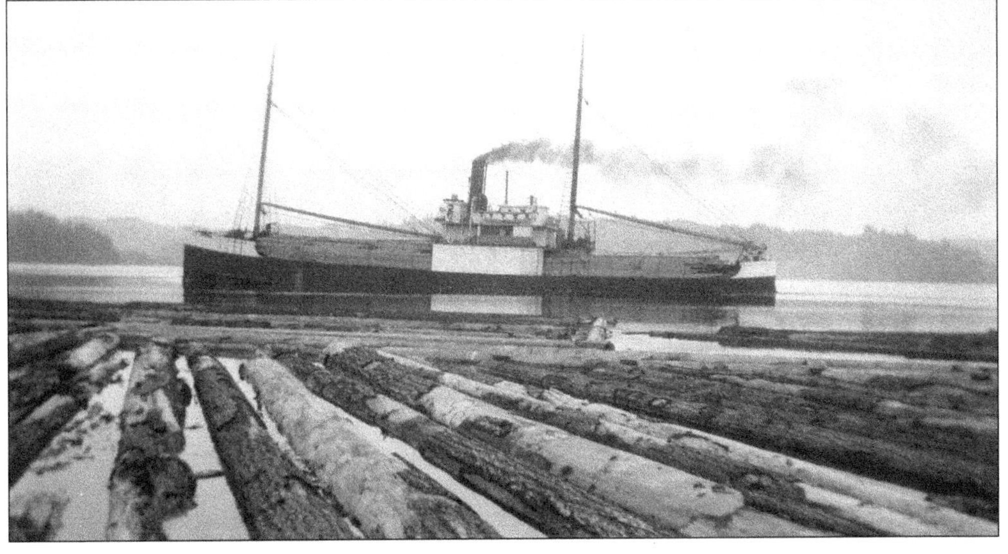

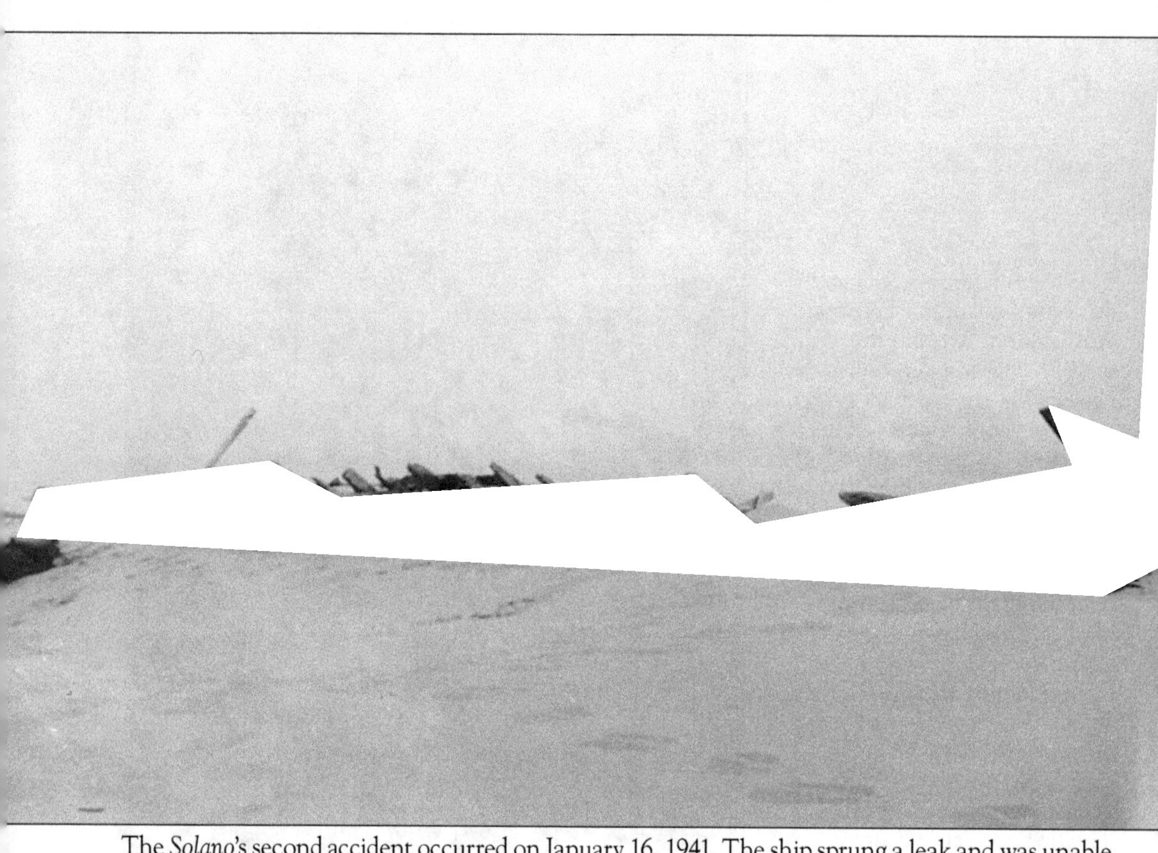

The *Solano*'s second accident occurred on January 16, 1941. The ship sprung a leak and was unable to make headway while traveling through a heavy storm off the Rogue River. The ship, under the command of Captain Johannsen, turned around and sought refuge on the Coos Bay and was repaired. The *Solano* had been en route from Grays Harbor to San Pedro with a cargo of lumber and shingles. After World War II, the *Solano* was scrapped. (Bandon Historical Society 14626.)

Bibliography

Belyk, Robert C. *Great Shipwrecks of the Pacific Coast.* New York: Wiley, 2001.

Boice, Meryl. *Gold Beach and South Curry County.* Charleston, SC: Arcadia Publishing, 2012.

Excerpts from Curry County Echoes, Volume I (1973–1974). Gold Beach, OR: Curry County Historical Society, 1973.

Excerpts from Curry County Echoes, Volume II (1975–1976). Gold Beach, OR: Curry County Historical Society, 1975.

Macdonald, Joseph F. *Macdonald's Steamboats & Steamships of the Pacific Northwest: A Directory of Steamboats & Steamships of the Pacific Northwest: Oregon, Washington, British Columbia, Alaska, Yukon Territory and Idaho, and Include(s) Lists of Crew Members, Owners, Companies and Builders (Vol. I & II).* Milwaukie, OR: Joemac Press, 2004.

Gibbs, James. *Shipwrecks of the Pacific Coast.* Portland, OR: Binfords & Mort, 1957.

Gibbs, Jim. *Peril at Sea.* West Chester, PA: Schiffer Publishing, 1986.

Grover, David H. *The Unforgiving Coast.* Corvallis, OR: Oregon State University Press, 2002.

Marshall, Don B. *Oregon Shipwrecks.* Portland, OR: Binford & Mort Publishing, 1984.

Masterson, Patrick. *Port Orford: A History.* Wilsonville, OR: Book Partners, 1994.

McCash, William. *Bombs Over Brookings.* Corvallis, OR: Maverick Publications, 2005.

Nelson, Shirley. *Port Orford and North Curry County.* Charleston, SC: Arcadia Publishing, 2010.

Osborne, Ernest L. *Men of Action.* Bandon, OR: Bandon Historical Society Press, 1981.

Pinyerd, David. *Lighthouses & Lifesaving on the Oregon Coast.* Charleston, SC: Arcadia Publishing, 2007.

www.ingramcontent.com/pod-product-compliance
Lightning Source LLC
LaVergne TN
LVHW081555100826
845153LV00004B/390